C000243796

Time, Consumption and Everyday Life

Cultures of Consumption Series

Series Editor: Frank Trentmann

ISSN 1744-5876

Previously Published Titles

The Making of the Consumer
Knowledge, Power and Identity in the Modern World
Edited by Frank Trentmann

Consuming Cultures, Global Perspectives
Historical Trajectories, Transnational Exchanges
Edited by John Brewer and Frank Trentmann

Fashion's World Cities
Edited by Christopher Breward and David Gilbert

The Khat Controversy
Stimulating the Debate on Drugs
David Anderson, Susan Beckerleg, Degol Hailu and Axel Klein

The Design of Everyday Life
Elizabeth Shove, Matthew Watson, Jack Ingram and Martin Hand

Food and Globalization
Consumption, Markets and Politics in the Modern World
Edited by Alexander Nützenadel and Frank Trentmann

Reconnecting Producers, Consumers and Food
Exploring Alternatives
Moya Kneafsey, Rosie Cox, Lewis Holloway, Elizabeth Dowler, Laura Venn and
    Helena Tuomainen

Forthcoming Titles

Governing Consumption
New Spaces of Consumer Politics
Clive Barnett, Nick Clarke, Paul Cloke and Alice Malpass

Time, Consumption and Everyday Life

Practice, Materiality and Culture

Edited by
**Elizabeth Shove,
Frank Trentmann and
Richard Wilk**

BLOOMSBURY

LONDON • NEW DELHI • NEW YORK • SYDNEY

Bloomsbury Academic
An imprint of Bloomsbury Publishing Plc

50 Bedford Square	1385 Broadway
London	New York
WC1B 3DP	NY 10018
UK	USA

www.bloomsbury.com

First published in 2009 by Berg
Reprinted by Bloomsbury Academic 2013

© Elizabeth Shove, Frank Trentmann and Richard Wilk 2009

Elizabeth Shove, Frank Trentmann and Richard Wilk have asserted their right under the Copyright, Designs and Patents Act, 1988, to be identified as Authors of this work.

All rights reserved. No part of this publication may be reproduced or transmitted in any form or by any means, electronic or mechanical, including photocopying, recording, or any information storage or retrieval system, without prior permission in writing from the publishers.

No responsibility for loss caused to any individual or organization acting on or refraining from action as a result of the material in this publication can be accepted by Bloomsbury or the author.

British Library Cataloguing-in-Publication Data
A catalogue record for this book is available from the British Library.

ISBN: HB: 978-1-8478-8365-0
PB: 978-1-8478-8364-3

Library of Congress Cataloging-in-Publication Data
A catalog record for this book is available from the Library of Congress.

Typeset by JS Typesetting Ltd, Porthcawl, Mid Glamorgan
Printed and bound in Great Britain

Contents

Section III: Rhythms, Patterns and Temporal Cycles of Consumption

Section IV: The Temporalities of Stuff

List of Tables and Figures

Tables

Figures

List of Contributors

Inge Daniels is a Lecturer in Social Anthropology at the University of Oxford. Her book *The Japanese House: Material Culture in the Modern Home* is due to be published by Berg in 2010.

Billy Ehn is Professor of European Ethnology at the University of Umeå. He has published a number of books on different aspects of everyday life, including *Vad konstigt: Om undran och oförståelse* (How Odd: On Curioisity and Disbelief; Studentlitteratur, 2005) and *När ingenting särskilt händer* (with Orvar Löfgren, Brutus Östlings Bokförlag Symposion, 2007, Engl. translation: *The Secret World of Doing Nothing*, University of California Press, in press).

Güliz Ger is Professor of Marketing at Bilkent University, Ankara. Her research interests involve issues of consumption, culture and globalization. She has co-authored 'Constructing and Representing the Islamic Consumer in Turkey', in *Fashion Theory* (2007), 'Aesthetics, Ethics and the Politics of the Turkish Headscarf', in Suzanne Kuechler and Daniel Miller, eds, *Clothing as Material Culture* (Berg, 2005), and 'The Fire of Desire: A Multi-sited Inquiry into Consumer Passion', in *Journal of Consumer Research* (2003).

Jukka Gronow is Professor of Sociology at the University of Uppsala. He has written widely on consumption, taste and style, including *Sociology of Taste* (Routledge, 1997) and *Caviar with Champagne* (Berg, 2003).

Mikko Jalas is a Research Fellow in Organization and Management at the Helsinki School of Economics. His work has focused on environmental policy and the politics of time and temporality in everyday life. He has published articles in *Time & Society* and *Ecological Economics*.

Olga Kravets is an Assistant Professor of Marketing at Bilkent University, Ankara. She has worked at A.C. Nielsen Australia, a market research company, as well as conducting academic research on consumption and marketing in transitional economies.

Orvar Löfgren is Professor of European Ethnology at the University of Lund. Among his recent books are *Off the Edge: Experiments in Cultural Analysis* (edited with Rick Wilk; Museum Tusculanum Press, 2006) and *Magic, Culture and the New Economy* (edited with Robert Willim; Berg, 2005).

Daniel Miller is Professor of Material Culture at the Department of Anthropology, University College London. Recent publications include *The Comfort of Things* (Polity, 2008), *The Cell Phone* (with Heather Horst; Berg, 2006) and the edited volume *Materiality* (Duke University Press, 2005).

Marina Moskowitz is a Reader in History and American Studies at the University of Glasgow. She focuses on the intersection of culture and business in American history, which she has explored in *Standard of Living: The Measure of the Middle Class in Modern America* (Johns Hopkins University Press, 2004) and the collection *Cultures of Commerce: Representation and American Business Culture, 1877–1960* (edited with Elspeth Brown and Catherine Gudis; Palgrave Macmillan, 2006).

Tom O'Dell is Professor in the Department of Service Management, Lund University, Campus Helsingborg. He is the author of *Culture Unbound: Americanization and Everyday Life in Sweden* (Nordic Academic Press, 1997) and has also edited several volumes on tourism and the experience economy, including *Upplevelsens materialitet* (Studentlitteratur, 2002) and *Experiencescapes: Tourism, Culture, and Economy* (with Peter Billing; Copenhagen Business School Press, 2004).

Ted Schatzki is Professor of Philosophy and Dean of Faculty in the College of Arts and Sciences at the University of Kentucky. He has written much on social philosophy and the theory of human activity and is author of *Social Practices* (Cambridge University Press, 1996), *The Site of the Social* (Penn State Press, 2002), and *Martin Heidegger: Theorist of Space* (Steiner Verlag, 2007).

Elizabeth Shove is Professor of Sociology at Lancaster University. Recent publications include *The Design of Everyday Life* (with Matt Watson, Martin Hand and Jack Ingram; Berg, 2007), *Infrastructures of Consumption* (with Bas Van Vliet and Heather Chappells; Earthscan, 2005) and *Comfort, Cleanliness and Convenience* (Berg, 2003).

Don Slater is Reader in Sociology at the London School of Economics. His research interests include new media and development; markets and consumer culture; and visual sociology. Publications include *Consumer Culture and Modernity* (Polity, 1997), *The Internet: An Ethnographic Approach* (with Daniel Miller; Berg 2000) and *The Technological Economy* (with Andrew Barry; Routledge, 2005).

Dale Southerton is a Lecturer in Sociology at the University of Manchester. Recent publications include *Sustainable Consumption: The Implications of Changing Infrastructures of Provision* (co-edited with Heather Chappells and Bas Van Vliet; Edward Elgar, 2004) and 'Analysing the Temporal Organization of Daily Life: Social Constraints, Practices and their Allocation', in *Sociology* (2006).

Frank Trentmann is Professor of History at Birkbeck College, University of London. His recent publications include *Free Trade Nation: Commerce, Consumption and Civil Society in Modern Britain* (Oxford University Press, 2008), *Consuming Cultures, Global Perspectives* (edited with John Brewer; Berg, 2006) and *Citizenship and Consumption* (edited with Kate Soper; Palgrave, 2007).

Richard Wilk is Professor of Anthropology and Gender Studies at Indiana University. He has done research in the rainforest of Belize, in West African markets and in the wilds of suburban California. His most recent books are *Home Cooking in the Global Village* (Berg, 2006) and the edited *Fast Food/Slow Food* (AltaMira, 2006).

Acknowledgements

This volume is the product of an evolving series of creative experiments as well as more conventional preparations to capture the dynamics of time. Time has multiple rhythms, and there is no reason, beyond the routinized imperatives of academic culture, to believe that scholarship might not also be advanced by occasionally switching the rhythms of academic protocol. A first exploratory meeting was hosted at Birkbeck College, London, in the winter of 2005, where many ideas, approaches and methods were first aired, with the generous help of games, hands-on-exercises and good talk. In spring 2007, a group of scholars came back together to discuss illustrative cases in Florence at the European University Institute. We should like to thank all participants and researchers who contributed their thoughts to these meetings and kept our momentum going. That we were able to make maximum use of everyone's time was in no small part thanks to the administrative assistance offered by Stefanie Nixon in London and Sergio Amadei in Florence, where Professor Heinz-Gerhard Haupt kindly acted as our local host. The Cultures of Consumption research programme (ESRC–AHRC) generously offered help with travel and expenses to explore this neglected dimension of everyday consumption. We should also like to thank Sheena Ketchum for her help in preparing the final manuscript.

Introduction

Elizabeth Shove, Frank Trentmann and *Richard Wilk*

> I think mankind is more than waist-deep in daily routine. Countless inherited acts,
> accumulated pell-mell and repeated time after time to this very day, become habits
> that help us live, imprison us, and make decisions for us throughout our lives.
>
> Braudel 1979: 7

Time, Consumption and Everyday Life

'Time' has become a central topic of debate in the academy, just as it has in public
life. Experiences of time poverty and hurriedness, burnout and stress are staples of
popular discussion, media hype and political concern. Some commentators have
even go so far as to diagnose 'the arrival of time politics' (Mulgan 2005; Virilio 2006
[1977]). The scope of the debate is considerable, stretching from alarmist critiques
to more positive evaluations which revel in the busyness and fast pace of city life.
On one end are critics of hyper-consumerism, denouncing a 'too much, too fast'
life-style. Social movements are trying to slow down the speed of life, campaigning
for a new 'simplicity', for slow food, slow cities, slow conferences, even slow sex
(Christensen 2007; Elgin 1993; Honoré 2004; Parkins and Craig 2006). In this view,
material civilization in affluent, wealth-orientated consumer societies has been
spinning out of control, and the pace of life is becoming too fast for personal well-
being and environmental sustainability (Aldrich 2005; Schor 1999). On the other
end stands a view that sees busyness as a sign of full and active participation in
society, based on an historical analysis which shows people working less and having
much more leisure than ever before (Easterlin 2001).

   This book responds to these divergent positions and ambivalent perceptions,
seeing them as an entry into important unresolved issues about the direction of
global change and the texture of consumer culture. The authors of these chapters
undercut and challenge the easy dichotomies which link time to crisis or utopian
movements by looking in more detail into the complex temporal organization of
everyday life. Fast and slow turn out to be inadequate ways to describe past, present
and future (Mintz 2006).

   One reason for the cacophony of voices and feelings about the pace of life is
that time itself is a complex subject that touches on everyday experience in many

different ways. Time is about coordination and rhythm, but it also involves material, emotional, moral and political dimensions. Time is punctuated by extraordinary events like birth and death, but it is also organized through a range of ordinary routines, like sleeping, eating or watching the evening news. Though the passage of time is an experience shared by all, it has never been the exclusive property or singular focus of any one discipline in the humanities or social sciences. Writing on the topic is scattered across history, anthropology, philosophy, geography and sociology, as well as physics, literature and theology. Few scholars focus their entire career on the study of time and temporality in social life; it is usually a topic secondary to something else.

Eviatar Zerubavel's pioneering work shows how temporal cycles – the night shift, the academic year, the internship – overlap, as well as the way these periodic and episodic cycles order and are organized by practices of nursing, educating, getting better and falling ill (Zerubavel 1979, 1981, 1985). Norbert Elias (1969 [1939]) offered a longer term perspective – following 'civilizing' forms of ordering time and showing how they take hold at a societal level: permitting otherwise impossible forms of work, communication and traffic coordination, interchange and exchange. James Carey's work is especially important in showing how the regulation, synchronization and standardization of time was an essential tool used by the state and corporate capitalism to extend their material and cultural control over national landscapes and daily life (1989). For E.P. Thompson (1967) and Tamara Hareven (1982), a more general control of temporality was used by the modern state and industry to regulate the lives of citizens. Controlling the pace of time was the foundation of the Fordist revolution and later movements towards scientific 'efficiency' in Taylorism (Kanigel 1999).

In geography, Allen Pred has sought to conceptualize the relation between individual life courses (paths) as characterized and punctuated by collective goals (projects). When applied in a working environment, this analysis helps to show how the temporalities of personal career development and the typically longer term persistence and transformation of institutional and organizational forms overlap, intersect and constitute each other. Using a geological metaphor, recent historians have tried to reveal the shifting layers of time that became sedimented in the formations of modern history (Koselleck 2000; cf. Corfield 2007).

Anthropologists like Alfred Gell (1992) have further questioned the universality of the perception of time, trying to go beyond simple dichotomies of east and west, or modern and primitive, to reveal and number different dimensions of time perception and classification. Other anthropologists like Johannes Fabian (1983) argue that time is the basis for all academic depictions of cultural difference, turning 'the other' into 'the primitive', as in Conrad's *Heart of Darkness*, where the journey upstream becomes a chronological unravelling into the depths of time (also Wilk 1994).

Instead of integrating these different dimensions and approaches, each academic tradition has cut its own path using its own tools. While drawing on these diverse theoretical resources, the studies in this book build a raft of common ground through their continuing focus on empirical studies of daily life. They bridge disciplinary boundaries by drawing inspiration from multiple sources: from the fields of material culture and consumption, from science and technology studies, and from social theories of practice. Rather than viewing time in terms of minutes, hours or years and instead of treating it as a resource that can be stored, released and used up like a rechargeable battery, the contributions to this book emphasize the creative production, reproduction and consumption of *multiple* temporalities. In this book, the study of time becomes a way to transcend disciplines and methodological traditions.

Challenges

In taking this approach the chapters collected here challenge familiar formulations of the time 'problem', including those that place the blame on consumer society, on spiralling 'consumerist' pressures to work and spend (Offer 2006; Schor 2000), on individualization, and on the irresistible pull of material culture or 'luxury fever' (Frank 1999). They also take issue with interpretations in which infrastructures and artefacts script the duration and timing of events, episodes and long-term projects. They do so in three related ways.

1. Multiple Temporalities

Following Gell (1992), contributors to this volume question the implicit historical direction of time from ordered tradition to anarchic modernity, an assumption that rests on romantic but unfounded notions of timeless tradition. Many commentators who are worried about 'time poverty' presume an historic shift from a more balanced and healthier 'traditional' era to a more frantic 'modern' regime. Peasants were hardworking but jolly, following steady seasonal rhythms with bursts of collective festivities and pleasures; workers then were disciplined and regimented by industrial time (Thompson 1967; cf. Glennie and Thrift 2009); most recently, consumers are struggling to coordinate and multi-task an ever-expanding set of practices and choices driven by the material temptations on offer in a 24-hour society.

Rather than taking this thesis as a fact, we treat it with a scepticism informed by comparative ethnography and historical analysis. Instead of assuming a sequential shift from one temporal order to another, contributors to this volume reveal the coexistence of multiple periodicities, and by implication a lack of coordination between scales and registers of temporal order. Natural and commercial rhythms have co-evolved and often complemented each other in the modern period. Routine and rhythm, we show, are often interdependent, not rivals. Recognition of the parallel, symbiotic nature of different temporal orders creates an intellectual space for exploring the emotional and political ambivalence of temporal constraint and freedom. Having made this space, we can then ask why so many cultures perceive order in the past and disorder in the present, why routines can sometimes represent freedom, and at other times bondage and restraint.

In moving into this territory, several contributors argue that at any one point in time, societies are composed of a combination of overlapping rhythms. Instead of characterizing wholesale shifts from one temporal regime to another (e.g. from a traditional, habit-ridden mode to a modern society of endless flexibility), they notice that affluent countries continue to differ in their daily rhythms, their scale, flow and compositions. The French continue to indulge in long meals and Mexicans take their siestas, while Americans snack quickly and on the move. Italian children stay up late into the evening, whereas their German neighbours go to bed early. Eating, sleeping, working and many other daily practices follow significantly different rhythms, which cannot be ordered according to a scale of development or modernity. The diversity in the ordering, sequencing and frequency of everyday practices cannot be reduced to differences in class, culture, urbanism, economic organization or evolutionary stages. Rather than supposing some dramatic divide between consumer society and an earlier phase in which life was less complicated, more relaxed or more structured, the common challenge is to detail multiple scales – short-term cycles, seasonal patterns and processes that unfold over generations as well as weeks and days – and to describe episodes and experiences of chaos and frenzy alongside those of predictability and routine.

2. Making time

Popular and academic accounts routinely assume that experiences of time – and especially those of being hurried and harried – are shaped by external 'forces'. In so doing they overlook the extent to which temporalities are themselves continually reproduced, enacted and transformed through the sequencing and timing of daily practice. This is an important shift in perspective in that it suggests that consumption – the arch-villain in critiques of hurriedness – contributes to the *making* of time, and is not simply a drain, a sink which takes time away from living. Or, to put it more precisely, consumption, broadly defined as a bundle of various practices and the use of things, constitutes an arena in which daily life is woven together, often imperfectly, and sometimes with tears and breaks, but always in ways that configure and reproduce its temporal texture. In elaborating on this insight, the chapters collected here clear the way for further analysis of the temporal and spatial profiles of what people do and how these intersect to produce what Henri Lefebvre (2002 [1961]) referred to as the 'pulse' of society.

We are not the first to notice that temporal rhythms are actively reproduced in daily life. Lefebvre's *Rhythmanalysis*, originally published in 1992, completed a life-long exploration of everyday life that had started in the 1940s, which took him from an analysis of daily practices to their spatial and, eventually, their temporal dimensions (Lefebvre 1991, 2002 [1961], 2004). For Lefebvre, rhythms operated along several axes: they could be 'secret' (physiological rhythms; the said and the non-said) or 'public' (ceremonies, calendars); they could be 'fictional' (verbal rhythms, dreaming); and they could be 'dominating–dominated' (made up, with an effect beyond the rhythms itself). But he was especially interested in what made a rhythm tick as regulated time, its repetitions, its evolution and its more cyclical or more linear movement. In attempting to dissect the dimensions of rhythmic movement Lefebvre characterizes coexisting pulses and comments on how these modulate and amplify each other to produce a powerful temporal 'texture'. These textures are depicted as forms laid down, if not imposed, by social agencies and acted out by a populace unwittingly caught up in this enfolding mesh. The city, in particular, was singled out for disciplining its inhabitants into a rhythmic flow of walking and living (see also Moran 2007). There are similarities between Lefebvre's account of ordering rhythmic regimes and that of Michel de Certeau, who also emphasizes the realm of the everyday as a central site of social reproduction (Certeau 1984 [1974]). One key difference is that Certeau takes this to be a terrain of potential and actual resistance and subversion, rather than the arena of more passive compliance depicted by Lefebvre.

Most contributors to this book share an emphasis on the 'everyday', but rather than viewing temporalities as *outcomes* of ongoing tensions between relatively 'heroic' individuals and oppressive systems, they seek to understand the many processes and practices involved in reproducing regimes and routines. Examples range from commuting to hobbies. In addition, we look at discontinuous challenges to rhythmic processes, as in periods of turmoil, stress and disruption. Building on but also going beyond Lefebvre and Certeau, the common challenge is one of understanding how temporalities of practice are produced, altered and disrupted and with what political, emotional and ethical implications.

3. Materializing time

Many, perhaps even the majority, of the processes and practices implicated in making time – in the sense of giving it meaning, order and personal as well as collective qualities and characteristics – involve the use of things. Time is rich in material culture, and vice versa. We have already noted that rather than seeing consumption as a force that sucks time out of our lives, many practices and hence many interactions with material culture create temporal order (a topic only recently taken up by archaeologists like Murray [1999]). But the materiality of time goes further than this. Things age, and we and our memories and identities age with them. Objects can be signs of enduring or momentary experience (an heirloom that signifies family time; a present that triggers feelings of 'growing up' or 'childhood'). Objects play a critical role as a kind of compass or clock across our lifecourse. But they also have temporal orientations associated with them, such as an appeal to novelty, different careers of obsolescence and recycling, and the various kinds of wear and patina which signify age and interactions with people (McCracken 1988).

How, and how much, time is in an object raises sensitive questions of value and authenticity, as any participant or observer of antique shows knows. At the same time, 'age' and 'ageing' is not simply a natural process that can be dated with the help of a calendar or mark of origin. Commercial consumer culture plays an active role in creating new regimes of temporal value, as is evident in the market for vintage reproductions. Rather than seeing material objects as a distracting presence that injects stress and temporal frenzy into our lives, then, it is helpful to see them also as communicators and stabilizing devices which people employ to attain, reproduce and challenge temporal identities.

Themes and Methods

Inspired by these overarching challenges, contributors to this book provide ideas, resources and empirical research that help in understanding (a) how multiple temporalities co-evolve and intersect and (b) how patterns of time and space are reproduced in daily life, and (c) how material culture acts as a conduit in the production and consumption of time. This three-pronged approach allows us to capture and comment anew on how time is experienced, and on the emotions, politics and infrastructures of ordering and routine. There are a number of wa·ys we could organize the chapters in the volume, for they connect with one another along many dimensions; the next section describes some of the most important intersections.

Seasonal Cycles

As noted above, critiques of consumer society routinely presume a paradigmatic shift from natural, seasonal cycles to a commodified 'unseasoned' and more feverish rhythm. Marina Moskowitz's discussion of the seed trade in the USA complicates and in effect confounds a sharp distinction between natural and commercial seasons. She demonstrates that these two rhythms interacted and evolved in tandem in the course of the nineteenth century. Seed catalogues were published in January so that plants could bloom later in the year, a strategy in which seasonality was commercialized rather than exterminated.

Inge Daniels' chapter on the way that changing seasons are made and marked in contemporary Japanese homes provides further illustration of how material culture is enmeshed in an annual cycle of consumption. Mikko Jalas offers a case study of people renovating wooden boats, a pastime that attracts devoted followers in Scandinavian countries. Here natural processes like the rotting and decaying of timber intersect with the many social, cultural and material temporalities folded together in the practice of repairing and maintaining a wooden boat. The attraction of wooden boating arguably rests on its evocation of another time which was slower and based on the rhythms of seasons and hand labour, but the possession of an actual wooden boat drags the owner into deep time commitments and obligations which are far from the imagined leisure. Although the point is made in very different ways, these three chapters force readers to acknowledge specific *relations* between coexisting seasons and cycles of consumption and practice.

Circuits of Commodification

The question of how commercial circuits are made and materialized is taken up by Jukka Gronow, who deals directly with the unending reproduction of 'fashion'. Does fashion really produce 'novelty'? Gronow is sceptical. In distinguishing between cycles that really do go round in circles and forms of innovation that represent another kind of spiralling movement, Gronow points to a raft of neglected questions about novelty and the simultaneous production and destruction of value in material culture. These questions are explored further in Daniel Miller's discussion of how the 'past' is embodied and commodified in things that people buy and use. In moving between an analysis of 'distressed' jeans and antiques Miller shows how contrasting temporalities worm their way through consumer culture and how products serve to reproduce as well as to mark the passage of time. The lives of objects and the lives of people intersect, but it is never possible to say one is simply driving the other.

Temporal Processes

Another strand running right through this volume concerns the processes of making and using time. What looks like a temporal order from a distance is exposed here as an illusion of scale; as we move closer to the object we see complex patterns and shifts in the micro-organization of routine and habit. The relation between social practice and 'timespace' is addressed from different angles in several chapters. Ted Schatzki's contribution sets out a range of fundamental issues about the status of 'timespace' as a concept useful in understanding the dynamics of order and coordination. Elizabeth Shove experiments with similar ideas, wondering about how we might capture and characterize the extent and scale of synchronization, the rate at which practices evolve, and the spatial and temporal range of contemporary routines. In his chapter, Dale Southerton takes up some of these challenges using historical data to show how the rhythmic order of temporal coordination shifted in the course of the twentieth century. In comparing the ordering of domestic life in 1937 and 2000, he seeks to identify long-term change whilst also showing how routines hang together at different points in time.

How do moments and episodes of practice combine to form new configurations, and how do these combinations play out in the longer run? In addressing this question, chapters by Billy Ehn and Orvar Löfgren and by Tom O'Dell elaborate on a series of middle-range concepts like those of routine, career and generation. The daily rhythm of commuting exists before and persists beyond the 'career' of any single commuter – at the same time, that regular flow of people from home to work and back is felt in the precise timing of the bike ride to the station and in the seconds saved and spent along the way. These contributions provide us with insights into how micro-social temporalities, including the detailed scheduling of the day, play out across years, over decades and between generations.

Routine and Rupture

While much of the existing literature and some of the chapters included in this book concentrate on regularities of habit, ordering only makes sense in relation to processes or threats of disruption and fracture. Frank Trentmann consequently writes about daily life as a process in which permanently fragile orders are ruptured and restored – an approach that positions routine and habit as an outcome not of casual dis-attention but of concerted repair work. As he explains, greater material and technological interdependence has arguably increased the risk of breakdowns in everyday life, and our sensibility towards them. Ironically, the consequences of failure increase the more we rely upon systems and infrastructures designed to sustain the safe and secure flow of materials, resources and people.

In highlighting intriguing paradoxes in which security begets risk and in which routine and rupture are never far apart, Trentmann's contribution disturbs and disrupts conventional representations of time in which the mindless grind of habit is set against the energizing thrill of spontaneity. As Don Slater's chapter shows, we do not come to routines fresh. Routines are positioned, disclosed and evaluated within established ethical frameworks. Many traditions in the West, especially in the line stretching from Marx to the Frankfurt School, have presented routines as structural, non-reflexive processes that alienate individuals from their authentic, true self. Slater's comparison between the negative evaluation of hobbies in this tradition with quite different framings of meditation and technological routines in other contexts brings to light the considerable ideological and moral work that goes into how and what people see as routines.

Richard Wilk's essay extends this critique to the level of personal mind and action, showing that the extent to which regularity figures as comfort or constraint is in part a matter of subjective experience and perception. That 'choice' is rarely completely free or sovereign has been a mantra of much recent research. Similarly, we need to recognize that habits are not automatically a tool of disciplinary restraint. They can have liberating features too. It is probably unwise, Wilk argues, to look for different accounts of habitual and spontaneous action or to treat these as somehow separate domains, one marked by discipline the other by liberation, as has been common in much of the human sciences. In part, these chapters can be read as exercises in retrieval, pointing back to more organic treatments of habit and choice which recognized their creative interdependence, most notably exemplified in the works of the pragmatist philosophers William James (1890) and John Dewey (1922).

Space and Time

Studies of time tend to lose sight of the fact that rhythms and routines have spatial qualities and characteristics. In their contribution Güliz Ger and Olga Kravets describes the teabag's arrival in Turkey and the havoc it wrought in relation to established distinctions between slow and fast consumption. The teabag speeded up what had been a reliably time-consuming ritual, creating new and different associations between tea and time. It disrupted the daily gatherings, events and spatial movements of people which had been based on the samovar and the continual availability of tea in a particular spot. Other spatial temporalities crop up across this volume, for example in the circulation of seed catalogues across the USA; in efforts to synchronize social and spatial coordinates in rush hours and commuting; and in discussions of where as well as when practices are enacted. In this collection, Ted Schatzki addresses the integration of timespace head on, demonstrating how these dimensions of social life constitute each other. In his words, 'timespaces form a kind of infrastructure through which human activities coordinate and aggregate' – an infrastructure that is itself made by the activities in question.

Implications

A greater focus on multiple rhythms and on the processes of producing time is a promising way to start unravelling the complexity of social difference in space and time. This is particularly relevant for those pondering how to promote life-style change and more sustainable behaviour, but it concerns all agencies seeking to change the temporal order of everyday life, from education and transportation to working and shopping routines. Most discussions of time poverty and stress have been future-orientated: are we *becoming* a rat-race society? Is our behaviour making life unsustainable? While raising sensitive, thorny questions that deserve debate, these lines of inquiry are of limited value in helping us think about the future, since they have – as we have shown – a restricted and typically unsatis-factory understanding of the evolving rhythms underlying social practices, past and present.

The first implication from the studies assembled in this volume is that analysing rhythms and temporal change requires elements from a range of disciplines, including history, geography and social theory as well as sociology, philosophy and anthropology. Likewise, relevant questions range from the spatial dimensions to the politics and ethics of habit and disruption.

In producing this volume, we readily acknowledge that it has sometimes been easier to document than to explain shifts in cycles and temporal orders. Although they do not provide all the answers, the inquiries assembled here provide a starting point and suggest a number of paths towards a new synthesis. One such route involves closer interaction with theories of practice. In recent years, the theory of practice has attracted growing interest in the social sciences (Schatzki 2001; Shove and Pantzar 2005; Warde 2005; Warde et al. 2007). To date, empirical studies have tended to follow the development of individual practices over time. As discussed in several chapters, rhythms are usefully understood as bundles of everyday practices, or, to be precise, they are achievements of coordinating and stabilizing relationships between practices. A shift in one practice, say having a quick daily shower instead of a longer but only weekly bath, will impinge on this bundle. Understanding the rhythmic richness and modulations of everyday life therefore requires a move from single practices to a focus on their interactive dynamics and coordination. This raises questions about how practices with different rhythmic properties can amplify, enable or cancel out each other. In combination, these observations call for further research on the spectrum of rhythmic performance in everyday life, ranging from successful synchronization to tension and disruption.

A second implication for research arises from the recognition of rupture and stress as integral features of 'normality' as well as routine (see Löfgren and Wilk 2006). Everyday life, in this view, appears as a more open, fluid terrain that, to reproduce itself, requires and involves a lot of fixing, frustration and coping. This, perhaps, does not produce the picture of heroic resistance as envisaged by Certeau, but it does emphasize the role of agency and mentality, putting back into the frame individuals and their ways of coping with strain. Habits and routines, in this view, appear less as external forces that become absorbed through techniques of governmentality, as some Foucauldians would have it, and much more as the result of an interplay between internally produced rhythms, the strains resulting from coordination between practices themselves, and associated pressures and opportunities for temporal change arising from technologies and social agencies. If disruptions are unique moments that allow us to see the braiding and unbraiding of rhythmic achievements at times of stress, it is worth debating the merits of deliberate disruption as a kind of research strategy.

Time has the curious quality of being both a completely mundane everyday experience and a complete abstraction which cannot be easily or objectively described or explained. The overall goal of this book is to bring these two qualities of time closer together, to help us bridge the gap between common experience and high theory in a way which is productive of new insights. No single discipline, science or philosophy can achieve this connection on its own. The three editors of this collection, who come from history, sociology and anthropology, and all the diverse authors have worked together to construct a shared set of terms and concepts which establish a transdisciplinary (or supra-disciplinary) space where new ideas flourish. For all the participants, this has been perhaps the most valuable reward of the common project.

References

Aldrich, T., ed. (2005). *About Time: Speed, Society, People and the Environment*. Sheffield: Greenleaf.

Braudel, F. (1979). *Afterthoughts on Material Civilization and Capitalism*. Baltimore, MD: Johns Hopkins University Press.

Carey, J. (1989). *Communication as Culture: Essays on Media and Society*. Boston: Unwin Hyman.

Certeau, M. de (1984) [1974]. *The Practice of Everyday Life*. Berkeley: University of California Press.

Christensen, I. (2007). Green Conferences: Practice Guide #19. Louisville, KY: EPA Region 4 Center for Environmental Policy and Management.

Corfield, P.J. (2007). *Time and the Shape of History*. New Haven, CT: Yale University Press,

Dewey, J. (1922). *Human Nature and Conduct: An Introduction to Social Psychology*. New York: Henry Holt and Company.

Easterlin, R.A. (2001). Income and Happiness: Towards a Unified Theory. *The Economic Journal* 111: 465–484.

Elias, N. (1969) [1939]. *The Civilizing Process, Vol. I. The History of Manners*. Oxford: Blackwell.

Elgin, D. (1993). Voluntary Simplicity and the New Global Challenge. In *Voluntary Simplicity: Toward a Way of Life that is Outwardly Simple, Inwardly Rich*, ed. D. Elgin. New York: William Morrow & Co.

Fabian, J. (1983). *Time and the Other*. New York: Columbia University Press.

Frank, R.H. (1999). *Luxury Fever: Money and Happiness in an Era of Excess*. Princeton, NJ: Princeton University Press.

Gell, A. (1992). *The Anthropology of Time*. Oxford: Berg.

Glennie, P. and Thrift, N. (2009). *Shaping the Day: A History of Timekeeping in England and Wales 1300–1800*. Oxford: Oxford University Press.

Hareven, T. (1982). *Family Time and Industrial Time*. Cambridge: Cambridge University Press.

Honoré, C. (2004). *In Praise of Slowness: Challenging the Cult of Speed*. New York: Harper Collins.

James, W. (1890). *The Principles of Psychology, 2 Vols*. New York: Henry Holt and Company.

Kanigel, R. (1999). *The One Best Way: Frederick Winslow Taylor and the Enigma of Efficiency*. Harmondsworth: Penguin.

Koselleck, R. (2000). *Zeitschichten*. Frankfurt: Suhrkamp.

Lefebvre, H. (1991). *The Production of Space*. Oxford: Blackwell.

Lefebvre, H. (2002) [1961]. *Critique of Everyday Life: Foundations for a Sociology of the Everyday, Vol. II*. London: Verso.

Lefebvre, H. (2004). *Rhythmanalysis: Space, Time and Everyday Life*. London: Continuum.

Löfgren, O. and Wilk, R., eds (2006). *Off the Edge: Experiments in Cultural Analysis*. Copenhagen: Museum Tusculanum Press.

McCracken, G. (1988). *Culture and Consumption*. Bloomington: Indiana University Press.

Mintz, S. (2006). Food at Moderate Pace. In *Fast Food/ Slow Food: The Cultural Economy of the Global Food System*, ed. R. Wilk. Walnut Creek, CA: AltaMira.

Moran, J. (2007). *Queuing for Beginners: The Story of Daily Life from Breakfast to Bedtime*. London: Profile.

Mulgan, G. (2005). The Arrival of Time Politics. In *About Time: Speed, Society, People and the Environment*, ed. T. Aldrich. Sheffield: Greenleaf.

Murray, T. (1999). *Time and Archaeology*. London: Routledge.

Offer, A. (2006). *The Challenge of Affluence: Self-control and Well-being in the United States and Britain since 1950*. Oxford: Oxford University Press.

Parkins, W. and Craig, G. (2006). *Slow Living*. Oxford and New York: Berg.

Pred, A. (1981). Social Reproduction and the Time-geography of Everyday Life. *Geografiska Annaler* 63 B: 5–22.

Schatzki, T.R. (2001). Introduction: Practice Theory. In *The Practice Turn in Contemporary Theory*, eds T.R. Schatzki, K. Knorr-Cetina and E. von Savigny. London: Routledge.

Schor, J. (1999). *The Overspent American: Why We Want What We Don't Need*. New York: HarperPerennial.

Schor, J., ed. (2000). *Do Americans Shop Too Much? A New Democracy Forum*. Boston: Beacon.

Shove, E. and Pantzar, M. (2005). Consumers, Producers and Practices: Understanding the Invention and Reinvention of Nordic Walking. *Journal of Consumer Culture* 5(1): 43–64.

Thompson, E.P. (1967). Time, Work-Discipline, and Industrial Capitalism. *Past and Present* 38: 56–68.

Virilio, P. (2006) [1977]. *Speed and Politics: A History of the Present*. Los Angeles: Semiotext(e).

Warde, A. (2005). Consumption and Theories of Practice. *Journal of Consumer Culture* 5(2): 131–153.

Warde, A., Southerton, D., Cheng, S.-L. and Olsen, W. (2007). Changes in the Practice of Eating: A Comparative Analysis of Time-Use. *Acta Sociologica* 50(4): 363–385.

Wilk, R. (1994). Colonial Time and TV Time. *Visual Anthropology Review* 10(1): 94–102.

Zerubavel, E. (1979). *Patterns of Time in Hospital Life*. Chicago: University of Chicago Press.

Zerubavel, E. (1981). *Hidden Rhythms: Schedules and Calendars in Social Life*. Chicago: University of Chicago Press.

Zerubavel, E. (1985). *The Seven Day Circle: The History and Meaning of the Week*. Chicago and London: University of Chicago Press.

Section I
Time, Space and Practice

–1–

Everyday Practice and the Production and Consumption of Time
Elizabeth Shove

Everybody's in so much of a rush nowadays, now everybody's trying to make money, trying to get to places, they've got to get here, they've got to get there, they've got to do their shopping – this, that and the other, I think there's a lot more pressure, you haven't got the time to do as much as what you want in a day nowadays.

Hedges 2001, part 4: 14

a sense of social time is made and re-made according to social practices.

May and Thrift 2001: 5

Introduction

In this chapter the simple observation that things like sleeping, eating, working and playing all take time provides the starting point for a progressively more complicated discussion of how the micro and macro temporalities of daily life might be represented and conceptualized. In what follows I consider two broad approaches. The first relatively familiar view is that time is a scarce resource which practices consume. The second is that 'it is the rhythm of social life which is at the basis of the category of time' (Durkheim 1976: 440). In other words, temporal arrangements arise from the effective reproduction of everyday life, or, to put it more strongly, practices *make* time.

I suggest that these two orientations, one emphasizing the consumption, the other the production of time, justify and are sustained by different lines of inquiry and methods of research. In reviewing these approaches my aim is to identify promising but as yet under-developed ways of analysing the interweaving of personal and collective logistics. Rather than studying the temporal 'properties' of a single practice, or the life and times of a single practitioner, my aim is to explore the temporal implications of contemporary complexes of social practice. In the process, new questions arise: for example, what does the appropriate or competent reproduction of everyday practice (i.e. the sets of practices that make up everyday life) demand in terms of minutes, timing, sequence, coordination and career? How do temporal profiles of this kind emerge? How do they fit together and with what consequence now and for the future? In the last part of the chapter I speculate about how the practice-time characteristics of society might be described and represented. While there are points of connection between Lefebvre's work on 'rhythmanalysis' (Lefebvre 2004: 73–74) and the project of capturing the temporal qualities of always-changing, always-intersecting practices, this chapter plays down ready-made distinctions between natural/cyclical and social/linear time and concentrates instead on patterns of temporality as they emerge from the dynamic coordination of complex systems of practice.

The argument developed here builds upon an understanding of practice as a 'type of behaving and understanding that appears at different locales and at different points of time and is carried out by different body/minds' (Reckwitz 2002: 250). As Schatzki puts it, a practice is 'a temporally unfolding and spatially dispersed nexus of doings and sayings' (1996: 89). In this sense, practices exist as provisional but recognizable entities composed of also recognizable conventions, images and meanings; materials and forms of competence. At the same time, if they are to exist at all, practices require active reproduction and performance. In other words, people have to do them. More than that, it is through these doings that the contours of individual practices are defined, reproduced and constituted. Since people engage in many practices (during a day, a year or a lifetime), any discussion of the temporal texture of daily life has to take account of how practices intersect in time and in space. There are various ways in which one might approach this topic.

First, and as indicated above, many would agree that uses of time (as well as of energy, water, money, material goods and environmental resources) represent the detectable remains or traces of practice. By following these variously visible trails one can learn, in aggregate and occasionally in detail, about who does what, and about when and how this varies. Although good for retrospectively revealing trends and patterns, exercises of this kind are of limited value in understanding exactly how some practices emerge and others disappear. Since people have to make or find time in which to do – i.e. to perform – practices, it is reasonable to suppose that if new practices are to take hold, time has to be made for them at the expense of others which are no longer performed, or not performed as frequently as before. This reasoning points to a zero-sum model of daily life in which practices compete with each other for necessary temporal, as well as material and cognitive, resources. From this point of view, time-use data also tell us something about the relative successes of rival practices.

Ironically, those who follow the temporal traces of practice are obliged to gloss over the fragile nature of the always provisional entities they track and play down the endless processes of recruitment and learning that are inevitably involved. By contrast, those who concentrate on the details of doing make much of the point that experiences accumulate and identities evolve in ways that are collectively important not only for the careers and trajectories of the individuals involved, but also for the practices they carry and of which they are a part (Becker 1963; Jalas 2006). For example, Sudnow's (1978) study of becoming a jazz pianist demonstrates that as the novice's career develops, new possibilities and performances come within his or her reach. At the same time, the enterprise of jazz piano playing – the detail of what it involves and what there is to learn – depends upon and is defined and collectively reproduced by the variously experienced cohorts of those who do it. This work suggests that time-critical concepts like those of an unfolding career are made by dynamic, mutually constitutive relations between practice and practitioner.

Another feature, also revealed by close inspection of what practitioners do, is that *timing* frequently constitutes an aspect of competence and procedure integral to the effective accomplishment of practices like those of phoning, eating and sleeping. To have a three-course 'dinner' at 7 a.m. or to start with the sweet and end with soup is to challenge conventional procedures of formal dining. More pragmatically, sequences like those of first preparing and then cooking vegetables are difficult to circumvent. In other words, doing dinner is not just a process that takes time, it is also a process that is internally differentiated, structured and sequenced in ways that are part of and that are reproduced through the practice itself.

The mutually constitutive relation between time and practice is even more evident with respect to the doing of things that require or that are better done in the company of others. For example, eating together involves an allocation of minutes, the nifty sequencing of chopping and boiling *and* the momentary conjunction of individual paths in time and space. More telling still, recognizable infrastructures of objective time – the day, the week, the morning routine, the annual holiday – are made so because they are *made by* distinctive kinds of practice. The week-end *is* the week-end precisely because we do things on Saturdays and Sundays that we don't do on Mondays and Tuesdays.

In combination, these introductory comments hint at new questions and lines of inquiry strung between the study of time and practice. For example, should we interpret experiences of rushing around as the result not of a time squeeze but of practice compression, and if so, how might we identify and describe the processes involved? More abstractly, is it possible to characterize or compare the temporal and spatial qualities of the complex and often interlocking systems of practice that constitute society? I come back to these questions in the last part of the chapter, but begin by elaborating on the theoretical and methodological implications of thinking about practices as consumers of resources like time, energy and water.

Practices as Consumers: Of Time and Other Resources

The proposition that much consumption, not only of time but also of money and other material and natural resources, is occasioned by people's involvement in relationships, activities and taken-for-granted routines makes a lot of sense (Warde 2005). Whether we like it or not, much of what we do, individually and collectively, leaves behind a trail of variously sticky footprints.[1] Some of these indicators are more directly revealing than others. For example, records of the timing and duration of telephone calls provide a relatively clear picture of how phoning is located in the daily and weekly schedule. In Finland, telephone conversations tend to be longer in the countryside than in the city; winter Mondays are peak times for calling and the fewest calls are made on summer Sundays. By comparison, data from the UK Electricity Association's load research group imply that (averaged over the year) people are engaged in practices that require different forms of illumination at the week-end as compared with the week. In terms of energy consumption, this supports the rather diffuse conclusion that demand is an outcome of 'interplay between the activity of the occupants and the availability of daylight' (Stokes et al. 2006: 3). Getting up later seems to be part of the story, but because illumination is a prerequisite for doing so many different things, it is hard to glean much about the details of daily life from data showing when artificial light is being used.

Micro-metering of every tap and water outlet in the home (undertaken as part of the Anglian Golden 100 Survey) produces data showing how water-consuming habits vary over the year and how – and to what extent – household routines differ. For example, Figure 1.1 represents the water used in a two-person household known as T10149. The lines on the graph show that members of T10149 have both baths and showers, they make much use of the kitchen sink and their outdoor water consumption peaks in August. We don't know exactly what the outside tap

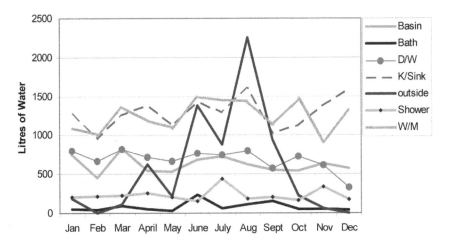

Figure 1.1 Water use of T10149 (a two-person household) in 2003. WC use not shown in graph. D/W = dishwasher; W/M = washing machine. *Source*: Anglian Golden 100. Thanks to Anglian Water for permission to use these data, which are based on micro-component studies of 100 households showing the use of each appliance recorded at 15-minute intervals.

is used for, how long these particular water-consuming practices take or why there is a sudden dip in July: did it rain, were the occupants on holiday? Whatever the explanation, time allocated to outside-tap-using-practices in the summer is spent doing something else in winter.

Should evidence like this exist for a large population and over a significant number of years, it would undoubtedly reveal changing habits on a massive scale. For example, the arrival of daily showering as opposed to weekly bathing would show up as traces both of time and of water consumption, with people now devoting more minutes and litres to 'personal hygiene' than before, and with these minutes now being spread more evenly across the week. Sure enough, data on each 'micro-component' of water use, gathered by Anglian Water since 1992, reveal increases in the proportions of water used for showering and a parallel decrease in bathing.

None of this is especially surprising, but these examples are useful in highlighting relevant differences between complex systems of practice and consumption in this case of energy, water and time. While the demand for energy and water increases and decreases over the year and during the day depending upon the resource intensity of what people do, this is not so of time. Strategies of multi-tasking arguably allow individuals to increase the intensity of time use and so extend the envelope of the day (a Yahoo–OMD study [2006] identified a 43-hour day made possible by multi-tasking), but a great many practices are mutually exclusive: doing them simply precludes doing something else at the same time.

It is because of this quality that data showing how the twenty-four hours of the day are on average allocated to specific activities (Figures 1.2 and 1.3) reveal interesting differences in the profile of what Finnish and French people do when, and in the homogeneity of the sample.

These graphs demonstrate that French respondents spent more time eating and that on a number of counts lunchtime is more pronounced than in Finland, a country in which food consumption is fairly evenly distributed across the day. They also illustrate the extent of collective variation, for example, in the duration of the normal working day, the spread of morning and evening rush hours and the level of societal synchronicity. I shall return to this issue of inter-personal scheduling, but for the moment it is enough to recognize that going to sleep and waking up are effectively collective processes – even for those who do them alone (Lefebvre 2004: 75).

Figures 1.2 and 1.3 are snapshots of a particular year (2000), so although they depict differences and similarities, they tell us little about how such arrangements come to be as they are. Providing it has been collected consistently over a number of years, time-use data can reveal changes in the profile of what people do. Based on a comparison of time-use studies from the Netherlands, Norway, France, UK and USA, Southerton et al. (2007) suggest that, contrary to popular opinion, reading practices are not converging, nor are rates of participation declining dramatically in the face of other competing activities. While this research gives a sense of the ebb and flow of specific ways of spending time, and hence the relative vitality of

Percent

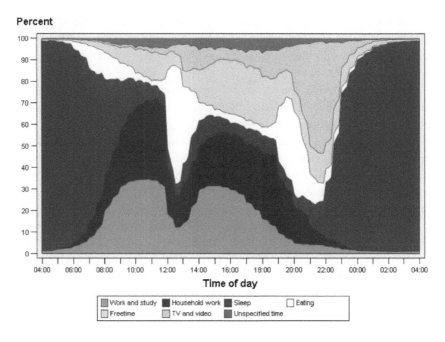

Figure 1.2 Time use, France, 2000. *Source*: Multinational Time Use Study, Version 5.5.2 (released 14 October 2005). Created by Jonathan Gershuny, Kimberly Fisher and Anne H. Gauthier, with Alyssa Borkosky, Anita Bortnik, Donna Dosman, Cara Fedick, Tyler Frederick, Sally Jones, Tingting Lu, Fiona Lui, Leslie MacRae, Berenice Monna, Monica Pauls, Cori Pawlak, Nuno Torres and Charlemaigne Victorino. ISER, University of Essex, Colchester, UK. http://www.timeuse.org/mtus/ (accessed 31 March 2009).

different practices, it does not show how discrete rivalries develop,[2] for example between print-based reading, TV viewing or reading on the internet.

If time is one amongst other resources that practices need to survive, it is important to think about how they capture and secure necessary minutes or hours of attention given the very many other things that people might do in a day. How do new practices enter the frame and how are others squeezed out or reconfigured?

Practices as Competitors: For Time and Other Resources

When focusing on relatively bounded populations, like those who enjoy winter sports, it may be possible to demonstrate the impact of new practices on those which are already established. For instance, snowboarding appears to have stolen energy and enthusiasm from people who previously concentrated on skiing (Franke and Shah 2003). More generally, it seems that the arrival of TV viewing challenged other forms of leisure. Newspaper articles reporting on a BBC daily life study conducted

Percent

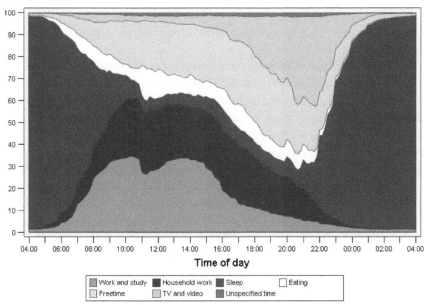

Figure 1.3 Time use, Finland, 2000. *Source*: Multinational Time Use Study, Version 5.5.2 (released 14 October 2005). Created by Jonathan Gershuny, Kimberly Fisher and Anne H. Gauthier, with Alyssa Borkosky, Anita Bortnik, Donna Dosman, Cara Fedick, Tyler Frederick, Sally Jones, Tingting Lu, Fiona Lui, Leslie MacRae, Berenice Monna, Monica Pauls, Cori Pawlak, Nuno Torres and Charlemaigne Victorino. ISER, University of Essex, Colchester, UK. http://www.timeuse.org/mtus/ (accessed 31 March 2009).

in 1952 refer to a running contest between gardening and TV watching: according to the *Daily Sketch*, 14 April 1952, 'Many people will watch television this afternoon and evening instead of going out. There will be few gardeners among them however. A BBC inquiry into the changes TV makes in family life reveals that it is seldom allowed to come between a man and his flowerbeds' (cited in Griffiths and Holden 2004). Gardening remains extremely popular in Britain today, but audience figures suggest that TV viewing has gained ground since 1952 and that flowerbeds have lost some of the prime time commitment they once commanded.

While some innovations add to the pressures of daily life (e.g. new practices have to be fitted into an already crowded schedule), others, like so-called 'labour-saving technologies', promise to release time for competing pursuits. Whether they have this effect or not (Cowan 1983; Hand and Shove 2007; Shove and Southerton 2000), the key point, at least in the context of the present discussion, is that such devices acquire value in relation to and as part of a struggle between competing practices. The nature of this struggle is coloured by the fact that concepts of effective accomplishment translate into seemingly necessary minutes of participation and powerful injunctions of timing. Although not undertaken with a discussion of time in mind, Kaufmann's (1998) study of 'Dirty Linen' points to two time-critical aspects of the practice wars of daily life, these being an understanding of appropriate performance and a related sense of compulsion.

By way of illustration, the respondents involved in Kaufmann's research discuss the feeling of being impelled to do the laundry or complete the ironing. For some, ironing had apparently acquired such a grip that they had 'no option' but to organize their schedules according to the demands of this particular practice (the boat owners studied by Jalas, this volume, describe much the same sort of experience). How much time ironing required, and when, differed depending upon related understandings of a minimum acceptable standard. Since there are always many things to do, the advantages of taking short-cuts or of deferring tasks are continually set against the demands of doing things 'properly'.[3] It is therefore no wonder that tensions between concepts of care and convenience (Warde 1997) run through the fine-grained juggling of domestic obligations (Thompson 1996) or that they result in strategies like those of deliberately rushing and hurrying some activities in order to make time for others (Southerton 2003). Exactly what these other pursuits might be is sure to differ and is likely to do so in ways that relate to a household's moral economy, the details of which, in turn, reflect the temporal embedding and disembedding of coexisting practices (Silverstone 1993). As Silverstone (1993) argues, the manner in which new technologies – specifically televisions, telephones, computers and videos – are appropriated, the kinds of practices they engender, and their impact on individual and collective schedules depends above all upon how they are defined in relation to existing habits and routines. For Silverstone, it is this relationality that matters in understanding how innovations in practice do and do not take hold.

Taking a step back, this line of argument suggests that discussions purporting to be about the use of time might be more appropriately framed as discussions about the relation between new, existing and competing practices. If so, the methodological challenge is to somehow represent these dynamic processes. Within any one household there might be ways of describing and perhaps analysing the re-sequencing of episodes and re-chaining of events (Ellegård 1999: 168) that goes on as new practices take hold and as others are edged out of the frame, but how to characterize the practice-time fabric of society as a whole? As indicated above, it is possible to imagine active forms of rivalry or competition between practices as they seek to capture recruits, resources and 'carriers' (Reckwitz 2002). It is – at least in theory – also possible to imagine tracking the temporal and material commitments that specific practices require of those who do them and somehow plotting the cumulative implications of such demands both for the diffusion of the practices in question and for consequent patterns of consumption, including the consumption of time. Anther way of approaching this question is to switch the balance of attention away from time as a resource and to see it instead as an integral part of the complex systems of practice in which we are all engaged.

Practice-Time Profiles

I use the term 'practice-time profiles' to refer to embedded conventions of duration, sequence and timing associated with the competent performance of a practice. As this hybrid phrase suggests, the details of everyday scheduling reflect and reproduce practice-based obligations and notions of propriety. These take various forms. Conventions of timing are important for doing and for interpreting a range of ordinary practices. In Zerubavel's words: '[W]e have relatively fixed notions of what constitutes "the proper time". It is almost inconceivable, for example, that an event such as a dance would be scheduled for the morning (even on non-working days)' (1981: 8). Likewise, phoning at 3 a.m. is itself a signal of some kind of emergency. 'During off-call times for the telephone (say before nine in the morning and after ten at night for adult members of the middle class) a phone ringing may cause alarm' (Goffman 1971: 300–301, cited in Zerubavel 1981: 23). While these arrangements are matters of social convention – in some sub-cultures it is perfectly normal to go dancing at dawn or to phone at night – other forms of scheduling intersect with natural rhythms of seasonality and decay: hence patterns of digging and harvesting garden crops and of painting woodwork before the rot sets in.

There are further senses in which timing is critical. The effective movement and coordination of the body is clearly vital for practices as varied as those of fixing of car engines, windsurfing or playing tennis. Dant and Bowles' (2002) study of the intricately sequenced work of car repair gives a sense the embodied and materialized ordering of process. They write as follows:

> The technician has within their body an understanding of how a task should proceed and rarely needs to consult other colleagues or manuals. Their approach to the task seems to have the structure of a sequence of actions that need to be completed: removal of road wheel, removal of brake disc etc. to get access to the constant velocity (CV) joint, removal of damaged CV boot, removal of contaminated grease, replacement with appropriate grease, replacement of boot, refitting of brake disc, road wheel etc. This sequenced pattern of action is largely determined by the designed-in properties of the objects involved. (Dant and Bowles 2002: 13)

In this instance, sequence is so much part of doing that a single error will spoil the entire performance. In other, more forgiving situations, taking too long, finishing too quickly or doing things in the wrong order signals incompetence but does not result in total failure. By way of illustration, the Mass Observation Study's report into the culture and organization of drinking in a UK town comments in detail on the phenomenon of 'drinking level' (Mass Observation 1987). Partly but not entirely due to the convention of buying rounds (each member of a party takes turns to buy drinks for everyone else), the rate at which an individual drinks is 'controlled' by a usually unstated but nonetheless effective convention of mutual synchronization. If anyone drinks 'too fast' or 'too slow', the balance of the whole is thrown out of kilter.

And so one could continue. The point is not to document all possible temporal dimensions of doing but rather to notice that they exist, that such characteristics are integral rather than coincidental features, and that these time-related qualities are themselves subject to change. Before turning to related but more complicated questions of coordination, I want to say a bit more about how practice-time profiles evolve and intersect.

How is it that arrangements previously defined as inappropriate short-cuts (e.g. the working lunch; regular use of ready-meals or reliance on instant coffee), or as exceptional rather than usual arrangements (e.g. taking a day trip from London to Brussels), have become the norm, at least for some? In reflecting on these questions, commentators write in rather general terms about the speeding up of society and the increasingly widespread experience of being hurried and harried (Southerton et al. 2001). In keeping with the view that time is part of practice, it makes sense to focus not on the pace of life or the shrinking of distance as such but on new combinations and configurations of doing – commuting, multi-tasking, day tripping – which take root around infrastructural affordances like those associated with mobile technologies or with faster means and modes of travel.

In addition, and as already mentioned, it is important to notice that the practice-time profiles of specific activities are shaped and influenced by each other and by deliberate efforts to structure routines and habits. For example, the very notion of 'prime-time TV' is itself an outcome of conscious programming (by producers) *and* of a co-evolving convention of settling down in front of the screen (by consumers) at a certain time of day.[4] As these comments indicate, interpretations of possible, potential and proper time and timing are critical for the ongoing reproduction (and transformation) of specific practices and for sometime supportive, sometimes uneasy relations between them.

Such considerations are also relevant for understandings of what it is to do and to be a practitioner, and hence for the recruitment and defection of specific populations of practice carriers. The idea that certain pursuits are appropriate to people of different age, gender or social class contributes to the persistence of a temporal ordering of propriety variously policed by laws (under-age drinking; sex) and social pressures of one kind or another (e.g. disapproval of 'mutton dressed as lamb'; norms of starting and stopping smoking, etc.).

As Philip Ariès's social history of childhood makes clear, such conventions are culturally and historically specific. In 1600, people beyond the age of three or four 'played the same games as the adult, either with other children or with adults' (Ariès 1962: 71). Over subsequent centuries, adults, especially of the upper classes, abandoned or transformed these games and in the process introduced and reproduced age-related distinctions and differences which had not existed before. According to Ariès, the cumulative result – not only of games playing, but also of other institutionalized ways of doing – is a society organised around increasingly precisely calibrated repertoires of distinct 'ways of life'.[5] Recognizable phases of life are distinguished one from another through the specification and enactment of appropriately 'childish' practices. The sociotemporal invention of childhood is consequently important in structuring the days and doings not only of young people, but of adults too. In so far as the same applies to other categories like those of class and gender, the terrain of practice-time is criss-crossed (and made) by the daily working out of all manner of distinctions (Bourdieu 1984).

These and other accounts of long-range societal transformation generally point in the direction of growing cultural and temporal fragmentation. In the next section, I turn this framing around and instead ask about the kinds of complexes and configurations of practice-time that might have these shattering effects and that might generate seemingly new challenges of coordination.

Coordinating Everyday Life

Some forms of coordination and synchronization emerge by virtue of what Zerubavel refers to as the 'social fact' (Zerubavel 1979: 107) of a sociotemporal order that exists beyond the individuals whose lives are organized and whose experiences are recalled and calibrated around it. Others require more deliberate planning and intervention. The significance of each form and the relation between them arguably depends upon the sum total of practice-time profiles within any one society, and on the manner in which they intersect.

Despite an apparent erosion of collective rhythms and schedules, the spreading of the day (thanks to electric lighting, and more recently to 24-hour opening) and the multiplication of discrete episodes, the extent of sociotemporal coordination remains impressive. The 'shoulders' of the London rush hour are getting broader and broader (according to Transport for London, the morning 'peak' now runs from 7 a.m. to 10 a.m.), yet Wright's account of the rhythm of this city remains instantly recognizable. In his words,

> Nine tenths of [the working force], despite some attempt to stagger office hours, start homeward within the same 90 minutes, queuing for buses in vacuous resignation, squeezing in indecent intimacy in the Underground, rather than linger awhile in park or café; for who will await the roomy 6:30 if he can just find standing room in the 5:45. (Wright 1968: 216, cited in Zerubavel 1981: 66)

Zerubavel highlights the infrastructural consequences of Wright's description of the 'almost complete identity between personal and collective schedules and rhythms', and the problems this presents for urban designers faced with 'unbearably congested peak periods around rush hours in the streets and in the public transportation systems, around mealtimes at restaurants, and during weekends and holidays on the road and on the beaches'. He goes on to note 'the implications of temporal symmetry

as a way of life on the consumption of energy (electricity, heating gas, and so on)'
(Zerubavel 1981: 66), and it is indeed the case that many elements of material
infrastructure – including ovens, cars, reservoirs and power stations[6] – are sized in
such a way as to cope with peak demands (Wilhite and Lutzenhiser 1999).

Given the economic and environmental costs of social synchronization, it is
perhaps not surprising that governments and others have sought to level these peaks
by setting lower tariffs for night-time electricity use or through more forceful methods
designed to spread the times at which people take their holidays. In the Netherlands,
for example, dates for school summer holidays are decided by the Ministry of
Education, which sets different periods for each of three regions. Although this
strategy might have advantages for the country as a whole, and for holiday resorts in
particular, such methods generate new problems of coordination for those who want
to enjoy the summer with people who live in another region.

While some forms of coordination 'just happen', the effective accomplishment of
many practices – like that of holidaying as a family – frequently requires deliberate
scheduling and synchronization. In documenting the growing importance of diaries
and, as they are so aptly named, 'personal organizers', Symes argues that their
popularity indicates a shift from highly structured 'industrial time', characterized
by a collective societal rhythm, to a more contingent form of 'professional time' in
which each individual has a timetable of his or her own (Symes 1999: 372). Whether
this distinction holds or not, a proliferation both of autonomy and of convenience
devices is likely to increase the sum total of arranging required to bring several
people, each locked into idiosyncratic schedules, together in the same place at the
same time.

Observations of this kind have led numerous commentators to claim that there
has been a loosening of shared temporal order, a decline in social capital and a
consequent loss of community (Putnam 2000). However popular and persuasive
these claims might be, it is difficult to put them to the test without first devising some
way of characterizing and comparing the practice-time complexion of different
societies and of showing how they change. In the final part of this chapter I speculate
somewhat wildly on what this might involve.

Characterizing Practice-Timescapes

In these last few paragraphs I stray beyond the limits of methodological plausibility
and fantasize about how practice-timescapes (these being composed of the
intersection of all coexisting practice-time profiles) might be represented, starting
with an imaginary societal synchronization index (SSI). Not quite the same as
a measure of organic or mechanical solidarity, but not entirely unrelated either,
such an index would capture the extent to which the practice complex of a given
society generates and requires synchronous performances. Assuming the SSI could

be deployed over time, it would show whether more solitary practices are edging collective ones out of the frame and taking more time than before. Based on Figures 1.2 and 1.3, and all other things being equal, one might expect France to score higher on such an index than Finland – especially at lunchtime. More fanciful still, a suitably subtle version of such an index (the SSSSI) might be sensitive enough to detect feedback circuits in the personal and collective logistics of daily life. Understandably enough, efforts to assess the social and temporal impact of London's congestion charging scheme[7] focused on the immediate aftermath. However, before and after surveys suggest that the scheme's effects are continually reconfigured as people adjust to the responses of others – for instance, visiting friends and family at the week-end, when charges do not apply, but resorting to other strategies when faced with the new problems of social coordination that arise now that everyone wants to visit at the week-end (MORI 2004). In effect, Londoners and visitors create and re-create the consequences of congestion charging as they respond not only to the scheme itself but also to the responses and reactions of other people. This results in ebbs and flows in the spatial and temporal distribution of practices and is in turn of consequence for competitive relations between them.

Accordingly, there is a sense in which it is difficult to interpret the SSI without also having a good understanding of the chart-atlas of contemporary practice (CACP). In so far as they constitute recognizable entities, practices have potentially identifiable spatial and temporal coordinates, that is, practice-time profiles. The CACP, which represents the totality of contemporary practices in terms of related injunctions or compulsions, minutes of attention required and associated features of sequence and timing, can also be used to plot the social-spatial distribution of specific practices. The CACP can, for example, reveal all those social groups and societies in which extremely time-hungry sports like golf are established and in which they exist as something that people routinely do. The latest versions of the CACP can be calibrated to represent a day or a lifetime and can be adjusted to produce formal estimates of practice squeeze.[8]

There are already precedents for the CACP, but on a much more limited scale. Oskar Korkman (2006) has, for example, sought to categorize the spatial and temporal qualities of the usefully limited array of possibilities open to families travelling on cruise ships between Finland and Sweden. This exercise, based on observation and interviews with literally captive respondents, suggested that the cruising experience was marked by tensions between the contrasting temporalities of child- and adult-orientated practices, and between activities properly undertaken together or alone. Korkman, who is a management consultant, makes a number of practical suggestions based on his analysis. Maybe the shipping line could reduce family frictions by introducing things to do that are not as temporally incompatible as the current array of practices on offer. The suggestion that organizations might get involved in what Korkman refers to as 'practice design'[9] is intriguing, as is the possibility that companies might deliberately scan contemporary configurations of practice-time looking for niches of opportunity in the current eco-system of daily life. Systematic studies, perhaps based on methods of time-space geography, might well reveal empty moments waiting to be colonized or point to gaps associated with the disappearance or modification of practices the effective accomplishment of which used to be especially demanding.

This possibility brings me to the fossilisation-innovation-transformation index (FITI), the third and final instrument in my imaginary tool-kit. Properly applied, the FITI gives a sense both of the rate at which practices are changing, and of the relative plasticity or rigidity (lock-in) of the interlocking systems of practice of which society is composed.

Although the SSI, the CACP and the FITI are the stuff of future fiction, something along these lines is arguably required if we are to build on May and Thrift's conclusion that 'a sense of social time is made and re-made according to social practices' (May and Thrift 2001: 5). Equally, and as my account of these three measures makes clear, operationalizing this idea on any scale seems to be an impossibly complicated task. Fortunately, all is not lost.

While the project of capturing the temporal qualities of always-changing, always-intersecting practices of everyday life does seem to be overwhelmingly ambitious, the process of thinking about it has served to crystallize a handful of more modest but plausible observations. The first of these concerns the limits of studying time and time use in ways that are detached from the dynamics and distributions of practice. Writing about rhythm and routine as if these could be separated from the specific details of doing seems misguided. Second, if the aim is to document the temporal configuration of daily life, matters of sequence and coordination are as significant as those of duration and deserve just as much attention. Third, those engaged in time-use studies should recognize that the practices they track and trail are far from stable and that it is important to keep a watchful eye on the changing composition of everyday life.

Notes

1. These include particularly indelible 'ecological' footprints (Wackernagel and Rees 1996).
2. And in any case, competitions between rival practices are likely to vary between people, e.g. different things will be given up.
3. Hence the rather moralistic saying, 'if a job is worth doing, it is worth doing well'.
4. Research designed to identify the audiences 'available' to watch TV at different time slots consequently reaches the somewhat circular conclusion that 'it is only at 7pm when prime time starts that TV switches for the majority from a secondary activity to the main focus of attention' (Griffiths and Holden 2004: 8).

5. Donzelot (1980) offers an explicitly Foucauldian account of similar transformations, underlining the political and economic significance of temporal structuring
   as a technique of disciplining and (self-)policing.
6. Large enough to take the Christmas turkey; to transport at least four people and
   their luggage; to meet all but the most extreme demands of winter or summer.
7. From February 2003, people driving a car into central London between 7 a.m. and
   6 p.m. have had to pay a congestion charge, initially of £5 and now of £8.
8. The respondent quoted at the start of this chapter gives a colloquial expression
   of this phenomenon when describing the challenge of fitting everything in and
   bemoaning the fact that 'you haven't got the time to do as much as what you want
   in a day nowadays'.
9. Korkman works for a management consultancy called Vectia. The following statements are taken from Vectia's website. 'Practices are defined as *ways of doing*.
   Examples of people's everyday practices in consumer markets are walking
   (shoes), eating (restaurants), working (IT support systems). Companies can gain
   significant benefits from exploring their markets in the terms of practices...
   Practice Design™ differs from traditional market research: instead of studying
   what customers think, feel and say, we concentrate on finding out what people
   actually do or what is really done in business' (http://www.vectia.com/?Deptid=
   2588, accessed 31 March 2009).

References

Ariès, P. (1962). *Centuries of Childhood.* New York: Vintage Books.
Becker, H. (1963). *Outsiders.* London: Free Press of Glencoe.
Bourdieu, P. (1984). *Distinction: A Social Critique of the Judgement of Taste.*
   London: Routledge & Kegan Paul.
Cowan, R.S. (1983). *More Work for Mother.* New York: Basic Books.
Dant, T. and Bowles, D. (2002). Car Care: The Professional Repair and Maintenance
   of the Private Car. Summary report available at: http://www.lancs.ac.uk/staff/
   dant/sumreport.pdf (accessed 31 March 2009).
Donzelot, J. (1980). *Policing of Families.* London: Hutchinson.
Durkheim, É. (1976). *Elementary Forms of Religious Life.* London: George Allen
   and Unwin.
Ellegård, K. (1999). A Time-Geographical Approach to the Study of Everyday Life
   of Individuals – A Challenge of Complexity. *GeoJournal* 48(3): 167–175.
Franke, N. and Shah, S. (2003). How Communities Support Innovative Activities:
   An Exploration of Assistance and Sharing among End-Users. *Research Policy*
   32(1): 157–178.
Goffman, E. (1971). *Relations in Public: Microstudies of the Public Order.* New
   York: Harper & Row.

Griffiths, G. and Holden, J. (2004). The Way We Live Now: Daily Life in the 21st Century. Available at: http://bbcdailylife.tns-global.com/ (accessed 31 March 2009).

Hand, M. and Shove, E. (2007). Condensing Practices: Ways of Living with a Freezer. *Journal of Consumer Culture* 7(1): 79–104.

Hedges, A. (2001). Perceptions of Congestion: Report on Qualitative Research Findings (part 4). Department for Transport. Available at: http://www.dft.gov.uk/pgr/roads/tpm/congestionresearch/perceptions/perceptionsofcongestionrepor4026 (accessed 31 March 2009).

Jalas, M. (2006). *Busy, Wise and Idle Time: A Study of the Temporalities of Consumption in the Environmental Debate*. Dissertation A-275. Helsinki: Helsinki School of Economics. Available at: http://hsepubl.lib.hse.fi/EN/diss/?cmd=show&dissid=306 (accessed 16 April 2009).

Kaufmann, J.C. (1998). *Dirty Linen: Couples and Their Laundry*. London: Middlesex University Press.

Korkman, O. (2006). Customer Value Formation in Practice – A Practice-Theoretical Approach. Ph.D. thesis, Swedish School of Economics and Business Administration.

Lefebvre, H. (2004). *Rhythmanalysis: Space, Time and Everyday Life*. London: Continuum.

Mass Observation (1987). *The Pub and the People: A Worktown Study*. London: Cresset.

May, J. and Thrift, N., eds (2001). *Timespace.* London: Routledge.

MORI (2004). *Central London Congestion Charging Scheme, Social Impacts Surveys 2002–2003*. Available at: http://www.tfl.gov.uk/assets/downloads/Social-Impacts-Report-TfL-Cover-Note(1).pdf (accessed 31 March 1999).

Putnam, R. (2000). *Bowling Alone: The Collapse and Revival of American Community.* New York: Simon & Schuster.

Reckwitz, A. (2002). Toward a Theory of Social Practices: A Development in Culturalist Theorizing. *European Journal of Social Theory* 5(2): 243–263.

Schatzki, T. (1996). *Social Practices: A Wittgensteinian Approach to Human Activity and the Social.* Cambridge: Cambridge University Press.

Shove, E. and Southerton, D. (2000). Defrosting the Freezer: From Novelty to Convenience. A Story of Normalization. *Journal of Material Culture* 5(3): 301–319.

Silverstone, R. (1993). Time, Information and Communication Technologies and the Household. *Time & Society* 2(3): 283–311.

Southerton, D. (2003). 'Squeezing Time': Allocating Practices, Coordinating Networks and Scheduling Society. *Time & Society* 12(1): 5–25.

Southerton, D., Shove, E. and Warde, A. (2001). Harried and Hurried: Time Shortage and the Coordination of Everyday Life. CRIC Discussion Paper 47, University of Manchester.

Southerton, D., Cheng, S.-L., Olsen, W. and Warde, A. (2007). Trajectories of Time Spent Reading as a Primary Activity: A Comparison of the Netherlands, Norway, France, UK and USA since the 1970s. University of Manchester, CRESC Working Paper No. 39.

Stokes, M., Crosbie, T. and Guy, S. (2006). Shedding Light on Domestic Energy Use: A Cross-Discipline Study of Lighting Homes. Proceedings of (COBRA, construction and building research) the annual research conference of the Royal Institution of Chartered Surveyors, 7–8 September, University College London.

Sudnow, D. (1978). *Ways of the Hand.* London: Routledge.

Symes, C. (1999). Chronicles of Labour: A Discourse Analysis of Diaries. *Time & Society* 8: 357–380.

Thompson, C. (1996). Caring Consumers: Gendered Consumption Meanings and the Juggling Lifestyle. *The Journal of Consumer Research* 22(4): 388–407.

Wackernagel, M. and Rees, W. (1996). *Our Ecological Footprint,* Gabriola Island, BC: New Society Publishers.

Warde, A. (1997). *Consumption, Food and Taste.* London: Sage.

Warde, A. (2005). Consumption and Theories of Practice. *Journal of Consumer Culture* 5: 131–153.

Wilhite, H. and Lutzenhiser, L. (1999). Social Loading and Sustainable Consumption. *Advances in Consumer Research* 26: 281–287.

Wright, L. (1968). *Clockwork Man.* London: Elzek Books.

Yahoo, OMD Research (2006). 'Family 2.0' Relies on Multi-tasking with Technology to Stay Close, Better Manage Busy '43-hour' Days. Available at: http://yhoo.client.shareholder.com/press/releasedetail.cfm?releaseid=212192 (accessed 31 March 2009).

Zerubavel, E. (1979). *Patterns of Time in Hospital Life.* Chicago: University of Chicago Press.

Zerubavel, E. (1981). *Hidden Rhythms: Schedules and Calendars in Social Life.* Chicago: University of Chicago Press.

–2–

Timespace and the Organization of Social Life
Ted Schatzki

Introduction

This chapter argues that timespace is central to the organization of social life. By 'timespace' I do not mean – as is usual – some combination of objective time and objective space. The timespace concerned is a phenomenon of human activity that is based in the teleological character of human life. It is also something largely overlooked in social thought. My thesis is that interwoven activity timespaces form a kind of infrastructure through which human activities coordinate and aggregate. Because coordinated and aggregated activities are essential to society, this infrastructure is fundamental to social life.

Analytics of Time and Space

When social theorists say 'time' or 'space', they, like most people, mean objective time or space. Objective time and space are time and space conceived of as features of reality that persist independently of human activity and understanding. Examples are the geometric arrangement of a room and the time it takes for a grape to ripen on the vine. Human activity and understanding can affect or comprehend objective times and spaces (as when humans rearrange a room or plant a vine in a greenhouse), but what they affect or comprehend persists independently of the activity and understanding. That feature of objective reality that is dubbed 'time', moreover, is succession: whenever events or instants occur before and after one another, there is succession – and time. Of course, different conceptions exist of this before and after ordering, including, most famously, absolute time, relational time and, on some interpretations, relativistic time.[1] Considerable dispute also exists regarding the entities whose succession constitutes time; events and instants are not the only candidates. Two prominent conceptions of objective space are, likewise, absolute space and relational space. Whereas absolute space is space construed as a container or arena in which events occur and entities exist, relational space is a collection of relations among entities (longer than, inside, etc.) and of properties based on those relations (length, position, etc.). Relativistic space also sometimes counts as a type of objective space.

Most social theories who consider time or space examine either time or space. Time and space, in other words, are taken to be separable matters, between which only contingent relations exist. Social theory is replete with accounts of either social time or social space that mostly ignore or elide the other phenomenon. In the past two or three decades, however, a variety of theorists have analysed social space-time, including Torsten Hägerstrand (1975), Don Parkes and Nigel Thrift (1980), Anthony Giddens (1984), David Harvey (1996), Tim Ingold (2002) and Henri Lefebvre (2004). Two features characterize their accounts. First, they usually, though not always, treat space-time as an objective phenomenon. Second, they always treat space-time as a conjunction of space and time conceived of as separable phenomena, that is, as phenomena that are not intrinsically related. According to these theorists, space-time is not unified; it exclusively embraces contingent connections between spatial and temporal phenomena or between the spatial and temporal properties of social phenomena.

I have no particular brief against most conceptions of social space-time. Social phenomena do have contingently related objective spatial and temporal properties, and grasping these properties can be important to understanding them. Social life, however, possesses another kind of space-time, or, better, timespace. Although this timespace is less noticeable than objective space and time, it is arguably at least as crucial to the existence of society as are the latter, if not more so. In fact, as indicated, interwoven timespaces are fundamental to human society.

The spatial dimension of timespace is familiar in the philosophy and geography literature, going under the names of 'phenomenological', 'existential' and 'lived' space. I will follow Heidegger and call it 'spatiality' (*Räumlichkeit*) so as to differentiate it from objective space. Spatiality is the world around (an actor) in its pertinence to and involvement in human activity. This world is pertinent to and involved in human activity in providing a platform for, and comprising entities that have places in, human activities. Spatiality, as a result, encompasses arrays of places and paths anchored in material entities. A place is a place to perform a particular activity, whereas a path is an avenue for getting from one place to another. A railing, for instance, can be a place to watch a horse race, whereas a grandstand exit passageway can be a path from the viewing stands to the betting windows, concessions and washrooms.[2] As a person goes through her day, she proceeds through arrays of places and paths that both reflect and determine her and others' activities; the passageway, for instance, is a path between stands and betting windows *because* people watch races and bet on them, and people use the passageway when they want to bet *because* it is such a path. As indicated, moreover, places and paths are anchored at objects: a place to watch the race can be anchored at a metal railing, whereas a path between stands and windows can be anchored at a cement passageway. The physical entity at which a path or place is anchored also yields the location in objective space where the path or place exists. Places and paths, finally, form arrays called 'settings'. Settings, in turn, form broader locales and regions: for instance, betting area, facilities under the viewing stand, the grandstand, Keeneland race track and the Bluegrass horse region. Which settings, locales and regions exist in a particular geographical area depends on the physical arrangements that exist there and what practices are carried on amid or in relation to those arrangements.

The temporal component of timespace is less familiar. Perhaps it will help clarify matters if I explain that my conception of this temporal component is heir to a tradition, beginning with Augustine, that affirms the idea of a human time. Twentieth-century notions of time that stand in this tradition include experiential time, lived time, existential time and the time of consciousness. My own conception of such a time derives from Heidegger's *Being and Time* (1962).

'Existential temporality', as Heidegger called it, is not succession. It does not consist in before and after orderings of events, instants or anything else. It is characterized, instead, by dimensionality, that is, by past, present and future. More specifically, existential temporality is the past, present and future of human existence. For present purposes, existence can be understood as human activity. Existential temporality is, thus, the past, present and future dimensions of human activity. Of course, past, present and future also characterize events (or instants): events belong to the present, past or future according to whether they are, are no more or are not yet. As dimensions of human activity, however, past, present and future do not order events or anything else. Rather, they are features *of* activity. As features of activity, moreover, they are so long as a person acts: the three dimensions of temporality occur simultaneously, 'at one stroke', as Bergson (1911: 309) put it. In this, the past, present and future of activity differ from past, present and future events. Past events are no more, while future events are not yet; only present events are. By contrast, the three dimensions of activity are and occur together so long as a person acts. If activity ceases, the three disappear together.

Heidegger famously analysed human existence as being-in-the-world, which he interpreted more expansively as projecting, thrown being-amid entities. Projection, thrownness and being-amid are, respectively, the future, past and present dimensions of human activity. Projection is acting for the sake of a way of being or state of affairs. Most of the time a person acts for the sake of something, and in doing so she comes towards that thing. This coming towards is the future dimension of her activity. Thrownness, meanwhile, is being situated. When a person acts, she almost always responds to or acts in the light of particular states of affairs. These states of affairs are that given which she does whatever she does. This departing, or coming, from particular states of affairs in acting is the past dimension of activity. Being-amid, finally, is having to do with entities: acting amid, towards and at (*bei*) them. It is the present dimension of activity, activity itself. In sum, a person, when acting, comes towards a way of being departing from certain states of affairs. This acting–coming towards–departing from is the temporal structure of activity.

This structure can be formulated in more familiar terms: the future dimension of activity is acting for an end, whereas its past dimension is acting because of something. The future is teleology and the past motivation. The present is acting itself. The temporality of activity is, thus, motivatedly acting teleologically.[3]

The spatiality of activity is also a teleological phenomenon. Which places and paths compose a setting (i.e. are anchored in a given arrangement of objects) rests both on the activities that people perform in (or in relation to) that setting and on the ends they pursue in so acting. That, for example, a railing is a place to watch a horse race and a passageway is a path to the refreshment kiosks rests on (1) the practices of watching horse races in grandstands and of imbibing while at the races and (2) the ends that people pursue in carrying out these practices (seeing who wins, being seen at the races, satisfying hunger, etc.). The determination of places and paths also rests on motivation; the passageway, for example, can be a path to the washroom or a path to the refreshment kiosk depending on what leads someone to head down it. The teleological foundation of spatiality is reflected in the fact that people set up settings and locales with an eye to the activities that will be performed there and the ends people will pursue in performing these actions. In the end, teleology underlies spatiality because spatiality is the pertinence that objects around have for human activity, and the pertinence of the world around for activity ultimately rests on the matters for the sake of which people act.[4]

Both the temporality and the spatiality of human activity are teleological phenomena. The teleological structure of human activity *is* the future of activity and *underlies* place-path arrays. Human activity thus institutes and bears a timespace whose temporal and spatial dimensions are connected inherently – and not contingently as with objective space-times. Indeed, the two dimensions are coordinately instituted together. This timespace, I claim, is key to the organization of social life.

I stress that timespace is not a substitute for, nor is it an alternative or competitor to, objective space-time, in particular, the conceptions of objective social space-time mentioned above. Social life amalgamates activity timespace and objective space-time: it is a temporalspatial spatial-temporal phenomenon. Myriad relations exist, moreover, between timespace and space-time. For instance, a transformation of what Erving Goffman (1959) called a back region into what he called a front region, or vice versa, can be understood as an objective temporal transformation of timespace: a coordinated nexus of ends, projects and places pursued amid or anchored at particular objects changes into a different nexus pursued amid or anchored at these objects. Similarly, a reorganization of the betting facilities at the race track designed, say, to increase efficiency can be described as an alteration of material arrangements and the spatialities anchored in them that is designed to change what people do when betting or to speed up those betting actions that survive the change.[5] In ways such as these, social changes can be understood as alterations in commixtures of timespace and space-time.

Timespace and Society

Timespace, strictly speaking, is a feature of an individual human life. It is, however, a *social* feature of an individual life, for much of it derives from and depends on social phenomena. Indeed, the timespaces of different lives substantially depend on the same social phenomena, namely social practices. Because of this, the timespaces of different lives are partly the same and partly different.

Most actions that a person performs are constituents of social practices. By a 'social practice', I mean an organized manifold of doings and sayings. (For more on practices, see Schatzki 2002.) The doings and sayings that compose a practice are organized by items of four types: (1) action understandings, which are abilities to carry out, recognize and respond to particular actions; (2) rules, which are formulated instructions, directives, admonishments, and the like; (3) teleoaffective structures, which contain enjoined and acceptable ends, enjoined and acceptable projects and actions to carry out for those ends, and enjoined and acceptable emotions; and (4) general understandings – of matters germane to the practice.

The timespaces of (the lives of) the people who participate in a practice derive from the practice because its organization circumscribes the teleologies – the end-project-action orderings – of these people's activities. A popular practice among visitors to Keeneland is betting on horse races. A variety of ends are deemed acceptable in betting practices, including maximizing winnings, being entertained, having fun, impressing a date and trying to beat the odds makers. Various projects and actions are enjoined or found acceptable in the practice for the sake of these ends, including studying the racing form, safeguarding a credit card with one's spouse, waiting until the last moment to bet, betting only on horses with green silks, standing in long lines and putting aside 10% of each winning. In participating in betting practices, people tend to act for the ends and to carry out the actions that fall within this normative range. This is the sense in which the teleological structure of the practice circumscribes the futures of those participating in it. This teleological structure also – together with the actions that compose the practice and the teleological structures of other practices that are carried on at the track (e.g. people gazing, eating, spectating, excretion) – underlies the spatialities of betters' lives. The past dimensions of their timespaces likewise overlap since participants in a practice often react to, or act in the light of, the same states of affairs.

Other components of practice organization also help shape participants' time-spaces. A sign (rule), for instance, might designate where people should line up before the betting windows open, just as an usher might tell people where they can stand to watch the race (another rule). Rules can also determine common pasts, as when the clerks who take bets are instructed to begin accepting them when a certain green light illuminates. A general understanding of courtesy, moreover, might pick out places where a person may stand to watch a race (and not obstruct others' views), just as in Keeneland corporation practices a general understanding of customer service or of pursuing profit might determine ends and projects for track managers and employees. Practices vary in which components of their organizations bear greatest responsibility for the futures, pasts and spatialities of their participants' lives.

The timespaces of those who participate in a practice are partly common, partly shared and partly idiosyncratic. Participant timespaces are common when particular teleologies, motivations and place-path layouts are enjoined. Track employees are enjoined to provide good service to visitors and to shut off betting when a red light comes on, just as grooms, prior to a race, are enjoined to walk their charges in view of onlookers in the interior paddock. Enjoinments of this sort lay down common futures and pasts for the individuals subject to them; they also dictate common places and paths for these individuals' activities. Common futures, pasts and spatialities also arise from the facts (1) that people often fall in with action regularities in a practice (participants encounter certain ends being regularly pursued, certain actions being regularly performed at certain places and people regularly acting for certain motivations) and (2) that in carrying out a given practice different individuals act in the same or similar material settings.

Participant timespaces are shared, meanwhile, when people act for the same end, react to the same state of affairs and understand the same places to be anchored at certain objects, but this sameness is not enjoined by practice organization. Nothing enjoins that a person aim to enjoy himself while at the track. On any given day, however, many visitors to Keeneland share this goal, just like they might share an understanding of a passageway entrance as a place to meet friends. Participant timespaces are idiosyncratic, finally, to the extent that people pursue ends, react to states of affairs and understand the world idiosyncratically.

As a person goes through her day, her actions bear futures and pasts and occur at places and paths that are parts of place-path arrays. She also thereby carries on this and that practice. Some of her futures, pasts and places will be common to and shared with the lives of other participants in the same practices. The organization, regularities and settings of a practice engender a net of interwoven timespaces, a net of interwoven jointly instituted futures-presents-pasts and place-path arrays. This net, incidentally, is a property of the practice. The activities of individual people are what possess futures and pasts and are performed at particular places and paths. *As a whole*, however, the net of interwoven timespaces that a practice's organization, regularities and settings engender is a property of the practice and not of individual lives. In sum, the social character of timespace consists in the dependency of (1) the timespace of a person's life and (2) the common and shared temporalspatial features of people's lives on the social practices they carry out.

Actions and practices also bear properties of objective time and space. Performances of actions often take time, performances of different actions can be simultaneous or occur before and after one another, and performances mostly occur at locations in objective space. The objective temporal and spatial properties of a practice include the rhythms, sequences and periodicities of its constituent actions as well as the geometric distribution of the locations where these actions are performed. Although I cannot defend the following claim in this chapter, I contend that many of these objective properties derive from the timespaces of actions and from the practices that actions compose. In particular, it might be emphasized, the rhythms and periodicities of practices such as betting, watching races and observing horses in the interior paddock reflect the timespace nets instituted in, and thus the organizations of, both these practices and practices related to them. In this sense, 'local' rhythms and routines of consumption rest on features of practices as wholes. More 'global' rhythms and routines of consumption require the interrelation of many more 'local' or wider practices spread out in time and space. These broader rhythms and routines are underpinned by local rhythms and routines (among other things) and likewise rest on the organizations of practices. Examining these dependencies is beyond the scope of this chapter.

As I have been writing, practices are carried on amid arrangements of objects. Promenading, betting, talking and watching races are carried out amid the arrangements of objects that form viewing stands, concessions, the trackside holding area, the interior paddock, and the passageways, staircases and doorways that permit movement between these. Practices, moreover, are tied to other practices and also bound up with other bundles of practices and arrangements more or less tightly or loosely. The practice–arrangement bundle at Keeneland on race day, for example, is bound up with (1) the bundles of the Keeneland corporation and of the taxi services that bring people to the track and (2) the bundles at Keeneland during annual horse sales or at other race tracks during their meets. The sum-total of linked practice–arrangement bundles at any moment forms a gigantic, intricate and constantly metamorphosing web that forms the overall site of social existence (see Schatzki 2002). This immense plenum also defines the total objective temporal and spatial spread of social life. Elsewhere (Schatzki 2002, 2003) I have argued that social phenomena can be understood as segments or configurations of this plenum of practices and arrangements. This claim entails that any social phenomenon consists either in a practice–arrangement bundle or in features of such bundles (racial prejudice, for example, consists in features of many bundles). What I want to argue in the remainder of this chapter is that interwoven timespaces form an infrastructure that pervades the practice–arrangement plenum, linking actions and tying practices together into the bundles that make up the site of the social. Stated in more familiar terms: timespace is crucial to the constitution of social phenomena. I will essay to make this claim plausible by sketching how timespaces underlie the coordination of action, the aggregation of practices and, in this sense, the integration of individual lives.

Action Coordination

Although there is more to social life than coordinated actions, coordination is obviously central. Examples of coordination include the following:

1. After the fourth race meeting someone at the top of the stairs that descend to the interior paddock.
2. A couple taking turns betting on races while the other person talks with friends in their box.
3. The jockeys lined up on their horses in the starting gate.
4. Employees changing behaviour in response to a management decision to provide better customer service communicated to them by letter.
5. The actions of grooms, auctioneers, bidders, ushers and announcers at a horse sale.

The coordination of actions is explained by the interwoven timespaces of the actions involved. For instance, the meeting at the head of the stairs rests on a common past (the completion of the fourth race) and a shared spatiality (the stairs as a place to meet); the behaviour of the convivial betting couple arises from a shared future (acting for the sake of combining betting and being social), common and shared pasts (e.g. that the race is finished, that you bet last time) and a common or shared spatiality that encompasses boxes, aisles, betting windows, and so on; and the fact that the jockeys sit in a line on their mounts reflects common futures and spatialities.

I have been treating the interwovenness of timespaces as a matter of commonality and sharing. In the above employee–management example, track employees and managers partly proceed through common or shared place-path arrays. It is not obvious, however, how common or shared their futures and pasts are. Regardless of how divergent their futures and pasts might be, however, these futures and pasts will often not be independent of one another. The fact, for example, that management acts for the sake of improving visitors' experiences is connected to the fact that employees have been acting out of indifference or disdain, or for the sake of heading home as quickly as possible. When people pursue ends and projects that differ from, but are not independent of, those that others pursue, I will say that their futures are 'orchestrated'. The futures of the activities of the grooms, auctioneers, bidders and announcers at the horse sale are orchestrated. The meeting at the stairs might also be orchestrated since the people meeting might do so for different, but interdependent, ends. Pasts, too, can be orchestrated. The fact, for example, that at the horse sale grooms lead their charges into the show ring at a signal from an usher is not independent of bidders turning towards the ring as the auctioneer begins to describe the next horse for sale. In short, timespaces are interwoven, not just through commonality and sharing, but also through orchestration. Notice, incidentally, that the coordination of action via interwoven timespaces can extend across practices; in the case of the horse sale, for example, across the practices of grooming, auctioning, bidding and announcing. I return to this phenomenon in the following section.

I claimed above that common and shared timespaces arise from (1) the organizations and regularities of practices and (2) common and similar settings. Orchestration, too, reflects these matters. Regardless, for instance, of whether the people meeting at the stairs do so for the same or interdependent ends, their ends are likely circumscribed by whatever practices they are carrying on (e.g. those of courtship, business, conviviality). The flow of events, too, contributes to the existence of shared and orchestrated timespaces. The people meeting at the stairs might be intentionally rendezvousing after bumping into one another earlier in the day or have accidentally run into each other on their way to meeting other people elsewhere. Myriad contingencies contribute to the interwoven timespaces through which actions are coordinated. Absent the interwoven timespaces, however, the coordination would not exist.

Coordination rests on interwoven timespaces. This means that such objective spatial-temporal features of coordinated actions as synchronized in the same location and sequenced in different locations (e.g. meeting someone at the top of the stairs and employees taking particular actions after management has made a decision) also rest on interwoven timespaces. At the same time, the interwovenness of timespaces occurs under the constraints of objective time and space. Nothing known can overcome or contradict the 'march' of objective time. Coordination must accommodate the fact of change and also conform to processes that conventionally function as markers of time such as the periodicity of environmental events (sunrises, animal migrations, seasons), the radioactive decay of caesium atoms, the turning of clock hands and the progression of digital numbers. Such processes are timing resources for managing coordination. The interwovenness of timespaces is also constrained by the materiality of things and their geometric distribution. This distribution determines where, in principle, places and paths can be anchored. The materiality and geometric distribution of things also constrains which places can be anchored at specific objects (a place to sleep cannot be anchored at a pen). Of course, within these underlying constraints, the *use* of objective time and space for purposes of coordination presupposes, and is often mediated by, interwoven timespaces. The use of clocks, for instance, presupposes the existence of temporalspatially interwoven lives whose further coordination it facilitates. Similarly, understanding a sunrise between two stones as seen from a specific vantage in a temple as signifying that people should gather to perform a particular ceremony presupposes common as well as shared futures and pasts.

To be distinguished from coordination is the phenomenon of harmonization. Harmonization exists when the actions of people who are simultaneously proceeding in the same or connected settings smoothly fit together through the contingent adjustment of each person's behaviour to what others are doing. Examples are traffic movement, people waiting in a queue to bet, the stream of people from the viewing stands to the betting windows, and the milling about of people who are watching the parade of horses in the interior paddock. One could treat phenomena such as these as instances of coordination. I distinguish them from coordination, however, because they achieve no overall result. Or, rather, the result they achieve is the absence of conflict, in other words, harmony. Regardless of how it is classified, harmonization resembles coordination in depending on interwoven timespaces. In most cases, for example, harmonization rests on common and shared spatialities (e.g. the road as path to work) and shared and common temporalities (e.g. the common futures of getting to one's destination and doing so safely). These identical spatialities and temporalities so sensitize people to one another that constant mutual adjustment almost automatically follows.

The opposite of harmonization is often conflict: car collisions, arguments about people's places in line, obstruction of crowd flow, people jostling for a view. Conflicts of this sort require interwoven timespaces – pursuing the same ends, reacting to the same state of affairs, the same place-path layouts. Conflicts of this sort are occasions when harmonization does not obtain because adjustments within common and shared timespaces break down. Many cases of conflict are not like this, however. Conflict often arises due to incompatible timespaces. For instance, conflict can arise because the same arrangement of objects anchors incompatible place-path arrays for different groups of people (as in disputes between developers and preservationists); or, more fully, because people, acting in partly shared and partly conflicting spatialities, pursue incompatible futures fuelled by divergent pasts. An example is disputes between Jews and Arabs concerning Jerusalem. I cannot pursue this line of analysis at present. The basic idea, however, is that conflict often results from the divided, divergent and/or incompatible features of either individual timespaces or the common or shared timespaces of different groups.

The Aggregation of Practices (and Arrangements)

A second key feature of social life is the aggregation of practices. Coordination is already a form of aggregation since it is a joining of actions through which a result ensues (e.g. a meeting at the head of the stairs comes off, betting coexists with conviviality, horses are sold). By 'the aggregation of practices', however, I mean practices hanging together in the constitution of social phenomena. Recall my claim that a social phenomenon is either a bundle of practices and material arrangements or features of such bundles. This claim implies that a social phenomenon embraces interconnected practices (and arrangements). Consider the following examples of a social organization, a social event and a social phenomenon:

1. Keeneland as economic enterprise: the interlocking of management, grounds keeping, betting, concession, public relations, sales and other Keeneland corporate practices in the interconnected material arrangements (offices, track, runways, betting corner, concession stands,etc.) where they occur.
2. Keeneland race day as an event: performances of actions belonging to the intertwined practices of race watching, betting, conviviality, people watching, entertainment, race track management, supervision, race preparation and horse grooming at interconnected stands, betting corners, boxes, walkways, TV rooms, offices, corners, barns, paddocks, and so on.
3. Goings-on in the boxes owned by wealthy horse farm owners as a social phenomenon: the joining of the practices of entertainment, flirtation, deal-making, horse observation and alcohol consumption in these boxes and in the aisles that connect them.

These three bundles overlap. This overlap reflects the fact that the corporation, the race day and the goings-on in the boxes are not substantially distinct matters in the world.

Practices bundle and thereby help constitute social phenomena through various sinews. Some of these sinews are the same as those through which timespaces interweave. Practices overlap, for instance, through common organizational elements (common ends, projects, rules, general understandings), some of which circumscribe timespaces. In the corporation, for instance, the end of making sufficient profit organizes management, public relations and sales practices in common. Much of what goes on in the luxury boxes, meanwhile, is keyed to events on the track (common pasts). Common or shared pasts exist, in fact, whenever people act on the same beliefs, expectations, perceptions or hopes. Practices can also bundle through the orchestration of timespace. The different ends and projects for which the people in the boxes act are often interconnected, as are those pursued by the people carrying on the practices that constitute the corporation. Orchestrated pasts occur when people interrelatedly react to, or in the light of, different states of affairs, for example when the hope of betters that they will win and the belief of track managers that visitors will continue to bet are not independent conditions.

Practices overlap not just through same and orchestrated temporalities (through same and orchestrated organizational elements generally), but also by virtue of doings and sayings belonging to more than one practice. Some of the actions that help make up race preparation also help compose entertainment (e.g. walking the horse in the interior paddock), just as some of the actions that help compose the observation of horses are also part of betting (e.g. watching films of past races). In these cases, practices bundle through the present dimension of activity. Practices are also linked via the present dimension whenever they are linked to one another via chains of action that embrace actions from multiple practices. As for spatiality, practices bundle when the arrays of places and paths at which their constituent actions are performed overlap, are orchestrated or refer to one another (an example of the latter is the customer affairs office being understood in betting practices as a place to demand that management alter its policies). Indeed, in so far as the practices of the Keeneland corporation, the race day and the luxury box goings-on are carried on amid the same material arrangements (the grandstands, the concessions area, the interior paddock, the boxes, etc.), the actions that compose them are performed amid the same arrays of places and paths. This common and shared spatiality strongly contributes to the bundling of practices that makes up each of these social phenomena; it also forms a background for the operation of other avenues through which the practices involved bundle.

These facts about materiality and spatiality, by the way, suggest that the designers and producers who make and lay out material arrangements have a special hand in configuring practices and their relations. These individuals enjoy the privilege of initiative – in constructing and laying out settings, they confront other people with *faits accompli* to which these others must accommodate themselves. Of course, the power of designers and producers in this regard is limited. How they build and arrange the world reflects existing practices and social matters. People, moreover, appropriate material arrangements in accord with the practices they already carry on. Still, the material spatialities that designers and producers set up form a background for the bundling of practices.

Bundled practices also possess significant objective temporal features. I will say nothing about these. My present aim is simply to suggest that interwoven timespaces form an important glue through which social affairs exist. Interwoven timespaces are not the only glue. For instance, the rules and general understandings through which practices bundle might have nothing to do with temporality or spatiality. I have said nothing, moreover, about the connections – including the technological connections – among material arrangements that are crucial for the existence of social phenomena.

Conclusion

This chapter has sought to make plausible that activity timespace is central to the organization of social life. In particular, I claimed, interwoven activity timespaces are essential to the coordination of action and key to the bundling of practices that helps constitute social organizations, events and phenomena. Theorists have often distinguished kinds of social linkage that work through the harmonization of actors' orientations from kinds of linkage that work, so to speak, behind their backs, for example through unintentional consequences of action. What these theorists dub 'actors' orientations' are inherently tied to what I am calling 'activity timespace'. Interwoven timespaces are crucial, however, not only to the social linkages that work through the harmonization of orientations, but also to those that work behind people's backs. The type of coordination that marks, say, an economic system rests significantly on common, shared and orchestrated timespaces. There is always more to the story than timespace, but timespace is an essential mediator of social existence.

Consider, for example, the following fact reported in Dale Southerton's contribution to this volume (see also Elizabeth Shove's chapter): that coordinated actions today rest more on interpersonal arrangement and scheduling and less on institutionally prescribed times and spaces than they did seventy years ago. The action coordination that arises from communication and accommodation among family members or coworkers clearly rests on interwoven timespaces. The same, however, is true of the institutionally effected coordination that used to be more prevalent. For instance, in so far as the fixed workplace starting and finishing times that Southerton discusses coordinate action, they do so by instigating common, shared and orchestrated temporalities and spatialities for both workers and the people closely related to them (e.g. family members). The coordination of action that derives from institutional events works through interwoven timespaces.

A different sort of example is the chain of actions, through which a few clicks of my computer mouse eventuates in the delivery of a package at my front door. No accommodation, communication or scheduling occurs between me and the other people whose actions, combined, lead to the package sitting on my front stoop; the action coordination in this example does not result from a harmonization of the orientations of the actors involved. Each pair of actions in the chain evinces, however, a configuration of interwoven timespaces. These configurations might or might not be enjoined or instigated by institutionally prescribed phenomena such as workplace starting and finishing times. Without these configurations, however, the links, and thus the chain, would not exist. Linkages among people's actions that do not work through the harmonization of orientations still rest on interwoven timespaces.

Notes

1. Conceptions of succession as a subjective and not an objective phenomenon also exist, but I will ignore these in the following.
2. All examples in this chapter are taken from Keeneland Race Course in Lexington, Kentucky, where the author has occasionally spent an afternoon consuming.
3. The structure of temporality resembles the temporal structure of motivation, as Schutz (e.g. 1962) conceived of it. Schutz, however, understood this structure as a configuration of objective time.
4. I acknowledge that the significance of the world for human beings need not be teleological. Examples are religious, symbolic and aesthetic significance. By themselves, however, significances of these sorts do not specify spatialities, that

is, place-path layouts. They instead, I believe, shape such layouts by determining and otherwise combining with the teleological orientation of human activity.
5. Cf. Elizabeth Shove's discussion of the reconfiguration of practice-time profiles in her contribution to this volume.

References

Bergson, H. (1911). *Creative Evolution*. New York: Henry Holt.
Giddens, A. (1984). *The Constitution of Society*. Berkeley, CA: University of California Press.
Goffman, E. (1959). *The Presentation of Self in Everyday Life*. Garden City, NY: Prentice Hall.
Hägerstrand, T. (1975). Space, Time and Human Conditions. In *Dynamic Allocation of Urban Space*, eds L. Lundqvist, A. Karlqvist and F. Snickars. Lexington, MA: Lexington Books.
Harvey, D. (1966). *Justice, Nature and the Geography of Difference*. Oxford: Blackwell.
Heidegger, M. (1962). *Being and Time*. Oxford: Blackwell.
Ingold, T. (2002). *The Perception of the Environment: Essays in Livelihood, Dwelling and Skill*. London: Routledge.
Lefebvre, H. (2004). *Rhythmanalysis: Space, Time and Everyday Life*. London: Verso.
Parkes, D. and Thrift, N. (1980). *Times, Spaces, and Places: A Chronogeographic Perspective*. Chichester: John Wiley.
Schatzki, T. (2002). *The Site of the Social: A Philosophical Exploration of the Constitution of Social Life and Change*. University Park, PA: State University of Pennsylvania Press.
Schatzki, T. (2003). A New Societist Social Ontology. *The Philosophy of the Social Sciences* 33(2): 174–202.
Schutz, A. (1962). Choosing among Projects of Action. In *The Problem of Social Reality: Collected Papers 1*. The Hague: Martinus Nijhoff.

–3–

Re-ordering Temporal Rhythms
Coordinating Daily Practices in the UK in 1937 and 2000
Dale Southerton

Introduction: The Paradox of Time Pressure

Time pressure is a contemporary malady for which a range of prescriptions have been spawned to alleviate the problem, including: self-help time management advice; convenience technologies and services; voluntary simplicity; and work–life balance policies. The underlying causes are identified in macro social processes that are deemed to re-order the temporalities of daily life. These include processes of consumer culture, the restructuring of labour markets, technological innovations and the cultural conditions of reflexive modernization. And the implications of time pressure are profound – well-being is compromised by the stress of being harried, social capital (or community) declines as people no longer have the time to participate in collective or public activities, families and friendships are torn asunder as we have no time to spend with those we care most about. Time pressure is, not surprisingly, a substantive concern that feeds into several influential theories of social change.

Many theoretical accounts attempt to explain the paradox that increasingly people feel time pressured despite time diary data consistently revealing that people have longer durations of free time today than did previous generations (Robinson and Godbey 1997). In the interest of brevity, five sets of theoretical accounts of the causes of time pressure will be outlined. The first can be described as 'economic restructuring' with particular reference to the impact of dual-earner families. These accounts highlight that women experience a 'dual burden' once they enter paid employment: the burden of 'juggling' domestic and workplace responsibilities (Sullivan 1997). One of the ways in which dual-earner households deal with 'juggling' is through reliance on domestic technologies which reduce the amount of time devoted to unpaid work – although the extent to which labour-saving technologies actually save time is debatable (Schwartz-Cowan 1983). This relates to a second set of accounts which suggest the further rationalization of time. Hochschild (1997) argues that as hours of paid work increase within households (what she calls the first shift), time for domestic matters (the second shift) is squeezed, and time devoted to emotional and inter-personal relationships becomes experienced as a 'third shift' subject to rationing and social planning. This is a process of rationalization because the principles of Taylorization, whereby tasks are broken down into their component parts (fragmented) and re-sequenced to maximize temporal efficiency, have become applied to domestic and inter-personal activities. For Hochschild, increasingly more spheres of daily life are regulated by the principles of efficient sequencing of tasks within designated slots of time, and it is this that generates experiences of time pressure.

The third, and most prominent, account of time pressure is Schor's (1992, 1998) 'work–spend' cycles. Schor explains the economic benefits for firms of training a limited number of employees who work long hours as opposed to a large number of employees who work limited hours. She also highlights the significance of consumer culture in 'ratcheting' upwards the hours people spend in paid work. Assuming people value their consumption relative to others and that a global consumer culture places the life-styles of the most affluent as the key consumer referent group, then 'the average individual needs to earn more money' (Schor 1998: 123). The logic of global capitalism is that people work more to consume more. The difficulty with this argument, and to some extent those of rationalization and economic restructuring, is that central to these theories is that people are spending more time in paid work. While this is (marginally) true for the professional middle classes during the period between the early 1980s and late 1990s, it is not the case for all social groups, and time diary evidence shows a significant and progressive decline of time spent in paid work over the course of the twentieth century (Gershuny 2000).

Given this empirical conundrum, the fourth group of accounts set out to explain why people may feel more time pressured even when time spent in paid and unpaid work appears to be on a long-term trajectory of decline. Linder's (1970) harried leisure class is the catalyst for a range of accounts which point to the intensification of leisure practices. Such accounts variously highlight how leisure has become less leisurely as people rush to cram more and more leisure activities into finite time. Gershuny (2005) goes so far as to claim that busyness has become a 'badge of honour'; a principal source of social status. Other accounts consider the impacts of reflexive modernization. Darier (1998) suggests that being busy is symbolic of a 'full' and 'valued' life. In his conceptualization of the problem, reflexive modernization and the requirement of individuals to narrate their identity through styles of consumption (see Bauman 1988 and Giddens 1991 for a detailed exposition of this theory) brings with it the demands of trying new and varied experiences, and it is this which leads individuals toward the infinite pursuit of more cultural practices. Being busy is hypothesized as a necessary requirement of reflexive identity formation.

The fifth and final set of accounts draws attention to transformations in the temporal ordering of social life. Innovations in communication technologies produce time-space compression where constraints related to time and space are progressively decoupled (Giddens 1991). Under such conditions, Rosa (2003) suggests that contemporary society is an experience of acceleration. With time and space no longer constraining communications and with more and more cultures opening up to be sampled and appropriated, everyday life comes to be experienced as one of acceleration – everything is faster because time and space no longer represent constraints on the tempo of activities.

The main, and crucial, difficulty with all these accounts is their assumption of 'past' temporal conditions. Theories are built around a vision of a society where everyone has time to spend with those whom they care most about, a time when everyday life was straightforward with fewer work, domestic and consumer-related time pressures. While this criticism may be read as a highly stylized characterization of a range of different theoretical accounts, the point that these accounts pay little attention to the empirical analysis of past daily lives is difficult to counter. In attempting to provide an empirically driven theoretical account of the changing temporal organization of daily life, this chapter takes 'day in the life of' diaries from 1937 and analyses them in relation to data collected in a research project that began in 2000. A practice-based analytical approach, which focuses on the temporal conditioning of what people 'do', is applied to both sets of data. A discussion of the data is followed by a brief overview of the key findings from the contemporary research project. The 1937 'day in the life of' diaries are then discussed in relation to four categories: temporal rhythms; negotiating time; relationships; and temporal experiences. In conclusion, it is argued that the mechanisms that organize temporalities in 2000 bear a strong resemblance to the mechanisms of temporal organization in 1937. What has changed is that institutionally timed events are no longer as fixed within the temporal rhythms of daily life such that the collective coordination of practices, particularly those connected with inter-personal relationships, has been undermined. In 2000, the personal coordination of practices was a central challenge to daily life; a challenge that was absent from the diaries of 1937.

Mass Observation 'Day in the Life of' Diaries and Household Interviews: A Practice-based Approach

The chapter employs two sources of data: household interviews from 2000 and 'day in the life of' diaries from 1937. Interviews were conducted with twenty households (a total of twenty-seven respondents) located in a suburb of Bristol, England. The sample comprised single households, couples with and without children, and the ages of respondents varied between 25 and 65 years. Some were dual-income households, some professionals and some retired, thus providing a range of demographic and socio-economic status groups. Respondents were contacted via letter sent to every other house in the most and least expensive streets of the town. The interviews were semi-structured, lasted, on average, two hours and the interviewer adopted a conversational approach (Douglas 1985). Respondents were asked whether they felt society, in general, was more time pressured than in the past, whether they felt pressed for time, to recount and reflect on the previous week and week-end day, and to describe how they organized the passage of time in their daily lives.

The Mass Observation project is a social scientific research organization established in 1937 with the aim of creating an 'Anthropology of Ourselves'. The original studies comprised a national panel of volunteers who responded on a regular basis to questionnaires and directives. On the coronation of King George VI (12 May 1937) the first 'day in the life of diaries' were collected as a directive to volunteers. Diarists were then asked to repeat the diary format on every twelfth day of the month thereafter. Five hundred people recorded diaries, although because the sample was based on volunteers it was not nationally representative.

The diaries analysed here were collected on two days in 1937: Saturday, 12 June and Monday, 12 July. Fourteen female diarists were selected on the basis of the legibility of the diaries on both days. Detailed socio-demographic variables of diarists were not collected to the degree that is common practice in contemporary social scientific research, but a crude breakdown of background variables was amenable. As Table 3.1 indicates, the diaries analysed were written by women of different ages, most of whom were 'housewives', married with children and two-thirds were middle class.

Table 3.1 Basic socio-demographic profile of sample diarists, Mass Observation Archive, 1937

Age		Occupation		Marital status		Children		Social class	
20–29	3	Housewife	11	Yes	10	Yes	9	Working class	5
30–39	7	Teacher	2	No	4	No	5	Middle class	9
40–49	3	Designer	1						
50–59	1								
60+	0	Part-time jobs							
		Designer	1						
		Elocutionist	1						

Given the format of the two datasets, it would be wrong to suggest they are comparable. At best, the two sets of data provide indications and tentative signs of changing temporal rhythms. Diarists were asked to record what they did and how they felt (their mood) on that particular day. This resulted in variations of the way the day was recorded. In some cases diarists recorded their day in the form of a time diary (e.g. 7.00 a.m. got out of bed; 7.10 a.m. made cup of tea); others wrote a paragraph outlining the rhythm of the day. By contrast, household interviews provided scope to explore temporalities of social practices in more detail. The interviews explored the length of time respondents allocated to particular practices (duration), the pace of the practice (tempo), whether the practice was performed simultaneously with other people or in conjunction with another practice (synchronization), how frequently the practice was performed (periodicity), and in what order (sequence). It was impossible to recover this detail of the temporalities of practices from the diaries.

Data analysis was informed by a Theory of Practice (see Southerton 2006 for a discussion of the application of a practice-based approach to the analysis of temporalities). The central principle is to examine the socio-economic, cultural and material configuration of the practices through which daily life is comprised. This requires taking practices rather than the 'individual' as the core unit of analysis. Critical to this approach is how practices of daily life relate to one another – how particular socio-economic, material and cultural constraints (and affordances) configure the performance of any given practice. By focusing attention on practices, analysis centres upon the ordering of daily life; on the way that the mundane and the extra-ordinary connect, are reconfigured and rendered meaningful. A practice-based approach represents a 'meso-level' analysis because it interrogates and reveals the ways that 'macro' processes (such as technological innovation, economic restructuring, changing cultural values) impact on the 'micro' detail (the performance and experience of practices) of everyday lives.

Changing Temporal Rhythms: 1937 and 2000

All respondents from the interviews conducted in 2000 were quick to suggest that contemporary society is characterized by an increasing shortage of time, and were particularly fluent in identifying generic time pressures that neatly mapped onto dominant discourses (pressures that result from consumption, workplace competition, family life and a fear of wasting time). However, when it came to discussing their own lives, senses of being harried were met with a degree of ambivalence. To not be harried was in some way regarded as not leading a full life. To be too harried was often seen as an admission that respondents didn't make enough time to spend with the people most important to them.

In negotiating this ambivalence, respondents described their daily lives as a roller-coaster ride with moments of harriedness and calm, of 'hot' and 'cold spots' of temporal activity. Hot and cold spots were differentiated according to the density and intensity of practices performed within designated time frames: hot spots having a high density and intensity of practices. The challenge as described by respondents was to coordinate within their networks so that cold spots, which were variously described as 'quality time' and 'family time', were aligned. They were mechanisms used by all respondents to manage the rhythms of their daily life. In a context where few institutionally timed events (e.g. work and meal times) fixed the temporal and spatial location of practices (with the important exception of school times), respondents re-instituted their own fixed events. These occurred around practices of co-participation, such as eating together, socializing by prior arrangement, participating in a team sport. Practices of consumption and work were presented as flexible in their temporal scheduling, but many of those practices came with sets of constraints and requirements (such as the co-participation of others) and this rendered coordination a contemporary challenge to the personal scheduling of work, domestic, consumption and inter-personal practices within daily life. Coordinating and scheduling practices were challenges that generated harriedness through the hot spots that were necessary if cold spots, which have come to symbolize togetherness, were to be achieved (Southerton 2003; Southerton and Tomlinson 2005).

Temporal Rhythms of Daily Life in 1937

The most notable difference between 1937 and 2000 was the amount of work (both paid and unpaid) conducted by women; the few mentions of time outside of domestic work were presented as fleeting moments of rest. This was illustrated by the extent to which paid and domestic work dominated the Saturday diaries. Table 3.2 provides a summary of all reported leisure activities for the total sixty-three observers on Saturday, 12 June.

Table 3.2 Reported leisure activities of sixty-three diarists, for Saturday, 12 June 1937

Activity	Number of diarists
Sport	12 (5 played, 7 watched)
Garden & home	10
Visits and outings	9
Reading	8
Radio	8
Art, theatres, etc.	5
Pubs	5
Country walks	4
Religious activities	3
Cinema	3
Garden fêtes	2
School speech day	1
Total	70

Source: Mass Observation Bulletin (1937).

Despite it appearing that, on average, each diarist enjoyed a leisure activity on the Saturday, and that eight of the fourteen sampled diarists stated Saturday to be a 'day of leisure', when leisure activities are read within context it becomes clear they were allocated around a variety of work practices. The breakdown of leisure practices for the entire sample appears relatively bountiful. However, when those practices are read within the context of each diary, moments of leisure, like for the Monday diaries, appeared fleeting or 'snatched'. Consider the complete diary for Saturday, 12 June (1937) of Mrs Beken (a married housewife with four children who lived in Kent and whose husband was a farm labourer).

5.45: Woke by birds.

5.55: Alarm clock rings and husband gets up to make tea – gas means no waiting about. I wonder whether I look fat and think about how much husband hates his job. After cup of tea make husband's lunch.

6.40: See him [husband] off to work.

6.50: Eldest son wakes up followed by the twins. Arrange flowers and send youngest back to their room to keep them out the way while I do house jobs but, better let come done and not whine, say I.

7.05: Sent Norman, my 9 year old son, to get milk from the dairy.

7.45: Start ironing. Must sandwich this in somehow with all the other jobs to do.

8.20: Eldest son goes to work.

8.30: Finished flowers, in between ironing and cutting bread and jam.

10.00: General tidying upstairs.

11.00: Clean dining room.

11.30: More ironing. Friend comes with fried fish for lunch, she [her neighbour] has made the last few years bearable.

12.20: Himself [her husband] comes home and demands his tea – but he does help with tidying.

1.05: Eldest son comes but I forgot he has to be back at work for two so had to rush some fried fish to the table and bread and jam for his afters. Tell him he can have pudding for tea. He says 'O.K'. Good job he's good tempered. Gives me his wages.

1.45: Family sit down for lunch.

2.20: Clear away lunch and husband washes up. I tidy dining room. Hectic scramble to wash twins. Wash and dress the children in best clothes.

3.10: Mother arrives.

4.00: Wash and change my clothes. Send Norman to get biscuits for tea as I have no time for scones as planned. Husband goes to local town.

5.30: Clear up tea, mother washes up and then asks for clothing that needs mending.

7.00: Put son's friend on bus to take him home and put twins to bed.

8.00: Fly along to little general shop for last minute shopping. Meet him [her husband] coming back from Bromley on bike.

9.30: Mother goes to bed, followed by Norman.

10.00: Go to pub with husband for one drink. Get home and have supper at same time as eldest son arrives home.

In contrast to 2000, where people talked in terms of hot and cold spots over which they have some capacity to manage and re-order practices, the diarists of 1937 present temporal rhythms that were dictated by the requirements of paid and unpaid work. Leisure and consumption fitted around work practices on all days; by 2000 there was a sense that leisure and work have their own rhythms which have equal weight or significance in the temporal organization of daily life.

It was not just work which acted to fix temporal rhythms. As demonstrated by Mrs Beken's diary, meal times were important in the ordering of daily practices, although the structure of meal times was very different to those of 2000. Without fail, breakfast was taken after getting up in the morning (usually between 7 and 8 on a weekday), lunch eaten between 12.00 and 12.40 for every diarist on a Monday (although on the Saturday lunch was taken between 12.30 and 2.00). Lunch was an important meal, with husbands and children returning from work or school in order to dine together. The evening meals that presented significant challenges of coordination in the households of 2000 were less significant in 1937. Rather, diarists reported 'tea' (light snacks) in the late afternoon of 'bread, apple and cheese' or 'bread, butter and banana'; and then a similar 'supper' taken later in the early evening. There were no discussions of eating together in the evening during the weekday diaries; rather each individual member of the household grabbed their pre-prepared (by the diarist) convenience food (e.g. apple, bread, cheese) and ate alone.

Despite the structure and timings of meals being different from those of today, there were some important similarities regarding snacking – the consumption of foods that require minimal preparation time and which are often eaten alone. This led to perhaps the main difference between the two years. Eating a cooked meal (rather than snacks) required much planning and preparation, including the timing of when to 'lay the kitchen fire', which for Mrs Friend (a married housewife aged 32, living in Norbury with no children) was best done to coincide with 'doing the Laundry' as the kitchen was warm and clothes could be 'dried if the weather turns bad'. For Mrs Friend, 'laying the kitchen fire' led to the coordination of a set of domestic practices, in addition to the laundry. Monday was 'bath day', 'laundry day' and also used to produce a stew (with Sunday's leftover meat). Such material constraints to the timing and coordination of domestic practices had a profound impact on the order of temporal rhythms in 1937. Monday's were laundry day because material infrastructures and cultural conventions acted to coordinate practices at a societal level.

The problems of coordination that affected the interview respondents of 2000 were less of a problem in 1937 because material constraints, working times and the local-ness of work meant that people within any given households came together at fixed times on a routine basis. The coordination of practices remained a mechanism that shaped the temporal organization of daily life in both years. However, in contrast to 2000, the coordination of practices in 1937 was less a matter of personal scheduling but structured around the fixed temporal constraints of institutionally timed events and the material hardware of daily life.

Negotiating Time

A range of strategies were employed by interview respondents when negotiating the coordination of practices in 2000 (Southerton 2003). In some cases respondents imposed predictable routines on day-to-day activities or created socio-temporal boundaries between day-time and evenings, between days or parts of the day for housework, and between times at work designated as breaks and productive time. The use of lists to detail the sequence in which practices should be conducted or to remember impending deadlines was a second strategy. Many respondents employed shared diaries and schedulers in order to coordinate the temporal schedules of household members, including combinations of individual diaries, household calendars, chalk boards and notes on fridges. A fourth strategy was the use of coordinating devices, such as mobile phones, e-mail and traffic warning systems; all being devices with a capacity to re-schedule personal arrangements at the last minute. Finally, everyone relied on time-saving and -shifting devices. Answering machines, VCRs and a variety of domestic appliances (including freezers, microwaves, dishwashers, automatic timing systems on ovens and washing machines) were deemed essential for shifting components of practices within time in ways that generated greater flexibility in personal schedules. In their various ways, such devices allowed respondents to by-pass conventional socio-temporal constraints. For example, the freezer–microwave combination re-sequences the temporalities of the practice of meal provisioning; food shopping can be done with less frequency, a meal can be cooked and stored for months before consumption, and a meal can be placed on the table subject to a few minutes of re-heating (Shove and Southerton 2000). All strategies provided greater personal flexibility in the allocation of practices within time. However, they also add another level of need for allocation and coordination.

As demonstrated by Mrs Friend's Monday routines surrounding 'laying the fire', technologies also played an important role in the negotiation of temporal rhythms in 1937. Yet, no diarist wrote of scheduling devices such as diaries, calendars or chalk boards in the kitchen; in 1937 there appeared little need to coordinate the movements in time and space of household members. Coordinating devices were not required because fixed institutional events such as meal and work times, or Monday as laundry day, structured temporal rhythms such that coordination was embedded in the routines of daily life. In all these ways, time was not negotiated in the same sense as in 2000: temporal rhythms were not malleable. Domestic tasks were fixed in time; there were some slippages in the schedules but a blueprint schedule remained firmly in place.

This is not to say that the diarists of 1937 did not plan or make mental notes about tasks that needed to be completed. Mrs Cotton (28 years old, married with a young child, housewife and elocutionist, living in Brighton) described in her Saturday diary how she 'planned the week-end menu' and ordered 'everything required up to Monday's breakfast'. At 12.30 p.m. on the same day, Mrs Hodson (38 years old, married housewife with one child, living in Marlow) began cooking the Sunday lunch of roast mutton, commenting that 'most working class people cook the joint on Sunday, but I cook on Saturday to lessen the work next day'. While the planning of activities was identifiable in 1937 diaries, there was little sense of the need purposefully to coordinate individual schedules of practices across social networks or to plan the sequence of those practices at the level of detail described by the interview respondents of 2000.

Whether the comparative lack of planning is a representation of a real change between the years or an artefact of the data is unclear. It is important to remember that diarists were not directly asked to comment on how they organize time; interview respondents were. However, the impression that temporal rhythms required less individual coordination in 1937 was further indicated by the absence of phrases such as 'quality' or 'family' time in the 1937 diaries, although some comments did imply the significance of togetherness. In Mrs Hodson's Saturday diary, she mentioned for a second time the importance of preparing Sunday lunch a day in advance, explaining that 'I like to make Sunday a day of leisure more or less. I particularly want to be as free as possible this Sunday, as my husband will be off duty, which is unusual'. Mrs Cotton described how, having made her list of groceries, Saturday morning presented the opportunity for the family to spend some time together, and she went 'straight down to the town front [she lived in Brighton], we went for a Donkey ride, stopped at a café for ice cream and returned home for 12.45'. After lunch the afternoon was then spend 'idling on the roof, where I sunbathed, the child played and my husband did his stamps (his hobby)'. While no diarist spoke directly of 'family time' or 'quality time', the notion that spending time together as a family was important and a normative obligation was clear. The difference was that time for togetherness required less purposeful coordination of individual schedules.

Relationships

In 2000, inter-personal relationships were critical to the temporal organization of daily practices. Anxiety was often expressed about the lack and poor quality of time spent with friends and family. Many efforts in negotiating time were directed toward making quality time. In 2000 the relationships that appeared to matter most were quality time with children, followed by partners and, to a lesser extent, friends and extended family. In 1937 the story was very different. The significance of togetherness was not absent in 1937, but it did not come across in the diaries as being a pervasive anxiety. This could be because temporal rhythms were more rigidly defined such that quality time was simply found in those moments outside of paid and unpaid work, and was therefore embedded within the temporal rhythms of daily life. Not having to make quality time may effectively remove the phrase from the discursive radar. To explore further, all comments referring to time spent with children, partners and friends or neighbours were examined.

Like in 2000, children were prominent in the narratives of diarists, including those who did not have children of their own. Many of the comments made by mothers about their children held strong similarities with some of the stories from the interviewees of 2000. Mrs Cotton lamented about how her daughter 'interrupted mostly every minute for help in brick building'. Several mothers spoke of the rush to get children ready for school. Mrs Beken commented on the difficulties of caring for children in school holidays: 'the woman next door has had to keep all 5 children off school due to whooping cough. ... The school holidays start in 2 weeks and she is really struggling with controlling and looking after all 7.' Other than the 'whooping cough' and sheer number of children, these are the kinds of difficulties associated with child care expressed by women in 2000.

Despite children having a strong presence in the diaries, there was no sense of an impending need to create time to spend together. Children were seen as household helpers. Take Mrs Beken's Saturday diary as an example: '7.05: Sent Norman, my 9 year old son, to get milk from the dairy'. At 4 p.m., Norman is off shopping again: 'Send Norman to get biscuits for tea as I have no time for scones as planned.' Children contributed (more so than men) to domestic chores within the home and there was no implication beyond Mrs Cotton's mention of 'donkey riding' that special measures were required to coordinate togetherness or quality time with children specifically.

More interesting, however, were relationships between partners. Diaries read almost as if partners engaged in separate practices during their day-to-day lives. Men went to work. When they were in the home they tended to engage in leisure activities alone. Eight of the women stated that on the evening their husband 'read', some listened to the 'wireless', Mr Cotton 'did his stamps'; others went out after 'tea' to 'the pub' or a 'Union meeting'. Mr and Mrs Cotton spent some time together during the Saturday day-time, two other couples went for a drink in the local pub on the Saturday evening, and one couple went out for a business meal with the husband's 'French acquaintances'. Compared with the interviews of 2000, where every couple spoke in great detail of the need to make time to spend with one's partner and took measures to achieve this objective, spending leisure time together in 1937 appeared less frequent and was largely taken for granted as something that just happened within the temporal rhythms of the day. Whether this was only the result of the rigidity of temporal rhythms or because what constitutes a close relationship between partners has changed is less clear. Certainly, many of the diarists wrote of strained relationships with their husbands, and any sense of a desire to achieve the perfect 'intimate' relationship (Giddens 1991) was absent. In this respect, 'making time' for intimate relationships can be regarded as a contemporary concern. The changing temporal rhythms of daily life are interrelated to changing cultural ideals surrounding relationship practices: the need to coordinate daily life because of the fragmentation of collective temporal rhythms both reinforces and facilitates cultural ideals of seeking the perfect 'intimate relationship', a relationship in which quality time is 'made' for one another.

The final set of inter-personal relationships that impact on the temporal organization of daily life are friendships and extended family. In the 2000 data, making and coordinating time to spend with friends was important for most respondents, especially those who were single. In the 1937 diaries, friendships were also important. Only one diarist, however, wrote of the need specifically to schedule and coordinate sociable practices with friends. Mrs Cotton commented that 'our friends phoned to cancel our arrangement for Sunday. I remarked to my husband that these particular friends were a Sunday Institution, as if anything came to interfere with either their visit to us, or us to them, they never suggested meeting during the week, or another day. Just waited for another Sunday.' Important here is the rigidity of the arrangement: Sundays only. In other cases, spontaneous visits to or from neighbours or members of the extended were referred to on numerous occasions.

Inter-personal relationships and temporal rhythms are mutually constituted. On the one hand, the temporal ordering of togetherness impacts on the extent to which network interactions need to be scheduled and managed. In 1937, the rigidity of temporal rhythms meant that moments of togetherness were routinely allocated within the temporal order of practices. On the other hand, the spatiality (or local-ness) of networks affected how practices of togetherness were performed. More localized networks made the need to coordinate and re-schedule practices less problematic in 1937. In this respect, the temporal organization of daily life shaped the form of interaction within inter-personal relationships, and the form of those inter-personal relationships shaped the ways in which people negotiated and experienced temporal rhythms.

Temporal Experiences: Harriedness and Anxiety

In the interviews conducted in 2000, respondents talked extensively of daily life as an experience of being 'rushed', 'harried', a matter of 'juggling' activities, of 'fitting it all in', and of not 'wasting time' on meaningless activities. As the following selection of quotations demonstrates, such temporal experiences were also a feature of life in 1937.

> 7.45: Start the ironing. Must sandwich this in somehow with all the other jobs to do. (Mrs Beken, Saturday, 12 June)
> 8.00: Fly along to little general shop for last minute shopping. (Mrs Beken Saturday, 12 June)
> 10.45: The market was much busier, but I hurried my shopping so that I did not miss the bus home. (Mrs Elliot, Saturday, 12 June)

While the language of rush and busyness was employed, it was not used as extensively in the 1937 diaries as in the 2000 interviews. Again, we must be cautious of the data. But, it does seem that few domestic tasks spilled over into other time frames in the same way as in 2000, where respondents talked of the problem that tasks always took longer than expected or that re-sequencing the order in which tasks were performed led to a constant 'flitting' between tasks. By contrast, the sequencing of practices in 1937 appeared almost 'seamless'. The above quotation of hurrying from Mrs Elliot (aged 48, married housewife with children, living in Burnley) can be read differently when taken in the context of her entire morning:

> 9.05: Caught the bus to Burnley. Went to the market which was quiet as it was early for shoppers and then to 'Woolworths' to buy cardboard box for sending a parcel in.
> 10.00: Go to get fruit and veg from the market before all the decent stock goes and then to the butchers for the same reason.
> 10.45: The market was much busier, but I hurried my shopping so that I did not miss the bus home.

While daily life in 1937 was an experience of moments of rush, this was a rush to keep within collective rhythms marked by numerous institutionally timed events – such as getting to market, meeting the bus, work and meal times, the laundry day. In 2000, harriedness was described in relation to the tension between managing the few remaining fixed institutional events (e.g. school times) and 'cramming' activities into self-designated 'hot spots' within one's personal schedule in order to free up 'cold spots' of togetherness at other times.

Conclusions

Similar mechanisms of temporal organization appeared significant in both years. Temporal structures were held together by a combination of fixed institutional events and constraints surrounding practices of domestic life, paid work, consumption and network interactions. The main differences were that by 2000 there were fewer fixed institutional events and the temporal boundaries of those events were less clearly defined. Second, constraints of coordination have shifted in tune with the changing materialities of daily life and spatialities of social networks. On these terms, the key social change is less to do with any radical overhaul of the temporal organization of daily life and more a re-ordering of the mechanisms through which temporal rhythms operate. Influential theories of social change that suggest daily life is speeding up, that we work more and are preoccupied with time spent consuming, and that all kinds of inter-personal relationships suffer as a result, miss the bigger point. What is at stake is better understanding how temporal rhythms are ordered and re-ordered.

Theories of consumer culture and post-industrial society place particular emphasis on the shift from a society ordered through production and work to a consumption and leisure society. In the process, a wider variety and greater flexibility of temporal rhythms in everyday life can be identified. The temporal rhythms of the contemporary period are characterized by the growing necessity for personal coordination of practices. Collective rhythms and routines of daily life remain, only they are not 'institutionally ordered' in the same way as they were in 1937. Indeed, the de-institutionalization of many times (work times, shopping times, meal times, laundry times) creates multiple and overlapping routines. Routines and rhythms are made and remade everyday, in micro and detailed ways. Those institutions which no longer dictate rhythms with such force still, however, act as constraints. Normative expectations of the timings of cultural practices, and the preservation of particular times for valued cultural practices of togetherness (Sundays, week-ends, evenings), continue to provide a basic structure pinned loosely around attempts to re-institute or re-routinize temporal rhythms. The respondents from the year 2000 were distinctive (when compared with the diarists of 1937) in the variety of strategies that they employed in order to re-sequence, juggle and coordinate practices across time and space. These strategies were largely dependent on material goods and infrastructures that make the progressive erosion of institutionally timed rhythms possible. By contrast, the materialities of daily life in 1937 acted to constrain and locate practices in time rather than afford their flexible and diverse allocation within personal schedules. To understand fully the re-ordering of temporal rhythms it is therefore necessary to examine how the temporalities of social practices change; and to do this requires analysis of the shifting relationships between the spatialities, materialities and network configurations (or co-presence) of practices, the interconnections between practices, and the ways in which practices are coordinated.

References

Bauman, Z. (1988). *Freedom.* Milton Keynes: Open University Press.
Darier, E. (1998). Time to be Lazy: Work, the Environment and Subjectivities. *Time & Society* 7(2): 193–208.
Douglas, D. (1985). *Creative Interviewing.* London: Sage.
Gershuny, J. (2000). *Changing Times: Work and Leisure in Postindustrial Society.* Oxford: Oxford University Press.
Gershuny, J. (2005). Busyness as the Badge of Honor for the New Superordinate Working Class. *Social Research* 72(2): 287–314.
Giddens, A. (1991). *Modernity and Self-identity.* Cambridge: Polity.
Hochschild, A.R. (1997). *The Time Bind: When Home Becomes Work and Work Becomes Home.* New York: Henry Holt.

Linder, S.B. (1970). *The Harried Leisure Class.* Columbia: Columbia University Press.

Robinson, J. and Godbey, G. (1997). *Time for Life: The Surprising Ways That Americans Use Their Time.* Pennsylvania: Pennsylvania State Press.

Rosa, H. (2003). Social Acceleration: Ethical and Political Consequences of a Desynchronized High-speed Society. *Constellations* 10(1): 3–33.

Schor, J. (1992). *The Overworked American: The Unexpected Decline of Leisure.* New York: Basic Books.

Schor, J. (1998). Work, Free Time and Consumption: Time, Labour and Consumption. Guest Editor's Introduction. *Time & Society* 7(1): 119–127.

Schwartz-Cowan, R. (1983). *More Work for Mother: The Ironies of Household Technology from the Open Hearth to the Microwave.* New York: Basic Books.

Shove, E. and Southerton, D. (2000). Defrosting the Freezer: From Novelty to Convenience. A Story of Normalization. *Journal of Material Culture* 5(3): 301–319.

Southerton, D. (2003). 'Squeezing Time': Allocating Practices, Coordinating Networks and Scheduling Society. *Time & Society* 12(1): 5–25.

Southerton, D. (2006). Analysing the Temporal Organization of Daily Life: Social Constraints, Practices and Their Allocation. *Sociology* 40(3): 435–454.

Southerton, D. and Tomlinson, M. (2005). 'Pressed for Time' – The Differential Impacts of a 'Time Squeeze'. *Sociological Review* 53(2): 215–239.

Sullivan, O. (1997). Time Waits for No (Wo)men: An Investigation of the Gendered Experience of Domestic Time. *Sociology* 31(2): 221–240.

Section II
Pace and Scale

Temporal Order and Disruption

–4–

Disruption is Normal

Blackouts, Breakdowns and the Elasticity of Everyday Life
Frank Trentmann

And there are blackouts in LA tonight
An evident lack of light tonight
An increase in desire, you'll catch me
Hanging out on a wire
Cutting the voltage to your power line
And the lights, go, out.

Now you cannot affect me
I feel no electricity
Now you cannot control me
I feel no electricity

And the lights, go, out

Hybrid, 'Blackout', from the album
Morning Sci-Fi (2003)

It was a stinking mess. In John Kyffin's draper's shop in London's East End the toilets were blocked and overflowing. Since the water company had cut back supply in July 1895, water had slowed to a trickle, leaving his toilets with 'no flushing remedy'. He and his shop assistants had nowhere to go; some were even taken ill. For Kyffin and other East Enders it was a return to ordinary life under drought ('Court Report', *Daily Chronicle*, 22 July 1895; Trentmann and Taylor 2006).

Breakdowns and shortages are a regular feature of everyday life. Indeed, some disruptions, like traffic jams and blackouts, have evolved into routines themselves. Others have had devastating consequences, bringing in their train mass migrations, disease and death, like the drought that ravaged the northern hemisphere in 1921, killing several million people in northern China and southern Russia. Disruptions, however, are not limited to developing societies, or to natural causes. John Kyffin lived in one of the most developed pockets of the world, the 'heart of empire', in a metropole that was amongst the first to have a network delivering a constant supply of water – except when it broke down, as it repeatedly did. In the last decade, water shortages have once again become a prominent feature of life in many affluent societies, disrupting the quotidian rhythms of bathing, gardening and other water-intensive practices. They are part of a broad range of interferences, ranging from serious natural disasters, like the Canadian icestorm of 1998, and technological accidents, such as at the Three Mile Island nuclear accident in Harrisburg, Pennsylvania, in 1979, to quotidian disruptions like congestion, electronic spam and power cuts. In Barcelona in the summer of 2007, for example, 350,000 inhabitants had no power for two days. Commuter trains stopped running. There were no traffic lights. In hospitals, the elevators were stuck. Shopkeepers had to sell by candlelight (*Neue Zürcher Zeitung*, 18/19 August 2007: 7). The blackout that swept across Ontario and the American East and Mid-West on 14 August 2003 affected 50 million people. Not all disruptions are this large and dramatic, however. In the United States, the average customer loses power every nine months for a total of 214 minutes, not counting the additional effects of storms or hurricanes (Apt et al. 2006: 51). Even more quotidian, in Italy the flickering of lights or a blown fuse are normal, as many homes are on lower tariff, low-wattage electric circuits that trip under the pressure of washing machines and other appliances.

Arguably, the advancing interdependence of technological systems and life-styles has made contemporary societies more prone to disruption than ever before. This is, in part, for technological reasons. Communication and transport systems all have increasingly come to depend on tightly coupled electricity networks and computer programs. Blackouts can demobilize sewage pumps, with serious consequences for public health, shut down the computers managing traffic controls and communication, set off fire alarms and deactivate electronic locks on garage doors. But it is also because increasingly complex rhythms of daily life have become more dependent on enabling technologies, making smooth coordination ever more difficult.

In many parts of life, disruption is becoming more frequent, not less. Traffic congestion is a good example. In the thirty-nine largest cities of the United States, the number of hours lost by travellers due to congestion has trebled in recent decades. In 1982, the average person driving in Boston or Chicago during peak hours (6–9 a.m. and 4–7 p.m.) lost twelve or fifteen hours a year. By 2005, it was an entire working week (forty-six hours each) (Texas Transportation Institute 2007: Table 4). One obvious way to reduce congestion would be for people to adopt car-sharing. That the take-up of such solutions has been so limited, traffic researchers recognize (Bhat et al. 2005), lies in no small part with people's increasingly flexible and frequent use of the car for non-work leisure and family activities. Disruption here is the price paid for the sake of coordinating an ever more complex life-style.

This chapter looks at disruption to illuminate the tenuous, fragile nature of everyday life. In contrast to most studies of blackouts and other shortages, where the focus is on how to manage disasters, I am turning to breakdowns here to open up the temporal fragility of habits and the elasticity of everyday life. Disruptions reveal the flexible side of habits and routines so often imagined as stable and stubborn.

They offer a snapshot of rhythms as they unravel and are braided back together again, capturing the work that is needed to keep them going. Disruptions, in this view, are not freak accidents or aberrations but natural, constitutive features of lived normality. It is important not to confuse disruption with disorder. Breakdowns may trigger individual road rage or anger at frozen food melting away during a blackout, but, collectively, communities are remarkably creative in producing alternative orders. Rhythms and habits are interspersed with disjunctures and connected via suspensions, interferences and repair work. Disruptions thus reveal the elasticity of everyday life. They also open up its politics. A power failure, a water shortage or a public transport system breaking down can raise questions about accountability (who is to blame), entitlement and social justice (who should get what) and, most profoundly, about 'normality' (how can or should members of a society live). Disruption therefore is a particularly useful way to explore connections between practices, politics and socio-technical systems.

Disruptions are as varied as they are plentiful. Accidents, breakdowns, a product flaw, strikes and disasters differ in scale, dynamic and effect. A flat tyre is not the sinking of the *Titanic*. The effects of a burst local water main are not those of a fire at a power station, which can plunge millions of people into darkness, as happened in Engköping, Sweden, on 27 December 1983. Some disruptions are small, like the newspaper that is again not delivered in time for breakfast, but can irritate people more than the much larger one-off damage caused by a flooded basement. Many disruptions are invisible, like the temporary hardware breakdowns of spam engines, and only brought to our attention by software alerting us to delays in email. Would a 30-second stop at a subway station in front of a red signal be experienced as a delay, before Tube conductors began to inform us about them as a matter of routine, apologizing for the 'disruption to our journey'? All these are, again, different from major disruptions of socio-economic cycles, like a depression and mass unemployment, which, as Marie Jahoda, Paul Lazarsfeld and colleagues showed in their pioneering study of Marienthal, Austria, in 1933, changed the most basic rhythms of bodily time and movement, leading people to walk more slowly and drift through the day (Jahoda et al. 1933).

'Disasters' have been the type of disruption that has received most attention, especially from experts on contingency, crisis management and the organizational risks of tightly coupled systems (Perrow 1999; Scanlon 2001). We can also, however, come to disasters from the other end, asking about how ordinary people cope with them. How do disruptions play themselves out, once they have struck? How do people respond? How (and how much) do disruptions transform the rhythms of everyday life, in the short- and in the long-run. It is easy to date when a disaster strikes. But it also carries a longer tail behind it, and its length depends on social and political dynamics, separate from whatever had triggered the initial breakdown in the first place. For example, a power outage hit Buenos Aires on 15 February

1999. It lasted eleven days, affecting 600,000 residents. Protests and battles over compensation, however, continued well after reconnection (Ullberg 2005). In other cases, the prevention of disasters can require deliberate smaller-scale disruption and the active participation of people willing to adapt their habits. Rolling blackouts or rota-cuts of water that hit certain groups of users sequentially can avoid a system-wide collapse. So, too, can campaigns to induce consumers to use less water and energy in expectation of a serious shortage. At this level, it becomes important how people think about the nature of the challenge. In the early 1970s, Americans who saw the energy shortage as the ploy of profit-hungry companies were less like to adopt energy-saving behaviour than those who believed it was a genuine geo-political or environmental crisis (Gottlieb and Matre 1976).

People's experience of disruption is relative and highly subjective, and this influences the elasticity of their responses and the resilience of systems. For some British commuters interviewed in 2005, 'congestion' meant standstill, whereas for others it was 'driving along at 20/30 miles an hour ... where you'd otherwise be bombing around at 90 miles an hour' (Department of Transport UK 2005: 41–42). Some drivers had come to hate congestion so much that they refused to visit their children during the day and instead would only drive the 20 miles in the evening. Others lived with congestion by turning their car into an office on wheels. Here are examples of how the rhythm of one practice (driving/congesting) impinges on others (socializing, working). It is important to stress that disruption is not automatically experienced as frustration or altogether negative. A survey of commuters in Austin, Texas, found a correlation between stress and highway mileage, but also noted that 37 per cent felt their commute was 'somewhat' or 'very enjoyable' (Bhat et al. 2005: 22). The privacy of the car, to be able to select the radio channel of one's choice or simply open and close the windows whenever one feels like it, makes congestion more acceptable to many than the noise and enforced intimacy of public transport (Department of Transport UK 2005: 70).

There are, then, good reasons for seeing the production and consumption of disruptions as entangled, not separate processes. The failure of public utilities offers a promising way to probe more deeply into this relationship. Because of their poten-tially devastating impact on public health, safety and order, power shortages have attracted considerable attention in disaster studies.[1] Here analyses of crowd behaviour loom large, in part because of the historical proximity of disaster studies to military and psychological concerns with panics and the collapse of authority during the Cold War and in the wake of the Kennedy and King assassinations. At the same time, electricity is also an 'enabling technology' for many quotidian practices (Nye 1998), so its disruption affects routines that are not strictly speaking matters of public order and safety, such as watching television, putting the toaster on or reading a book by lamplight. Just as there has been an ever-tighter coupling between organizational systems, so networks and practices have become increasingly entangled.

In Actor-Network-Studies, breakdowns like the *Columbia* shuttle disaster have appeared as illustrations of how easily 'objects flip-flop their mode of existence', from 'completely silent intermediaries' to 'full-blown mediators' (Latour 2005: 81). This line of thought might be extended to the nexus between technologies, users and practices. How easily do practices flip-flop? This is not just an academic question but touches on the basics of behaviour change. In addition to asking about the resilience of infrastructures – how much damage can a system withstand, and how easily is it repaired – we should also ask about the elasticity of rhythms. How far can rhythms be stretched, and for how long? Why do they snap in some contexts but not in others? These are timely questions as energy and water industries are beginning to look beyond supply-based solutions to modifying consumption in order to reduce stress on crisis-prone systems.

In addition to component failures and maintenance problems (considerable in the United States), power shortages register the growing number of technologies and activities powered by electricity. In Finland, for example, 40 per cent of all houses were still heated by wood in the 1960s; by 2006 this figure had dropped to a mere 10 per cent. Most homes are kept warm through district heating fed by combined heat and power plants. This is a relatively energy-efficient system (utilizing c. 85 per cent of the fuel energy value) compared to producing electricity separately (c. 45 per cent). But it also means a tight interdependence between electricity and heat, making Finland particularly vulnerable to a power shortage; at an outside temperature of –26 degrees Celsius, it takes less than forty-eight hours for the temperature to drop from +22 degrees Celsius to freezing point. The incidence of blackouts might therefore be rare (thirteen in rural, four in populated areas in 2006), but the consequences are disastrous; in November 2001 when two storms hit Finland, 800,000 people in total were affected, including 1,600 for more than five days (Landstedt and Holmstroem 2007).

In warmer regions, too, technologies have facilitated new cultures of comfort that have added pressure on energy systems. The spread of air-conditioners has been accompanied by an increasing rate of blackouts in India (Wilhite 2008: 117–121) but also in Italy. Mediterranean countries are becoming more vulnerable to public supply disasters during heatwaves. During the heatwave of 2003, the national grid in Italy introduced power cuts as early as June – the first in twenty years. In France, demand for electricity was almost 10 per cent above the previous year (IEA 2005: 39–41). This interweaving of technologies and habits takes place at the office as well as in the home. Coffee and Xerox machines are switched on routinely on arrival in the office, while computers are left on after departing in the evening. In eleven offices surveyed in San Francisco and Washington, DC, in 2000, a mere 44 per cent of computers and 32 per cent of monitors were switched off at night (IEA 2005: 81).

What have been the responses to blackouts and more generally to the difficult business of keeping supply running smoothly? After the 2003 heatwave, French organizations were heavily criticized for their habitual, mechanistic response (Lagadec 2004). But beyond such emergencies, recent power shortages also tell a story of considerable and creative effort to encourage people to change habits and consume less. 'If you sing in the shower, choose shorter songs' was a slogan during the 2003 electricity shortfall in New Zealand. In Japan, preparing for the summer peak in the same year, the Ministry of Economy, Trade and Industry set up an 'energy-saving team' of 1,350 women headed by a popular actress, who visited shops and companies to encourage them to set air-conditioners at higher temperatures and adopt other energy-saving measures (IEA 2005: 61).

The success of such strategies has varied significantly. Energy savings in France in 2003 were 0.5 per cent. In Brazil, two years earlier, the figure was 20 per cent. Whereas the French case points to the stickiness of habits, Brazil tells a tale of elasticity within vulnerability. Brazil depends for 80 per cent of its electricity on hydropower, making it extremely vulnerable to droughts, like the one in 2001. By May 2001 it was apparent that only serious reduction in energy use could save the country from repeated blackouts. The shortage lasted for ten months. The government responded with a stick-and-carrot policy. It combined mandatory energy savings (rationing) with a national awareness campaign and a mix of penalties and incentives. The biggest savings were in the public sector – street lighting alone dropped by 35 per cent. The commercial sector reduced its demand by 15 per cent – raising temperatures in cooling systems as well as introducing more efficient lighting systems and switching to gas-based equipment. But a good deal of the reduction came in private households. The government distributed over 5 million fluorescent lamps to the poor. However, it was affluent households with higher energy use which showed the main savings: households using more than 100 kWh/month dropped their energy consumption by 20 per cent, whereas those using less than 100 kWh/month did not change at all. Customers who used between 201 and 500 kWh but failed to meet the target of reducing their demand by 20 per cent were subject to temporary interruption. And they had to pay 50 per cent extra (IEA 2005: 24–30).

How were such targets implemented, and how much disruption to everyday life did they involve? The available evidence, such as the reports compiled by the International Energy Agency, is of an aggregate kind and unfortunately says little about how such savings were absorbed by particular consumers in their daily activities. Some of these dynamics, however, can be inferred. Poorer households found it much harder to lower their already moderate energy use. Households with greater demand also had greater elasticity for change. They achieved this in part by using existing technologies less, like air-conditioning, in part by changing the mix of consumer durables in use: middle-class households switched off their freezers. This alone amounted to a saving of 100 kWh/month. Ironically, the elasticity provided by freezers had been the result of another, earlier form of economizing behaviour. In the high-inflation 1980s and early 1990s it made good sense to invest in frozen food at the beginning of each month. Presumably, the arrival of the freezer led to fewer, more concentrated shopping trips, while unplugging it accelerated the rhythm. The response of Californians in the wake of the 2001 electricity crisis affords a point of contrast, in spite of a similar reward/incentive scheme. Here unplugging the second refrigerator was extremely rare (4 per cent). People were more likely to watch less TV (12 per cent), unplug their computers (15 per cent) or turn off the air-conditioner (30 per cent) and lights (62 per cent) (IEA 2005: 38).

Many changes to daily practices, however, are not voluntary and individual but collective and imposed. Shops, industries and services are important levers in modulating everyday rhythms. Most directly, energy shortages affect the rhythm of work. In Britain, in February 1972, over a million people were made idle on a single day by the power crisis resulting from the miners' strike (*Guardian*, 16 February 1972). During the 2001 blackout in Stockholm, Ericsson told its 11,500 employees to stay home on Monday (Deverell 2003: 59). In Tokyo, some industries have increased the number of shifts. In Ontario, the government responded to the major blackout of 14 August 2003 by closing down all non-essential parts of the provincial and federal government: more than half of federal employees did not go to work in the second half of August. During peak power demand, Beijing forced over 6,000 enterprises to take week-long vacations (IEA 2005: 52–53, 80) . Other evidence, such as in the wake of the 35-hour week adopted in France in 2000, suggests how the re-ordering of the workday significantly alters the rhythm of leisure and social activities, favouring longer, more intensive practices like reading and listening to music, as well as spending more time with family and children (Viard 2004). Studies show how difficult it is for people on shift-work to develop a healthy sleeping rhythm and to coordinate practices with people who are on a different schedule (Rudat 1978). It would be interesting to know more about how disruption-induced changes to working hours affect the rhythm of other practices.

It is especially practices depending on mobility and light that are affected by energy-saving measures. Car-free Sundays re-ordered the rhythm of the weekend during the energy crisis of the early 1970s. In more recent years, one frequent strategy to lower energy consumption has been to change shops' opening hours to save on heating, cooling and lighting costs; in Ontario, the department store chain Hudson's Bay Company cut its energy use by a third in 2003. What did people do in the time the shops were closed? We do not know. One group of hospitals and nursing homes responded to the Ontario power shortage with a set of measures that left barely any quotidian rhythm untouched. Outside lights were switched off – instead of walking alone to their cars, people walked together with escorts. Staff were encouraged to bring cold lunches. Patients were asked to switch off their television sets between 3 p.m. and 8 p.m., disrupting the routine of watching soaps. And people were urged to use the stairs instead of the elevator. The company saved 12 per cent of its usual energy in the week after the blackout (IEA 2005: 81–82).

How long would such measures have to be in force before new habits are internalized? The Brazilian case shows the difficulty of translating short-term adjustments – even when a power shortage lasted ten months – into long-term energy-reducing habits. By the beginning of 2003, electricity demand had almost returned to the same level as on the eve of the crisis. How much energy savings have resulted from changed habits, and how much from energy efficiency measures? In California, it is estimated that 70–75 per cent of the 4200 MW customer load reductions in the summer of 2001 came from life-style change, such as watching less TV or switching off the air-conditioning, 25–30 per cent from more energy-efficient equipment, appliances and buildings. It is the latter that are expected to have a life-long effect. Whether the former can perpetuate themselves is more doubtful (Goldman et al. 2002).

So far we have focused on measures aimed at avoiding serious blackouts. But what and who exactly is disrupted when the lights go out? One of the earliest detailed accounts of people's reactions comes from the blackout that spread across the eastern seaboard of the United States in the late afternoon of 9 November 1965, affecting 25 million people. Six days after the breakdown, the National Opinion Research Centre (NORC) began to interview 1,313 people, offering a nuanced picture of where people were and how they reacted to the blackout, analysing groups by class, gender and location (children were curiously neglected). Significantly, this study was framed by a general interest in public reactions to national crises, reflecting concerns about potential panic and a vacuum of authority in the wake of the Cuban missile crisis in 1962 and the Kennedy assassination the following year; the report was commissioned by the Office of Civilian Defense (NORC 1966).

In fact, NORC researchers found that most people were not the least alarmed by the blackout. Two-thirds had experienced earlier power failures in their neighbourhood and initially thought it was an 'ordinary', localized event (NORC 1966: 10–11). People mainly learned of the seriousness of the event from neighbours, family and radio; most television stations were disabled throughout the blackout. There was no panic. '[W]ithout knowledge of its vast scope,' the NORC concluded, 'people could incorporate the blackout into their preformed conceptions of permissible permutations in their situations' (NORC 1966: 13). Americans in 1965, in other words, did not expect ordinary life to be always running smoothly. They lived with an in-built degree of elasticity. Breakdowns were just part of normality.

What was the emotional response to the blackout? The majority reported that strangers were unusually helpful and friendly to each other. Only a small minority (3.6 per cent) felt that people were taking unfair advantage of each other. For a significant number, the blackout was an occasion to break with their normal routines and 'make a holiday' – 11.9 per cent total, rising to 26 per cent after 4 a.m. (NORC 1966: 24). Emotional responses diverged considerably, however. When interviewed, 31 per cent of men and 21 per cent of women said they 'enjoyed it'. Interestingly, the rate of enjoyment went up the longer the blackout lasted. Interviewers noted the social dynamics of observed 'mirth making': joy was contagious. Fright, by contrast, was far less so. Only a quarter of women said they were frightened at some stage that others might 'misbehave'. They were 'so restless they couldn't sit long in a chair'. But these feelings were short-lived and relatively 'mild'. The dominant negative feeling was boredom and a sense of enforced passivity. Around one-fifth of people felt 'bored'. Almost half the men and women interviewed were 'annoyed' that they could not do the things they wanted to (NORC 1966: 24, 50, 52–67).

Above all, the blackout affected rhythms of communication and social interaction. The New York Telephone Company reported an all-time record of calls; it operated a full service with the help of diesel generators. Between 5 and 6 p.m., local calls shot up by 800 per cent. Interestingly, hardly anyone called the police, the electric company or the telephone operator. Most calls were to relatives other than household members (NORC 1966: ch. 4). And, instead of turning for information to City Hall or formal organizations, people turned to local 'public affairs' leaders in the neighbourhood, mainly men with higher income and education and links to voluntary organizations. The blackout, according to NORC researchers, demonstrated how disasters generated their own 'nascent emergency system' as the 'social bases of the social system ... spring to life' (NORC 1966: 31, 37)

How a democratic society copes with disasters that immobilize formal social and political structures was a defining question for research in the 1960s. Studies since have broadly agreed that disasters do not tend to produce panic or normless anarchy (Scanlon 2001). Some researchers have gone so far as to postulate a timeless model of rational human behaviour: 'The modern citizen responds to disasters in the same fashion as his ancestor.' Citizens do not panic, they act as rationally today as they did when they had to protect themselves against harsh winters, failing crops or infectious disease without the help of modern technologies and medicine (Helsloot and Ruitenberg 2004: 98).

The problem with this view is simple. It fails to take into account that what is rational behaviour is shaped by the context in which people act, and this in turn varies, itself the result of social norms, institutions and the technological systems with which they are connected. Many disasters have sparked altruism. Two million volunteers flocked to Mexico City after the 1985 earthquake. In fact, too much altruism can set off more disruption: in 1999, when an earthquake hit the Turkish city of Golcuk, volunteers produced a 32-kilometre-long traffic jam obstacle for rescue vehicles. But disasters can also create an opening for bottled-up social conflict, resulting in open violence and looting. Vulnerability and the social resources for coping with disruption are unevenly distributed. The Chicago heatwave of 1995, which killed 700 people, for instance, hit elderly and poor African-Americans disproportionally hard, because of run-down buildings and infrastructure combined with isolation bred by crime and commercial decline; the Latino Little Village, by contrast, was a busy social and commercial district that facilitated inclusion (Klinenberg 2002: 91).

And the elasticity of everyday life changes over time. It can snap. When the next major blackout struck New York on a blistering hot 13 July 1977 – this time affecting 6 million people – it hit a community scarred by recession, austerity and racial tensions. At Shea Stadium, play stopped in the sixth inning, with the Mets trailing the Cubs 2 to 1. In the heat, the 22,000 fans sang along for almost an hour to the Organist playing 'White Christmas'. Elsewhere the atmosphere was less cool and convivial. In the ghettos, unemployment amongst young African-Americans stood at 40 per cent, more than double that in 1965. As in other disasters, many alarms of theft or fire proved false, but there also was real looting and arson. Firemen had to fight 1,037 fires – six times the average. In Bedford-Stuyvesant, 'bands of determined men, women and even little children' were roving the streets with crowbars, smashing shop windows and helping themselves to clothing, TV sets, liquor and furniture. In the Bronx, looters broke into the Ace Pontiac showroom and drove off with fifty new cars. On 125th street in Harlem, people walked off with bags full of steaks from a meat market. Altogether 2,000 stores were plundered and the police arrested more than 3,500 people, eight times the number during the 1964 and 1968 riots (*Time*, 25 July 1977: 12–26).[2]

Perceptions of what counts as 'normal' and what as unacceptable disruption have likewise changed over time. Technological systems, and the expectations of functional order surrounding them, have transformed the sense of what is an ordinary and what an avoidable breakdown. These values, in turn, are also shaped by politics that inform assumptions about the working order of society, about accountability, and about what people can and should do when things go wrong. Together, these factors influence how disruptions play themselves out. Disruption, in other words, alerts us to how rhythms need to be situated within both technological and political cultures. Three short examples illustrate the different dynamics at work.

The first example comes from a developed country with an unusually distinguished record of things breaking down or not materializing: socialist East Germany. The GDR was not a 'consumer society' in the classic sense, but people here too had a lot of stuff. The difference was that many private goods and services were scarce and shoddy or required 'connections' and many years of patience. Everyday life moved to the rhythms of queuing, making-do, things breaking down and trying to fix them. The case of the Sparwasser family of Oranienburg tells a sad, familiar tale. They were a family of seven with a disabled mother. Having waited for twenty years for a car, the family was finally able to jump the queue in 1986. After picking up the car from the VEB works in Magdeburg, the Dacia 1310 developed one fault after another. At 690 kilometres the radiator and speedometer ceased to function. Thirty kilometres later Mrs Sparwasser had to return it again because the starter would not work. At 3,200 kilometres the gear unit gave up. By 3,600 kilometres the ball-bearings had become defective. Two hundred kilometres later, the clutch went. Mrs Sparwasser was exasperated. Each time she went back to the VEB works she was told the problem had been fixed and everything was fine. Now the warranty was coming to an end. The family's routines were thrown into chaos. The Sparwassers avoided longer trips and, like so many people in East Germany, had to use up their holidays to return and collect their defective product from the factory (Bundesarchiv Berlin 1986).

This saga of breakdowns was more than a string of personal bad luck. What makes these cases interesting, and why we know about them, is that these private frustrations had a public outlet. The GDR had an elaborate petitioning system (even encouraged it), where citizens could voice their complaints or suggestions to the heads of the regime. Historians have mainly viewed this system as an instrument to contain political opposition, if with diminishing success over time. But it also worked as a channel for the frustrations of daily life. The endless wait for the telephone, the queuing for children's clothes, or, in the case of the Sparwassers, sitting once again on the side of the road in a broken-down car – the petitioning process amplified a sense that life was not ticking according to its proper rhythm, that the regime was failing on its promise to bring material comfort to all. Through the petitioning system, breakdowns exposed the dysfunctionality of the regime. The thick documentation of letters and complaints to the VEB works that the Sparwassers prepared was a kind of quotidian politics of disruption, about the rights of the little man to things running smoothly, and to redress where they don't – in short, of not having to put up with repeated breakdown. As Mrs Sparwasser put it bluntly: this 'cannot be normal'.

The second episode is from contemporary Canada and concerns the normalization of disruption. For families who had lived in Manitoba for generations, the frequent flooding of the Red River was part of their culture. When newcomers began to prepare for the risk by moving possessions to higher floors or storage, they were disparaged by locals for being 'excessive'. Floods happened. There was nothing that human intervention, adaptation or planning could do to change that. In this case, the habit of naturalizing flood made for such a high degree of elasticity in people's behaviour that, when a major flood struck in 1997, many were unwilling to evacuate or move their animals to higher ground, with devastating consequences (Scanlon 2001: 1–2).

The breakdown of the Hongkong Mass Transit Railway (HMTR) on 6 May 1996 shows the opposite force at work: the denormalization of disruption. Instead of being normal, the public came to view disruption as exceptional and avoidable, the result of human error and mismanagement. On the morning of 6 May 1996, a track-circuit defect near one station escalated into a delay that held up sixty-six trains for almost an hour. When trains resumed at 11 a.m., 156,000 commuters were late for work. Forty-four people had to be hospitalized, including three pregnant women. The incident is interesting because it occurred in one of the world's most intensely used and most reliable transport systems. The HMTR carries 800 million passengers a year. In 1995, a mere 0.1 per cent of its 717,000 journeys had an incident, that is, less than one potentially accident-causing incident for every million passengers.

The breakdown nicely illustrates the inherent tensions in tightly coupled, interactive systems that require decentralization as well as centralization but cannot have both. It is also revealing for the mismatch between objective performance and subjective expectations, or, to be precise, between the operator's idea of routine behaviour during a delay and that of many passengers. For it was the number of people pressing alarm-plungers that created the domino-effect of a technical fault tuning into serious delays and overcrowding. The immediate response of the transport operator was to blame passengers for the inappropriate use of the alarm-plungers, which had been designed for serious emergency use only. The railway expert in charge of the inquiry gave the HMTR a clean sheet of health. The system's safety and reliability were as high as possible, he found. The system broke down because so many alarms were set off – 109 in total – 'petty actions by disgruntled passengers'. The public was outraged. The delay was unacceptable, a sign of inefficiency and incompetency. Newspapers attacked the subway system as 'suited to a Third World backwater', 'flabby and frayed around the edges' (Ellis 1998).

What these cases point to is a dilemma of vulnerability. Groups that view disruptions and disasters as 'normal', acts of God or things that 'just happen' are less likely to challenge authorities, demand redress or radically alter their habits. This can defuse potentially conflictual situations; one reason why there was not more anger during the 2001 blackout in Stockholm, it has been argued, was that the district most affected had a high percentage of immigrants used to power shortages (Deverell 2003). But this also leaves groups disproportionally vulnerable to disruptions that are of a more extreme force or of a different kind than the 'normal' one. By contrast, groups with a low threshold of tolerance will place much higher demands on social and technological systems to run smoothly. This makes political authorities and social organizations more vulnerable to frustration and may create unrealistic expectations of a normality without breakdowns.

How people respond to breakdowns is further shaped by political economy. It is not that in capitalist societies things do not break down. Consumer movements in the 1960s and 1970s fought many battles over cars that would not start or exploded on impact. Notwithstanding decades of improved standards, people continue to complain about faulty products and services, especially computers, public services, electrical goods and car repairs; in Australia, 73 per cent of households complain about these an average 3.4 times per year, to be precise (SOCAP 1994). Rather, the difference lies in the ways in which frustration with breakdown is channelled. In market societies, complaints are directed at particular companies, not the government or the market system as such. Frustrations, accountability and influence are diffused, whereas they were bundled and laid at the door of the regime in socialist societies.

The question is how these structural traits have played themselves out historically. Have they enabled market-based societies to live with disruptions more or less well? How do societies perform that depend more on familial and social networks in absorbing the pressure of breakdowns and repair than others? When are breakdowns accepted in silence, when do they feed back information that might improve the performance of systems? There are parallels here to Hirschman's distinction between exit and voice (Hirschman 1970). The complexity of modern technological systems adds further to the dilemma of mobilizing voice. In a society where disruptions are accepted as relatively normal, what are the incentives to make life run more smoothly? Making people more demanding, giving them more outlets to vent their frustration (complaints management) and posting performance targets creates higher pressures for accountability and performance. But it may also initiate a vicious cycle of ever-higher expectations of perfect functionality. In a competitive marketplace, a company might put customer service to good use to gain an edge over rivals: fly with us, we have fewer delays and do not lose as many bags. However, in the world of public transport, motorways, energy and other natural monopolies where there is no choice but through which so many rhythms of everyday life are coordinated in the first place, this force is much weaker.

The challenge of managing disruption has been amplified by the historical promise of networks to bring smooth flow and universal access to all. We except to have running water on demand, day and night, and have light when we flick a switch. It is useful to recall how recent such expectations are in the developed world, and how unusual they remain elsewhere. In British cities, constant water supply was only introduced from the 1860s, but even then the system was prone to temporary suspensions, as in the shortages of the mid-1890s with which we began our discussion. Victorian engineers and urban reformers had optimistic views of the efficiency and durability of their networks. Yet these gained their true public force in the social-democratic vision of public services, as suggested by the case of London, where water was municipalized in 1902. Public control of public services, so the assumption, would put an end to shortages. There would be a civic contract between citizens and the state. The state agreed to increase the scope and level of consumption – by expanding networks, connecting the countryside and bringing everyone into the realm of a civilized existence. Consumers, in return, were expected to be good citizens and not waste water (Taylor and Trentmann forthcoming).

On the eve of the Second World War, progressive leaders in Britain openly mused that municipalization had made droughts a thing of the past. This was fantasy. There were major shortages in 1921 and 1933–4. But now such disruptions tended to be externalized, blamed on temporary, external variants. They were not part of normality. The association of rising levels of water consumption with civilization and progress made it difficult to acknowledge the pressures internal to the system caused by consumers' expanding and intensifying practices of bathing, gardening, washing the car and, after the Second World War, using a washing machine. The civic contract inevitably limited the scope of action in response to shortages, favouring the expansion of supply through reservoirs and transfers between networks at the expense of modulating consumption in the long-term. It prioritized appeals to voluntary restraint during serious drought – be a good citizen and do not water your garden, please, drive a dirty car as a sign that you care for the community, and so on. But these were only momentary signals, and with mixed effect. As one critic pointed out during the 1934 drought, appeals to consume less water were of doubtful value when people had for years been encouraged to consume more in the pursuit of cleanliness and civilization (Taylor et al. in press).[3]

Reprivatization in the last two decades has not put an end to shortages or black-outs, but it has changed the political constellation between consumers and producers. On the one hand, it has made disruptions once again politically more sensitive and confrontational. As in nineteenth-century London, the fact that companies were making profits while their customers went without services created public anger and conflict (Morgan and Trentmann 2006). After the blackout in Buenos Aires in 1999, people took to the streets and burned tyres in protest. The situation was only defused when the electricity company Edesur accepted liability and began to compensate users (Ullberg 2005). More recently, some commuters have set trains on fire near Buenos Aires in protest against delays during rush-hours. Likewise in Soweto, privatization in 1999 has made the utility company Eskom a target in grass-roots battles over cut-offs (Egan and Wafer 2004).

On the other hand, the move to private ownership has come with a new recognition that consumers are not just recipients but co-producers, whose behaviour is vital for managing shortages. In Britain, in 2006–7, water companies defused criticism of 'fat-cat profits' through a consumer-orientated campaign with information on expected shortages and water-saving tips. The Californian 'Flex Your Power' campaign in 2006 told consumers that they had it in their power to resolve the power shortage collectively (Todd and Wood 2006). It could be argued that we see here a general trend of providers trying to recruit users to assist with maintenance, repair, monitoring and servicing, already widespread in the commercial service sector (self-service, customer service) but also reaching into public services which seek to capitalize on users' competence and voice (Clarke et al. 2007).

Disruptions deserve more respect than they tend to be given. If it were unwise to romanticize breakdowns, it would be equally wrong to see them purely as a temporary, external intrusion or an irritating nuisance. Breakdowns are a systemic part of everyday life. Consumers are not only their victims. They play an active role in absorbing and coordinating them, in some cases even generating them. Breakdowns can serve as a temporary flashlight, illuminating dynamics of everyday life that lie obscured in more continuous and holistic accounts of consumer culture. There are synergies here with an older intellectual tradition, that of pragmatism, which recognized the insights to be gleaned during irregular moments when habits are broken or switched. Looking at a landscape with our head upside down, William James argued, makes the colours grow richer and more varied, and the contrasts between light and shade more marked (James 1890: 81; see also Brown 2003: 74–80).

Most disruptions in social life are not as deliberate, nor do they turn the world upside down, but they disturb habitual ways of doing things. Disruptions disturb the conventional view of consumer culture, which has been painted either as a paradise of choice and freedom or as a smooth materialistic machine that has turned active citizens into docile, privatized consumers. Quite the opposite, the more consumption, the more breakdown, tension and patchwork. Disruption reveals the material world as tenuous and fragile, one that involves a lot of energy, maintenance and adjustments from consumers.

Reactions to disruption stretch from fury to a sense of liberation, but, beyond individual responses, we should also appreciate the social and political energies created in moments when collective habits suffer from interference. Disruptions trigger new social processes and political consciousness. The hope to create perfectly functional systems is therefore as unhelpful as an attitude of powerless resignation that simply treats all interferences as unavoidable. A more realistic attitude would be to recognize disruptions as a creative as well as destructive part of normality. This brings us back to poor John Kyffin, the London shopkeeper with whom we began, who had his water supply interrupted in 1895. Kyffin first took the water company to court. Then, after his case was thrown out, he mobilized citizens in his neighbourhood and led a deputation to the local government demanding stiff penalties against the water companies in compensation for the shortages they had suffered. It is debatable whether a world without disruptions would be a more desirable place.

Acknowledgements

Thanks to the Economic and Social Research Council for grant RES-052-27-002 and to Heather Chappells for research assistance.

Notes

1. 'Power shortage', again, involves different phases and degrees. In Finland, providers distinguish between 'strained power balance' (forecasts showing insufficient supplies), 'power shortage' (requiring that fast disturbance reserves are activated and obliging producers to offer electricity during the peak loan period) and 'serious power shortage' (consumption is restricted) (Landstedt and Holmstroem 2007).
2. Looting and homicide have also followed other distasters like the poison gas accident in Bhopal in 1984.
3. In 1934, people briefly saved 10 per cent of their regular water consumption. However, such campaigns could also backfire, as in 1921, when, in advance of warnings of the coming drought, many people resorted to previous strategies of

coping with shortages and filled up their bathtubs and other vessels in advance, thus worsening the problem. Direct interference with consumers' habits was a last resort, and only came after industry had its water rationed, as in the 1959 drought, when 170,000 people in the Irwell Valley were prohibited from using their washing machines and even the bath.

References

Apt, J., Lave, L.B. and Morgan, M.G. (2006). Power Play: A More Reliable US Electric System. *Issues in Science and Technology* 22: 51–58.

Bhat, C., Sivakumar, A., Sen, S., Guo, J. and Copperman, R. (2005). Austin Commuter Survey. Center for Transportation Research, Austin: Research Report SWUTC/05/167240-1.

Brown, B. (2003). *A Sense of Things: The Object Matter of American Literature.* Chicago: University of Chicago Press.

Bundesarchiv Berlin, Bundesarchiv Berlin/Hoppegarten: DG 7/1769 Buergeingaben an den Ministerrat der DDR, Abt. Handel und Versorgung, 1986, E 886/86, 13 September 1986 [name changed].

Clarke, J., Newman, J.E., Smith, N., Vidler, E. and Westmarland, L. (2007). *Creating Citizen-Consumers: Changing Publics and Changing Public Services.* London: Sage.

Department of Transport UK. (2005). *Perceptions of Congestion.* London: Department of Transport UK.

Deverell, E. (2003). *The 2001 Kista Blackout: Corporate Crisis and Urban Contingency.* Stockholm: Swedish National Defence College.

Egan, A. and Wafer, A. (2004). *The Soweto Electricity Crisis Committee: A Case Study for the UKZN Project Entitled: Globalization, Marginalization and New Social Movements in Post-Apartheid South Africa.* Durban.

Ellis, P. (1998). Chaos in the Underground: Spontaneous Collapse in a Tightly Coupled System. *Journal of Contingencies and Crisis Management* 6(3): 137–152.

Goldman, C., Barbose, G.L. and Eto, J.H. (2002). California Customer Load Reductions during the Electricity Crisis: Did They Help to Keep the Lights On? *Journal of Industry, Competition and Trade* 2(1/2): 113–142.

Gottlieb, D. and Matre, M. (1976). Conceptions of Energy Shortages and Energy Conserving Behaviour. *Social Science Quarterly* 57(2): 421–429.

Helsloot, I. and Ruitenberg, A. (2004). Citizen Responses to Disasters: A Literature Review and Some Practical Implications. *Journal of Contingencies and Crisis Management* 12(3): 98–111.

Hirschman, A.O. 1970. *Exit, Voice, and Loyalty: Responses to Decline in Firms, Organizations, and States.* Cambridge, MA: Harvard University Press.

IEA, International Energy Agency (2005). *Saving Electricity in a Hurry: Dealing with Temporary Shortfalls in Electricity Supplies.* Paris: OECD/IEA.

Jahoda, M., Lazarsfeld, P.F. and Zeisel, H. (1933). *Die Arbeitslosen von Marienthal. Ein Soziographischer Versuch über die Wirkungen Langdauernder Arbeitslosigkeit.* Leipzig: S. Hirzel.

James, W. (1890). *The Principles of Psychology,* Vol. 2. New York: Henry Holt and Co.

Klinenberg, E. 2002. *Heat Wave: A Social Autopsy of Disaster in Chicago.* Chicago: University of Chicago Press.

Lagadec, P. (2004). Understanding the French 2003 Heat Wave Experience: Beyond the Heat a Multi-layered Challenge. *Journal of Contingencies and Crisis Management* 12(4): 160–169.

Landstedt, J. and Holmstroem, P. (2007). Electric Power Systems Blackouts and the Rescue Services: The Case of Finland. Civil Protection Network (CIVPRO) Working Paper 1.

Latour, B. (2005). *Reassembling the Social: An Introduction to Actor-Network-Theory.* Oxford: Oxford University Press.

Morgan, B. and Trentmann, F., eds (2006). *Journal of Consumer Policy.* Special Issue: The Politics of Necessity 29(4): 345–488.

NORC, National Opinion Research Centre (1966). *Public Response to the Northeastern Power Blackout.* Chicago.

Nye, D.E. (1998). *Consuming Power: A Social History of American Energies.* Cambridge, MA: MIT Press.

Perrow, C. (1999). *Normal Accidents: Living with High-risk Technologies.* Princeton, NJ: Princeton University Press.

Rudat, R. (1978). *Freizeitmoeglichkeiten von Nacht-, Schicht-, Sonn- und Feiertagsarbeitern.* Stuttgart: Kohlhammer.

Scanlon, J. (2001). Lessons Learned or Lessons Forgotten: The Canadian Disaster Experience. Institute for Catastrophic Loss Reduction (Paper no. 1).

SOCAP, Society of Consumer Affairs Professionals in Business Australia (1994). Study of Complaint Handling in Australia, Report 1.

Taylor, V. and Trentmann, F. (forthcoming). Liquid Politics: Water and the Politics of Everyday Life in the Modern City.

Taylor, V., Chappells, H., Medd, W. and Trentmann, F. (in press). Drought is Normal: The Socio-technical Evolution of Drought and Water Demand in England and Wales, 1893–2006. *Journal of Historical Geography.*

Texas Transportation Institute (2007). Annual Urban Mobility Report.

Todd, A.M. and Wood, A. (2006). 'Flex Your Power': Energy Crises and the Shifting Rhetoric of the Grid. *Atlantic Journal of Communication* 14(4): 211–228.

Trentmann, F. and Taylor, V. (2006). From Users to Consumers: Water Politics in Nineteenth-Century London. In *The Making of the Consumer*, ed. F. Trentmann. Oxford: Berg.

Ullberg, S. (2005). *The Buenos Aires Blackout: Argentine Crisis Management across the Public–Private Divide*. Stockholm: CM Europe Volume Series.

Viard, J. (2004). *Le Sacre du Temps Libre: La Société des 35 Heures*. La Tour d'Aigues: L'aube.

Wilhite, H. (2008). *Consumption and the Transformation of Everyday Life: A View from South India*. Basingstoke: Palgrave Macmillan.

–5–

My Soul for a Seat

Commuting and the Routines of Mobility
Tom O'Dell

Introduction

Home, 7:32 a.m., a February morning. That's where I was a few minutes ago. Two minutes behind schedule. I'm biking down a dark and snowy path towards the train station. On my way I will pass three clocks: two outside the offices of two different opticians, and one by the train station. I have one traffic light as a potential obstacle in my flow between these clocks. Each clock is a marker of how my day is going to be. I don't know why I am so stressed about being two minutes behind schedule... I've actually set my watch five minutes ahead of time, so I know I'm actually three minutes ahead of schedule. But in my own mind, my ideal time for leaving for the train is two minutes behind me. I bike a little harder. If there is one thing I hate, it's standing on the train platform, and watching my train leave. It always happens when I am most certain that I am on time – or just a little uncertain.

This is the beginning of my commute to work. It's basically the same routine every day. Same bike path. Same clocks. Same tension. No matter how early I leave home. At times it may feel like a necessary evil, but usually commuting to work is, like most routines, something which I, and millions of other people, 'just do' on a daily basis. At first glance it is tempting to view commuting as a very distinctive and particular type of routine due to its public nature. As people make their way from home to work and back again they handle a series of boundaries between themselves and the surrounding world. And this is a phenomenon which I shall reflect upon shortly. But commuting also shares a number of characteristics with many other types of routines (such as making meals, doing the laundry or housecleaning) which people engage in on a regular basis. It is, for example, stretched out over time (taking anywhere from a few minutes to a few hours of time to perform each day), and composed of a series of practices that are linked together. Very often these practices are not only linked together, but even coordinated with other activities, and organized in a very particular serial order.

Daily routines have long been characterized as the epitome of that which is grey, bland and stifling. These are the black holes of joy, spontaneity and inspiration from which scholars have all too often presumed we need to escape (Cohen and Taylor 1992) – simple, mindless activities which we do over and over again. But this perspective belies the fact that most routines, particularly those which are serially linked, involve polyrhythmic fluctuations of activity and non-activity which, while subtle, can be complexly organized, and highly meaningful aspects of people's daily lives (Seigworth and Gardiner 2004: 141).

Taking this position as a point of departure, the following text uses commuting as an empirical prism through which to problematize daily routines and their rhythms while simultaneously challenging the perception of them as being static, uniform and empty of meaning. In order to do this, the chapter begins by outlining some of the ways in which the routines of commuting are important to people. It then proceeds by interrogating the issue of structure and the manner in which people creatively and ritualistically use routines at times to provide order to their lives, while at other times they find themselves longing to break out of existing patterns of behaviour. As part of this discussion, the text argues that routines do not just unfold in a simple predetermined and mechanical fashion; they have tempos and rhythms of their own that make them susceptible to change, but that even help people *adapt to* the ever-changing context of everyday life. As a means of exemplifying this, the chapter closes by examining the particularities of the commute as a public endeavour in which people continuously use routines as vehicles of boundary control – ever moving back and forth between states of public and private; work and leisure; and home and away.

In order to address these issues, the work in hand draws upon a several different forms of methods and materials. In part, it is anchored in a combination of short interviews conducted with commuters, and materials gathered from local Swedish newspapers about commuting.[1] But more importantly, larger portions of the following text are the products of phenomenologically orientated empirical observations I have made over the past seven years on my own commute between Lund and Helsingborg. These observations constitute a form of auto-ethnography in which I have allowed my own experiences as a commuter to work as a point of departure for portions of the analysis. The choice to introduce auto-ethnographic materials was motivated by my desire to move the analysis from beyond the bounds of what people say they are doing, and into the realm of the actual rhythms, tempos and practices of commuting.[2]

The Drama of the Undramatic

It's actually gotten to the point that passengers have gotten into fist fights on the bus... Things are difficult.

Bus driver in Åtvidaberg[3]

I don't dare go on the bus again in Åtvidaberg since I was yelled at by elderly passengers the one time when I happened to take my sick child and baby carriage on the bus to the hospital…

Mother in Åtvidaberg[4]

The field of mobility has become a vital arena of research activity in the humanities and social sciences over the course of the past decade. This is a subject of study in which vast amounts of work have already been conducted on subjects ranging from international migration and the life circumstances of migrant laborers to tourism and transnational travel. However, in light of how much time most people spend commuting, a review of the literature reveals that this is an activity (and form of mobility) which has attracted surprisingly little scholarly attention.[5] At least part of the reason for this can be found in a comment made by an anthropological colleague when the subject was broached recently. As he said, 'The problem with studying commuting is that it is just so damn boring.' The problem here, however, is not an issue of boredom. It is an issue of moving into, and challenging, the realm of the taken for granted.

As Elizabeth Shove has argued (2003: 1), social scientists have been highly preoccupied with studying that which is explicit and dramatic, but less interested in the inconspicuous routines and praxes that saturate daily life. Turning our attention to the routines and rhythms of daily life implies a shift in focus that takes us into the world of what Joe Moran (drawing upon Georges Perec) has called the 'infra-ordinary: that part of our lives that is so routine as to become almost invisible, like infrared light' (2007: 3). And as Edward T. Hall has demonstrated (1990), it is a world that has been ritually organized to the degree that, if it seems to be invisible, it is because the rituals we engage in have nearly become embedded in our biological being and sense of self. But make no mistake about it. The rituals and rhythms of activities we are dealing with here are not genetically inherited or passed down. To the contrary, while they may produce actions that seem nearly instinctive, they are thoroughly cultural. And if commuting seems like a dreadfully boring subject for the anthropologist to approach, it is because the organization of these rituals is so thoroughly complete that it usually works to disguise the dramas and tensions ever implicit in the commute – dramas which can become vividly apparent when one least expects it.

Take, for example, the local commuter buses in Åtvidaberg, a small, economically hard-pressed, rural mining town in Sweden. Over a period of nearly four years, the municipal authorities had provided the local population with free bus services. These services proved to be highly popular, particularly (but not exclusively) amongst the elderly, who otherwise found it difficult to travel into the centre of town to purchase food and conduct their errands. But by October 2006 the situation on the buses had gotten out of control as people began fighting over the seats and standing space within the buses. As the local paper reported on the tensions surrounding the buses, the cultural dynamics of the commute quickly came into view. Among other things, arguments erupted as to who was the most 'handicapped' and thereby had the rights to the special seats designated for the physically impaired. Mothers with small children complained about the verbal abuse they encountered as they brought their children and baby carriages onto the bus – taking valuable space which could otherwise have been used by people with walkers and impeding the ability of everyone to enter and exit the bus. Others were accused of joyriding and just using the buses as a means of killing time. And finally there were those passengers who wondered if it was really fair that youths used the buses, taking seats, and thereby forcing some elderly to stand with their walkers. At issue here were questions concerning such things as rights of access to transportation, personal identity in relation to specific places and spaces, and presumptions about particular rhythms of the commute (such as those related to the processes of entering and exiting the bus, finding or giving up a seat, or for determining the 'appropriate' duration of time for which one could 'fairly' claim a space on the bus).

Ultimately, in an attempt to regain control over the situation, the municipality of Åtvidaberg opted to cease providing the local community with free bus services and replaced them with fee-based services. But the complaints and criticisms coming out of Åtvidaberg remind us of the degree to which routines, such as the particular practices associated with regularly performed commutes, can come to have such meaning to people that they are willing to fight over them when those routines become disrupted, and the identities associated with them are thereby brought into question.[6] Beyond this, the example from Åtvidaberg also points to the fact that commutes are embedded in a wealth of ritualized activities that we normally take for granted (concerning such practices as boarding buses, finding seats, maintaining social distance, etc.) that need to be maintained even in shifting conditions, such as those caused by overcrowding. Without them, even the most routinized forms of travel quickly degenerate into chaos. The question is: how is all of this structured, and how can any semblance of order be maintained in light of the fact that no two commutes can ever be exactly the same? In order to approach this question, let me turn to the specifics of the train ride between Lund and Helsingborg.

My Soul for a Seat

> Taking the train to work every day takes an enormous amount of energy. Two hours of glum faces, crowdedness and sweat, and on top of it all, a lot of worry – you sit there like a sardine in a can, if something should ever happen...!
>
> Anna

I think it's tragic that you have to pay 2000 Swedish Crowns every month to stand two hours a day, and you just don't stand. Usually you have some unknown person's breath working as a fan in your face, and in the morning it's not all that fresh. I can promise you.

Johanna[7]

Commuting by train is not a phenomenon that many people regard very highly – if you ask them. Some may speak appreciatively of being able to bike or walk to the train, of getting fresh air, and perhaps even a little exercise. But press people on their experiences of commuter trains, and one enters a realm of frustrating delays, crowded cars, obnoxious passengers and uncomfortable proximities. From this perspective, the commute is a 'necessary evil' of sorts, whose negative reputation has long been reinforced and further denigrated by a prevalent flora of popular representations found in films and books in which commuting works as the ultimate symbol of drudgery: a space of flow inhabited by ashen grey and alienated faces, staring blankly into nothingness. This is a morally charged genre of popular folklore wherein train lines are all too easily likened to zones of transit in which machines transport the empty husks of humanity, so ravaged by the pressures of work and the intensities of the rat race that their bodies are hardly capable of registering the impulses to which they are exposed. The train is here not only a means of transportation, but also a jungle of micro-mobilities in which the social order and the sanctity of one's own identity are ever threatened, and on the brink of oblivion, as bodies are jammed together, jarred around, intermixed and hurled forward along the trajectory of the tracks.

But implicit in images of the rat race are not only notions of the threat of flux and disorientation, but even the overwhelming and crushing weight of structure as people engage in the exact same routines day after day. This is also an aspect of life on the rails to which Michel de Certeau has drawn attention. His observations were based upon rail travel in general and not commuter travel specifically; nonetheless, his insights can work as a fruitful point of departure for a consideration of the role that structure plays in relation to routines. In Certeau's view, trains were anything but chaotic; to the contrary, train travel was a phenomenon he referred to as 'Travelling incarceration':

Immobile inside the train... The unchanging traveller is pigeonholed, numbered, and regulated in the grid of the railway car, which is a perfect actualization of the rational utopia. Control and food move from pigeonhole to pigeonhole: 'Tickets, please...' 'Sandwiches? Beer? Coffee?...' Only the restrooms offer an escape from the closed system. (1984: 111)

In Certeau's eyes, the railroad car was little more than a rolling tyrannical prison. Once aboard, there was little chance for escape. Everyone had an assigned place, and the conductor carefully checked to make sure that everyone was in the right place and remained there.

Listening to complaints coming from passengers on the Lund–Helsingborg line (as well as those coming from the buses in Åtvidaberg), it is interesting to note that most of the grievances that are voiced focus upon the moments in which the flow of daily routines break down and cease to comply with any laws of predictability. Day after day, people like me leave their homes at approximately the same time,[8] have a more or less predetermined tempo with which they proceed to the station, and even specific places on the platform at which they stand and wait for the train. But the rhythm of the commute is broken here, and a moment of unpredictability is injected into the routine as commuters stand anticipating the train. As the train approaches, the cultural energy on the platform thickens. Newspapers are folded, bags are picked up and idle daydreams dissipate.

Ben Highmore has described the daily commute as a phenomenon which people engage in 'as if on autopilot' (2004: 310), but as the train approaches, commuters in Lund seem collectively to shut off their autopilots. While each person's commute may be an individual project, this is the point at which it becomes tangibly entangled in a larger collective movement. People draw together and collect in front of the train's closed doors waiting for them to open – rubbing, touching and pushing one another. The normal boundaries of what Edward T. Hall described as 'personal distance … [the] small protective sphere or bubble that an organism maintains between itself and others' (1990 [1969]: 119) collapse into 'intimate distance' (the distance at which the presence of another person is 'overwhelming' (1990 [1969]: 116). With the sanctity of one's personal space disrupted, the atmosphere on the platform shifts from the lull of waiting, to a more competitive and aggressive mode. But even here, in the chaotic moments before the doors open, ritualized rules of engagement still apply. Backpacks, bags and elbows are all employed strategically to ensure an optimal position, but only within clear limits (physically brushing someone aside is allowed, inflicting pain is not). The eyes of commuters remain either fixed on the doors, refusing to acknowledge the presence of the bodies that at this range must be included in peripheral fields of vision, or peer directly into the necks and backs of heads of those directly in front of them who have successfully jostled their way into the best positions in front of the train's doors.[9]

It is the presence of the train which catalyses the sudden burst of activity on the platform, but in order fully to understand the cultural mechanisms behind this tightening emotional atmosphere, an appreciation of the materiality of the train is necessary. For as it turns out, the trains along the Lund–Helsingborg line feature padded and upholstered seats with retractable trays; they lack hand straps, or poles to hold onto for those who might have to remain on their feet. While commuters in many parts of the world generally expect to stand (and just hope to be able to get on the train), the success of the commute in southern Sweden is entirely dependent upon one's ability to quickly find a seat, claim it and thereby reconstitute the boundaries of one's personal space. Indeed, when one of the local newspapers ran a critical series of articles on the state of the commuter services in the region, it was immediately bombarded by readers' complaints – and their number one complaint was the lack of seating that forced many people to stand on their way to and from work. The commuter rail authorities responded by lengthening the trains, providing much more seating.

Nonetheless, the rush for seats still exists. Commuters can hardly do more than shuffle aboard, but these are the few seconds in which the commute really is a race. And it is the anticipated opening of the doors that releases this unique cultural energy, emanating from the upholstered seats within. Somewhat ironically, these are seats that were placed on the trains to make passengers' trips more comfortable and relaxing, but which paradoxically have a haunting effect upon everyone boarding the train.

As Kevin Hetherington (2004) has pointed out, consumption is not just about processes of acquisition, use and having. It also concerns issues of absence and disposal (see Munro 2001). And the seats within the commuter train constitute a sort of disposable good that consumers strive to acquire every morning, but which they gladly forfeit every day (twice a day) upon arriving at their destination. But unlike paper plates and Styrofoam cups, which we generally think of as 'disappearing' after we have used them, train seats are relinquished in a way that we hope will only be temporary. The seats are, in other words, perpetually entering and exiting states of 'secondhandedness' (Hetherington 2004: 170–172), of allure and 'used-upness'. They haunt the bodies of passengers through the corporeal memory of how it feels to stand the distance of the commute as opposed to sinking down into a soft seat. And even as commuters get off the train, and leave their seats behind, they presume at some level that the seat (or its equivalent) remains stored on their monthly passes – ready to be reclaimed and pulled out of storage upon the pass's re-invocation at the end of the day. In a sense, the pattern of consumption here is a perpetually cyclical one of acquisition, divestment, longing and attempted reacquisition, in which the dynamics of return are as important an aspect of the consumption process as the actual acquisition and use of the object in question (the seat).

Rituals of Transformation: Between Home and Work

Once on the train the rhythm and intensity of the commuter's routines shifts yet again. As Christena Nippert-Eng (1996) has argued, this phase of the commute provides people in the morning with the opportunity to re-orientate themselves away from the home and the routines of the private sphere towards work – and the process reverses itself in the evening in a manner that is highly visible.

Take the commute home from work, for example. Compared to the morning commute, this is an emotionally 'lighter' trip. While the morning commute may be characterized by people getting ready for work, reading papers, working on laptops, consuming coffee to get them focused and ready for the hours ahead, the evening commute features buttoned-down collars and loosened ties (which are immediately jettisoned and replaced by leisure clothing upon arrival home). This is a commute in which alcoholic beverages tend to replace caffeinated ones (more so in the US than Sweden), as people talk, joke and prepare themselves mentally for the arrival home (Nippert-Eng 1996: 125–135).

In Nippert-Eng's view, the commute is a liminal experience, something of a bridge between home and work, in which a wide range of 'transitional activities' (1996: 113) take place as people move from one place and realm of daily life to another. It is, in other words, a very important corridor for ritualized processes of identity transformation. Indeed, as one listens to the phone conversations people engage in on the evening trip home, it is obvious that the commuter train is a vessel of anticipation as people coordinate dinner dates and evening get-togethers. But it is also the equivalent of an airport control tower as parents endeavour to locate children and spouses, plan the evening meal, delegate chores and coordinate the shuttle schedule between hockey practice and riding school. To some extent this is indeed a liminal space between home and work in which people begin to shift their mental disposition as they leave one sphere of daily life and proceed to enter another. But to some extent it is also more than this, as the boundaries between home and work are perhaps more blurred than is acknowledged in Nippert-Eng's writing (cf. Tietze and Musson 2002).

Mobile Homes

> It's a blurring of the line separating public and private space... There are women who paint their nails and those who strip them of paint with cotton balls soaked in pungent polish remover... And then there are the clippers, a class of men and women given away by the unmistakable ping in otherwise silent subway cars. Emilia Kelley ... watched a woman finish clipping her fingernails only to move on to her toenails one summer morning on the Red Line. 'She slipped off her shoe, pulled up her foot and started clipping away.'
>
> Layton, quoted in Letherby and Reynolds 2005: 168

Underscoring this fact, it is always surprising to note how readily commuters seem to be able to make themselves at home on a rush-hour train. Rather than being incarcerated in a seat, as Certeau described the situation, the taking of the seat can, I would argue, also be seen as the point at which the micro-processes of home-making are activated. Borders are quickly erected, and flexibly defined personal spaces are established. Closed eyelids, open newspapers, worn earphones, are all effective barriers to the surrounding world, but this is the last line of defence. There are both subtler and more complex processes at work here. As Deleuze and Guattari have pointed out when reflecting upon the notion of home and processes of home-making, 'home does not pre-exist: it was necessary to draw a circle around that uncertain and fragile center, to organize a limited space. Many, very diverse, components have a part in this, landmarks and marks of all kinds' (1987: 311).

Here I am reminded of the events which unfolded around me on one particular morning commute. One of the last available seats on the train was occupied by a young woman's book bag. The woman who owned the bag made no effort to move it as I stood before the seat, and only did so reluctantly after I asked if I could have the seat – whereupon she moved the bag down to the floor between the two chairs, where it continued to work as a divide. Before I arrived she had already folded down the table tray in front of her, and placed a book and a notebook on it. As the train departed from Lund, she sat and listened to an iPod through headphones, and, having momentarily looked at the book, wrote '50 cl = 500 ml, 30 cl = 300 ml' in her notebook. After this she picked up her cell phone from her lap, and pressed a few buttons. A few seconds later she looked at her telephone again and wrote some more in her notebook. To my surprise, I realized that she was not alone. She was doing her homework with someone else I could not see. We were on a train, but we could have just as well been sitting at a kitchen table.

Her activities were not unique, but part of a larger flexible pattern of routines which most commuters engage in ceremoniously on each commute as they stake out public space and convert it into semi-private space by furnishing it with their personal possessions. In this sense, iPods, laptops, cell phones, books, cups of coffee and papers from work do not just help people orientate themselves towards the home or work. They also help to 'warm' (cf. Ger 2005) public space (in ever-shifting contexts), and make it more hospitable to the needs and wants of the individual commuter. But they also do more than just warm space and make it seem more home-like. Part of their ability to make this space feel more hospitable is derived from their propensity to work as conduits of what Erving Goffman referred to as 'civil inattention' (1971: 209, 219), the process through which people can engage with one another in an ordered but seemingly disengaged manner. Working as cultural attractors of attention, they implicitly help to define everyone and everything else in our immediate surroundings as incidental and of peripheral interest. They are in other words both buffering tools of disengagement and symbolic fences demarcating the difference between the here and the there of commuter space. And it is perhaps for this reason that I felt slightly uncomfortable as I watched the woman beside me.

On my commute over the years I have watched hundreds of people send SMS messages, and always wondered what they were discussing, and with whom. Planning the evening's activities? Receiving a grocery list? Announcing an arrival time? This, however, was the first time I had ever partaken of another person's SMS correspondence, and understood its content. I was surprised by my own response. I felt slightly uneasy and dirty. Like a voyeur. Like someone who had secretly opened someone else's mail. All of this reminded me of how I felt a few years earlier when I began overhearing other people's private cell phone conversations. In those days I tried not to hear. I even turned my head away from the speaker, as if that would diminish my ability to listen (strangely enough, I still do this).

From Novelty to Routine

The cell phone worked in new ways to destabilize the boundary between public and private, home and away. As it spread through society, people quickly developed new cultural competencies for handling this border (Caron and Caronia 2007). Here, people speaking on cell phones learned to create walls separating them from the outside world by turning their backs, sinking their voices, speaking while staring into empty space, and avoiding eye contact with others. And while many of these techniques have proven to be effective while using a cell phone on a street corner, they have proven to be of limited use within the confines of a railway car. Here, unwritten rules have slowly begun to take shape, defining how loudly, long and intimately one should speak on the phone. But the routines associated with the cell phone remain something of a contested arena of cultural praxis. The soundscape of the cell phone conversation freely invades the private space of all within earshot. Speakers take hostages, who at times start their own uprisings and protests, or seek refuge in the growing number of cell phone-free railway cars that are appearing on transit lines. At the heart of these tensions lies the simple question of 'whose space is this, and what rights do I command over in *my* space'?

'Overhearing' my neighbour's SMS actualized many of these issues and suddenly placed a number of inconspicuous details that I had largely taken for granted in a new light. I tried more than ever to be polite, and not watch her doing her homework. As I did so, however, I found myself accidentally overhearing the other conversations around me. And between us still lay the book bag with which it all began. The bag, as it turns out, was more important in the context of this trip than I had first realized, because in moving the book bag, the woman next to me had opened part of the space on the train that she had reserved for herself. At some level, this was a very small and simple gesture of hospitality – and without reflection we had entered a vaguely defined guest–host relation. After all, she had opened part of the space she had staked out for herself to me, and I had gladly accepted this hospitable gesture – and in so doing proceeded to embark upon the cultural journey that would transform me from a competitor (a person racing to find a seat) to a visitor (claiming my right temporarily to inhabit this space). My discomfort over having 'overheard' her SMS (no matter how impersonal it was) was somehow linked to this first gesture – perhaps even by the fact that we had both created small home spaces so close to one another, but that I had then peered over my neighbour's fence. In so doing, like a guest going through his host's bedroom drawers, I had transgressed the laws of privacy governing hospitality. As Derrida has pointed out (2000, 2001), hospitality is both fragile and complex:

> Nowadays, a reflection on hospitality presupposes, among other things, the possibility of a rigorous delimitation of thresholds or frontiers: between the familial and the non-familial, between the foreign and the non-foreign, the citizen and the non-citizen, but first of all between the private and the public, private and public law, etc. (2000: 47–49)

And he continues,

> I want to be master at home…, to be able to receive whomever I like there. Anyone who encroaches on my 'at home,' on my ipseity, on my power of hospitality, on my sovereignty as host, I start to regard as an undesirable foreigner, and virtually as an enemy. This other becomes a hostile subject, and I risk becoming their hostage. (2000: 53–55)

Train seats do not make for spacious homes, but, nonetheless, notions of home (of having one's own space and privacy) work as an important 'cultural backdraft' (O'Dell 2006) informing the rules governing life on the tracks. Commuting may be readily equated with the rat race, but once on the train, people tend to demonstrate high levels of tolerance for one another. This works as long as the laws of hospitality are respected. The risk of exceeding the implicit bounds of hospitality always exists, but as Derrida argued (2000, 2001), hostility and violence are inevitably built-in components of hospitality. Absolute hospitality seems to be an impossibility. Hosts always set limits. They do not just accept anyone, for any length of time, to doing whatever they like. And guests always have the potential of becoming threats. This is the dilemma of hospitality, and this is part of the tension built into the commute.

In this sense, aspects of the train commute are more similar to the workings of a motel or apartment building than the prison to which Certeau alluded. It is a place in which 'room' is rented by the minute rather the hour or day, and in which neighbours meet briefly before moving on. And perhaps it is this aspect of the commute that so readily lends itself to a whole genre of lore concerning chance meetings and found loves. It is a world in which many neighbours will never get to know one another, but in which the simple movement of a bag has the possibility of leading to bigger things. Seats here are more than pigeonholes, and their proximity to one another is more than incarcerating or claustrophobic. It also throws people into vaguely defined relationships with one another that can be the basis for loose-knit communities of repetition and recognition. 'There's the woman who gets off in Landskrona,' 'Oh no. That's the guy who ALWAYS talks on the cell phone. I'm not sitting near him today!,' and so on. This type of knowledge that commuters have of one another may seem superficial, but the results of accumulative and repetitive observations do play a role in the production of a sense of both space and belonging. Their presence is a confirmation of the fact that the rules of the game we engaged in yesterday will still apply today – and at some level I understand what this means in this specific context. It is a reassuring and anxiety-diminishing aspect of the structure of the commute.

Terminus

Commuting may not be an activity that many people actually look forward to, or initially speak of appreciatively, but as one speaks with commuters in southern Sweden, it turns out that most people are actually fairly content with their commutes, and even go so far as to say they would not like to live a life without any commute at all. They may bemoan the pressures which the train's timetable places upon them, or the unreliable degree to which the trains keep their schedules. But by and large, the commute is an important segment of time in the rhythm of people's days. And while it is tempting to view commuting as a monotonous, mindless activity, or as dead or wasted time, the empirical evidence offers a much more complex picture.

This is a world that is not only strung together by a series of small routines with very different rhythms and tempos of their own, it is also a world which people have come to adapt to their own needs as best they can – and which they expect to encounter. It is a world of micro-calculations, each of which may seem meaningless at first glance, but which come to be highly meaningful when woven together in the pulse of daily life. And this is not an insignificant insight. In a time in which employers are increasingly 'allowing' their employees to work from home, and politicians are prepared to expend millions of dollars to shorten people's commutes by a few minutes, there is reason to pause, and reflect not only upon the significance commuting may have in people's lives, but, as social scientists, also upon the state of our understanding of the most elementary activities in which people engage – the routines of daily life. It is here, I would argue, that the structure of the larger cultural world starts to take form. And if the study of rather inconspicuous routines seems trivial or uninteresting, the problem is not the field of study, but our perspective on it. This is where the drama of daily life is anchored, and understandings of it begin to emerge.

Notes

1. Here I would like to thank Susanne Ewert, who, through the auspices of the Folk Life Archives in Lund, spent the better part of two months travelling the local commuter lines, conducting interviews with train personnel and passengers, and photographically documenting 'the daily commute'.
2. In the eyes of some, this may raise questions concerning subjectivity and the gendered position of the scholar. My choice to include other materials than my own personal commuting observations is an attempt to address this concern, but,

clearly, these are questions that are not completely resolved through polyphony, and which therefore need to be borne in mind. See Reed-Danahay (1997) and Marcus (1998: 246) for a larger philosophical and methodological discussion of auto-ethnography.

3. http://archive.corren.se/archive/2006/10/27/ix6llnpjjto6z9d.xml (accessed 3 April 2009). I have translated all quotes which originally appeared in Swedish.
4. http://www.corren.se/asikter/forum/archive/2006/10/43/ix6lndqpfwc4n7t. xml?category1=1097835189-26&category2=1100702641-0& (accessed 3 April 2009).
5. Admittedly, the car, and act of commuting by car, has received a growing degree of scholarly attention in recent years (Laurier 2004; Miller 2001; O'Dell 1997; Thrift 2004); however, the cultural dynamics surrounding commuter trains and buses has remained largely overlooked in the literature (although see Evans and Wener 2006 for a psychological consideration of stress amongst rail commuters). In contrast, there is a great deal of literature of a more technical nature focusing on such things as air quality in trains, risk management, engineering advances, and so on (see, e.g., Letherby and Reynolds 2005).
6. For example, fights over the seats for the physically disabled were, if nothing else, fights over the cultural identity of being not only 'disabled' but even 'most disabled'.
7. In November and December 2006, one of the local newspapers in southern Sweden carried a series of articles that critically described the crowded conditions on the commuter trains running in the region. The two quotes presented here are parts of letters that were sent to the newspaper in response to their articles, and later published on the newspaper's homepage (see http://sydsvenskan.se/skane/article199243.ece?context=print, accessed 3 April 2009).
8. This ritual of departure is so exact that some of the people the Folk Life Archive in Lund interviewed reported that they even set their clocks and daily rhythms based upon the departure time of neighbours (see Ewert 2007).
9. It is interesting to note that while Swedes generally regard themselves as a conflict-avoiding people (see Daun 1996), the ritualized form of aggressivity expressed here is strongly bound to the public sphere in times of crowding. It would never be tolerated in the home or amongst friends.

References

Caron, A. and Caronia, L. (2007). *Moving Cultures: Mobile Communication in Everyday Life*. Montreal: McGill-Queen's University Press.

Certeau, M. de (1988). *The Practice of Everyday Life*. Berkeley: University of California Press.

Cohen, S. and Taylor, L. (1992). *Escape Attempts: The Theory and Practice of Resistance to Everyday Life*. London: Routledge.

Daun, Å. (1996). *Swedish Mentality*. University Park: Pennsylvania State University.

Deleuze, G. and Guattari, F. (1987). *A Thousand Plateaus: Capitalism and Schizophrenia*. Minneapolis: University of Minnesota Press.

Derrida, J. (2000). *Of Hospitality*. Stanford: Stanford University Press.

Derrida, J. (2001). *On Cosmopolitanism and Forgiveness*. London: Routledge.

Evans, G. and Wener, R. (2006). Rail Commuting Duration and Passenger Stress. *Health Psychology* 25(3): 408–412.

Ewert, S. (2007). Känna sig hemma: Pendlarens vardagsstrategier. Unpublished report. Lund: Department of European Ethnology.

Ger, G. (2005). Warming: Making the New Familiar and Moral. *Ethnologia Europaea: Journal of European Ethnology* 35(1/2): 19–22.

Goffman, E. (1971). *Relations in Public: Microstudies of the Public Order*. New York: Basic Books.

Hall, E.T. (1990) [1969]. *The Hidden Dimension*. New York: Anchor Books.

Hetherington, K. (2004). Secondhandedness: Consumption, Disposal, and Absent Presence. *Environment and Planning D: Society and Space* 22: 157–173.

Highmore, B. (2004). Homework: Routine, Social Aesthetics and the Ambiguity of Everyday Life. *Cultural Studies* 18(2/3): 306–327.

Laurier, E. (2004). Doing Office Work on the Motorway. *Theory, Culture & Society* 21(4/5): 261–277.

Letherby, G. and Reynolds, G. (2005). *Train Tracks: Work, Play and Politics on the Railways*. Oxford: Berg.

Marcus, G. (1998). *Ethnography through Thick and Thin*. Princeton, NJ: Princeton University Press.

Miller, D. (2001). *Car Cultures*. Oxford: Berg.

Moran, J. (2007). *Queuing for Beginners: The Story of Daily Life from Breakfast to Bedtime*. London: Profile.

Munro, R. (2001). Disposal of the Body: Upending Postmodernism. *Ephemera: Critical Dialogues on Organization* 1(2): 108–130.

Nippert-Eng, C. (1996). *Home and Work: Negotiating Boundaries through Everyday Life*. Chicago: University of Chicago Press

O'Dell, T. (1997). *Culture Unbound: Americanization and Everyday Life in Sweden*. Lund: Nordic Academic Press.

O'Dell, T. (2006). Cultural Backdraft. *Ethnologia Europea* 35(1/2): 113–118.

Reed-Danahay, D. (1997). *Auto/Ethnography: Rewriting the Self and the Social*. Oxford: Berg.

Seigworth, G. and Gardiner, M. (2004). Rethinking Everyday Life: And Then Nothing Turns Itself Inside Out. *Cultural Studies* 18(2/3): 139–159.

Shove, E. (2003). *Comfort, Cleanliness + Convenience: The Social Organization of Normality*. Oxford: Berg.

Thrift, N. (2004). Driving in the City. *Theory, Culture & Society* 21(4/5): 41–59.

Tietze, S. and Musson, G. (2002). When 'Work' Meets 'Home': Temporal Flexibility as a Lived Experience. *Time & Society* 11(2/3): 315–334.

–6–

Routines – Made and Unmade
Billy Ehn and *Orvar Löfgren*

Introduction

> – So what did you do today?
> – Nothing, just the usual things . . . .

Such an exchange presents a challenge for cultural analysis. What's going on when nothing seems to happen? If you ask people to narrate what they have done during the day, they might answer like this or just mention something that happened out of the ordinary. It is rare that people start listing all the minor routines that carried them from the bed to work, and if they did, all the details would probably feel extremely tedious. If we were really persistent ethnographers, trying to either observe or interview about such routines, the chances are that even then we would miss many of the small micro-routines, bodily reactions or examples of 'just going through the movements', which seem more like reflexes than culturally learned habits.

Doing Nothing?

This problematic has been a starting point for a research project titled *The Secret World of Doing Nothing* (see Ehn and Löfgren 2007, in press). In this chapter we draw on our ongoing work, looking at the large undercurrent of routines, creating rhythms and temporalities in everyday life, rarely noticed or reflected upon. We want to explore some aspects of how this undercurrent is made visible or slowly sinks into invisibility. How is an activity routinized into a habit? Why is it that some activities form more or less unnoticed platforms for other, more conscious activities? In many everyday situations the autopilot takes care of the routines and sets the body or mind free for other parallel activities.

Routines are interesting because their seeming insignificance or invisibility may hide questions of power, freedom and control, for example in the power play of 'my routines, your bad habits'. By looking ethnographically closer at certain routines, we also want to destabilize the notion that they are about 'just going through the same movements'. The repetitious nature of routines often hides important micro-changes that eventually may transform them into something else.

The word 'routine' is actually the diminutive of route, the making of small paths in everyday lives, and this metaphor can be useful to remember. When is a chosen route repeated enough to become a trail, and how are trails redirected, narrowed or broadened in ways that slowly may change them? One important aspect of comparing routines with paths is that once the path is established the moment of conscious choice is diminished. Most routines are likewise usually performed without second thoughts. But if you stop people and ask why and how they walk a certain trail or perform their mundane tasks, they are ready to answer you in detail.

There is a striking vagueness in the terminology surrounding the spaces between choice and ingrained habit. The classic discussions of routines and habituation in the works of scholars like Gregory Bateson (1973), Pierre Bourdieu (1977), Michel de Certeau (1984) and Norbert Elias (1978 [1939]) may be contrasted with some more recent studies of the field undertaken by Jean-Claude Kaufmann (1997), Elizabeth Shove (2003; Shove et al. 2007) and Ben Highmore (2004), who all try to develop a more nuanced understanding of how routines work in our daily lives.

The concepts of routine and habit have a specific Western history. The old world was seen as a system where 'custom was king', keeping people in the grip of unchangeable traditions. Habits belonged to the reform project of modernity. Bad ones should be exchanged for better ones, new routines should reorganize and discipline the everyday clutter of activities (see, for example, the discussion in Ehn and Löfgren 2007 and Highmore 2004). There are still moral or value charges in these concepts. Just think about the differences between sexual routines, which sound rather dull and mechanic, sexual habits, which may contain whatever one can imagine, and sexual rituals, which point to something more symbolically coded than a simple question of lust and desire.

For most people routines are linked to order, predictability and control, or, as Richard Sennett has put it: 'To imagine a life of momentary impulses, of short-term action, devoid of sustainable routines, a life without habits, is to imagine indeed a mindless existence' (1998: 44). They can be seen as tools for organizing the flow of time, and in this process create temporal rhythms and patterns, by sequencing and synchronization. They can also be seen as manuals for what has to be done in everyday life or as maps of our lives where some activities are charted in detail. As economizing devices they may help us to avoid making a myriad choices or reflect about alternatives in recurring situations, something that otherwise may drive us crazy.

Routines are of course much more than a survival technique; they constitute a cultural field full of tensions and paradoxes. What kinds of meanings and values are hidden in daily routines, and how are they related to questions of power, control or freedom? Routines can often provoke conflicts, but again their invisibility or taken-for-grantedness often makes such conflicts difficult to grasp and handle.

Polarities

We would like to start our discussion by exploring some of these polarities. The first one is the juxtaposition of routines as either constraining straitjackets or supportive corsets. There are routines described as (self-made) prisons of ingrained and inflexible habits that constrain actors or prevent people from changing their life, and then there is the opposite view of routines as a comforting and helpful supportive structure that offers security and predictability as well as making it possible to combine many tasks with other activities – from daydreaming to other kinds of multi-tasking. Routines thus may work as a liberating force, providing energy for other things.

Another polarity takes the degree of conscious reflection as a starting point. There is a continuum from mechanical – reflex-like – routines over to emotionally charged habits, collective traditions and symbolically elaborated rituals. Mundane activities can change both ways: rituals can turn into mindless reflexes, and even the most trivial routines may be transformed into more conscious acts, something people experience as reassuring, and comforting or give some symbolic meaning.

The third polarity has to do with ideas of routines as collective patterns as opposed to intensely personal ones. Habits may be described as sets of shared practices that make society possible – as something we are forced to do. Then there is the kind of routines that are described as intensely personal – a secret or mystical world that people create on their own and that become a central part of their self-definition.

Our point is that polarities like the ones above may hide the constant possibilities of transformation found in routines. We are interested in the ways in which an unnoticed routine may become an everyday ritual, or how a routine can be transformed from a feeling of security to one of constraint. How may an unproblematic habit develop into a heatedly contested practice, and how may routines that are seen as intensely personal also show some striking collective, cultural patterns?

Questions like these call for an analysis of situations of transformation, crisis or confrontation, and our approach is to focus on at two major kinds of change: routines made or un-made.

Integrating and absorbing new tasks, skills, objects and ideas into the patterns of everyday affairs is a basic process in individual and social life. By repetition these novelties turn into effortless activities, slowly sinking into the unconscious – but how?

One way of approaching this question would be to develop detailed ethnographies. By observing and describing routines in detail, we ought to find out how they are put together and coordinated, how they are synchronized with other tasks and become part of a daily rhythm. From such ethnography we could move on to explore how they have been learned, perfected or changed.

How is a routine born? As the path we earlier mentioned, one step followed by the next, and the next…, as a practical solution to a specific problem, or as a way of ordering the rhythms of the day, week, year, life? Every new choice or willed action may be the starting point for creating a new habit that sooner or later will turn the task into something taken for granted, as Colin Campbell (1996) has pointed out.

By turning the viewpoint and instead studying situations in which self-evident routines become visible and problematic, we may learn more about the hidden meanings of seemingly inconspicuous everyday behaviour. In situations of crisis the routines of the ordinary day are lost and may be strongly missed. In extreme situations of war and catastrophe people try to reconstruct whatever they can of normal life, but they may also discover how important some of these seemingly trivial routines were in their former lives.

Morning Routines

If you ask people about their routines, they often start with their morning habits, and this is not only because it feels like a natural start. Morning routines are about staggering from sleep to awakening, to get body and mind ready for a new day. Mornings are vulnerable times.

'What is so loaded about morning routines?', the sociologist Christina Nippert-Eng asked in her interview study of how Americans organize their lives between home and work. If we are preparing ourselves for a new working day, routines may work as a warming-up, she says. They ease the daily shifts between home and work. The mindless activities prepare us for the mindful ones (Nippert-Eng 1996: 113ff.). For some people this passage is always demanding, and calls for small tricks of mental reframing. Already before they have left the breakfast table the rest of the family may feel that they are long gone – mentally they are already out of the house.

One of the informants, June, needs to vacuum the kitchen floor before leaving, others keep checking their tie knot or shine their shoes in anticipation of the raid into public life. When Nippert-Eng listens to these morning stories she thinks of the anthropologist Evans-Pritchard's classic study of the ways the Nuer used ceremonial spears that many men carried with them, not as weapons but as mental supports. Where do we find such ceremonial spears in American life, she asks, and decides on the coffee mug carried in a firm grip on the journey to work.

One could, however, have chosen other examples. Let us take up one of them: the morning routine of putting on make-up. This is a practice with complex meanings that calls for a lot of learning before it can be turned into a mechanical routine. It is also a habit charged with different content, from the daily minutes in front of the mirror, to situations where this routine becomes a very conscious and well-planned ritual, as when you are preparing for a new exciting date or an important public appearance.

This is how one woman describes her daily make-up, which usually takes 10–15 minutes of work every morning and maybe later some extra moments with the compact during the rest of the day. For those who are part of the same routine this is a well-known territory, for others it may seem more exotic. In the interview this woman was struck by how little she usually reflected over her morning session and all its complexity, the many elements that have to be organized into a detailed order and rhythm: cleaning the face, putting on foundation, shadows for the eye-lids, a brush for the eye-lashes, mascara pen for the eye-brows, and finally lipstick and rouge, to name a few of the basic details. The hands move fast and confident in the heap of tools, containers and other props in the make-up bag, searching for the right ingredients, colours and mixes. 'Even if I have done this a thousand times,' the woman said, 'it still calls for concentration and a steady hand.' But this does not prevent her mind from wandering. Putting on make-up is for her a moment of daydreaming and planning.

This is a morning situation where both the body and the mind are prepared for the coming day and the raid out into public life. It is a routine that calls for certain choices, about colours and clothes, improvisation or perfection. Do you have to put on make-up for days at home or during vacations? 'It happens that I forget to put on make-up', the woman continues, 'but never if it is a day for work or a party. When I was younger make-up could feel like a must, something my social environment demanded of me, but as an adult I can feel OK without make-up.'

Many women remember strongly how they learned to master this routine, starting out with make-up experiments on dolls or having secret sessions with friends. This particular woman started as an 11-year-old, being taught by her older sister. She remembers the excitement because it felt like a rebellion against the teachers, who had forbidden make-up in school. Make-up has always been surrounded by many unwritten rules, moral judgements and taboos. What level is too much, thus vulgar or just right? What constitutes discreet make-up, and who decides the rules? Should women use make-up at all? You just have to enter the internet to follow the intense discussions about right and wrong, a very complex moral and even ideological universe, linking the private routine both to the multinational cosmetics industry and to debates over gender struggles.

Back to our informant – why does she put on make-up? 'It's a way of feeling good', she answers, 'you wake up feeling pale and greyish, but afterwards you suddenly look alert and nice, with rouge and all that other stuff.' Your skin also grows accustomed to this daily treatment, she says, and you become dependent on moisturizing creams.

Make-up is thus a double act of organizing time by using cosmetics: directed outwards, something done, with the help of more or less expensive goods, to look better and get the appreciation of others, but also a more inward-directed, private and meditative activity where you may be pondering about existential questions of meaning, identity and beauty. In this morning routine the personal and the cultural aspects are intertwined in a number of acquired skills of repetition, the self is strengthened and is at the same time connected to millions of other women.

When we asked a few hundred female students, mainly between 20 and 40, to write down their morning make-up habits, we got very diverse answers. For many of the students this act is very important for their appearance and self-esteem, 'the most important 10 minutes of the day', while others think it is a waste of time and money; for them it is better to look 'natural'. Some women reported that they love to put on make-up, it is a cherished moment of stillness and self-absorption, while others said that they hate it as a stressing and demanding time-thief. They complained that they were usually hardly awake and that they should be running for the bus or subway. In some cases the stress got worse by small children, teenagers or a partner competing for the bathroom space. While some women felt that they were painting their face in order to emphasize their 'true self', others said that they painted a mask to hide themselves.

This routine can be intensely private and solitary, but also a collective act, going to make-up parties, a beauty salon or engaged in together with one's best friend. Make-up also provides a popular topic for conversation between women, trading tips of new brands or techniques, commenting on the looks of others.

A detailed ethnography of make-up teaches us much about how routines are made and changed, according to the context. It also focuses on the ways in which a routine may move on a continuum from an insignificant mundane activity to an act with strong symbolic charges. On the one hand it can be experienced as a banal activity, on the other as a cultural practice full of meanings and evaluations concerning gender, body, power, control and the politics of beauty.

Even less striking routines, for example brushing your teeth, have a similar complexity, and are transformed by time and context. Just the same old routine, day after day, year after year – but yet not. The technology may change; you might experiment with a new toothpaste. At the same time many people look in the mirror at a person constantly changing, a face that some mornings seem very familiar and other days rather unfamiliar. Some people even feel that they are losing control of their life when they do not brush their teeth or have forgotten their brush. An act of personal hygiene is transformed into a kind of moral rearmament. And what about the feelings that are aroused when your partner never learns to put back the cap on the toothpaste tube?

My Routines, Your Bad Habits

Our interest is directed to situations where routines all of a sudden become visible. Changes in the life cycle may bring them up to the surface in different ways. One such transformation is couple making. Two individuals with each their own set of ingrained habits have to negotiate a shared household or everyday life. My normal routines are confronted with your strange habits.

The French sociologist Jean-Claude Kaufmann (2002) has analysed the first step in this process in an interview study about 'the first morning' of a new relationship. People are remembering how it felt to wake up in a new setting in what may be the start of a life-long relationship or just a temporary love affair. As two strangers start to share a morning together they often find themselves manoeuvring in a mine-field, where the tiniest routine may become endearing or provocative. For some of the interviewed couples the magic of new romance makes anything acceptable, while others start looking at the new partner's morning routines in order to find out if this is a kind of person they are ready to share their life with.

Colombine remembers that first morning like this: 'In the beginning this was an unknown house, with strange drawers and food you normally wouldn't eat – it was a journey of discovery, a total discovery.' With eyes wide open she enters the bathroom, checks the fridge and secretly glances at the photos on the desk. As a guest in this new morning universe she is cautious and lets her new partner get the breakfast things and give the morning its shape and rhythm.

Anna wakes up surrounded by her new partner's family. In spite of the friendly atmosphere, she is trying to make herself as invisible as possible, all the time afraid she will lose her face. Every gadget or task seems like a potential trap.

It was not until the third day that Vincent realized he had committed a deadly sin by using the wash basin to the left in the bathroom. It was strictly reserved for the father in the house and the rest of the family had to use the one on the right. 'I thought this was comical, I just couldn't get it,' he remembers.

The new couple watches each other's behaviour, adapts or feels provoked. Many feel petty in their judgements of the other person's habits; even the smallest detail gathers great importance. Is it important to shower before breakfast? Can one blow one's nose on a piece of toilet paper? What is seen as cute and what seems awkward or perhaps even revolting?

As morning follows morning a de- or reroutinization takes place. What kinds of morning routines are you ready to compromise about? As the first intense passion fades away, the tolerance for what is seen as strange behaviour diminishes. You no longer want to live as a guest.

When Isa visited Tristan she felt like a different woman who accepted the strangest habits, like having spaghetti and cheese for breakfast, or going along with the very slow rhythm of her new boyfriend's morning routines. But the day she decided to move in with him, she started to see his habits with new eyes: 'As I opened my suitcase I felt like changing everything according to my own needs.' Others tell that it was through confrontations like these they realized how obsessed they were with their own routines. Why were they so immensely important?

A Cultural Battleground

As new couples try to build up routines together, they synchronize interests and habits. When they create a shared choreography of working together in the kitchen, and keeping a certain order in the bathroom, another aspect of routines comes into the foreground: their potential as a battleground.

The derogatory dimension of a word like routine or habit (see the discussion in Highmore 2002) can be used to ignore or devalue the activities of others. 'It's only a habit' can be stated with a shrug of the shoulders, 'nothing to fight about'. On the contrary it is the taken-for-grantedness of routines and the ways in which they are anchored in our bodies that make them important. 'They are just a part of me!' If they are challenged or questioned, as often happens in a new domestic partnership, this is no little thing.

In her study of couple making Sarah Holst Kjær (2009) discusses the ways in which everyday routines easily are transformed into my good habits and your bad ones. She follows young couples from the kitchen sink to the TV-sofa and the bathroom and shows how important it is for them to synchronize their individual habits into common routines. They try to find a shared rhythm and get into a lot of discussions about what kinds of everyday behaviour they find 'immensely irritating'.

At the same time stereotypes of male and female are reproduced and often used as argument for what is important or not. Who takes the role of the expert of how things should be done in the kitchen and what kinds of arguments about right or wrong are used? In this early manoeuvring, life-long divisions of labour or hierarchies of the importance of routines may be established. (For other discussions of such domestic conflicts, see Kaufmann 2006 and Pink 2004.) Again, we may follow how certain routines are seen as crucial or central to people's ideas about what kind of person they really are.

As households and families develop steady routines, there are still challenges that can make even the tiniest difference irritating. You can hear who is coming or going by just listening to the way the door is closed, and there might be endless negotiations about what doors should be kept open or closed. In a study of conjugal conflicts there was the couple who waged a constant battle about the door to the kitchen (Lindvall 1983). As sure as the husband kept it open, the wife closed it with an irritating slam. Their different routines turned out to have to do with their class background. He had grown up in a working-class family where the kitchen was the centre of the home, where everybody congregated and all kinds of activities occurred. In her upper-class childhood the kitchen was a territory strictly reserved for cooking and the smell of food seeping in through the rest of the flat was a sign of vulgarity. Everything must have its own place and time!

Sarah Holst Kjær recounts another situation. She is visiting an older woman whose husband has just died. The woman is sitting at the kitchen table with bruises on her forehead and tells Sarah that it is only now she realizes that her husband silently went around and closed all the kitchen cabinet doors that she used to leave wide open.

When Everyday Life Collapses

What happens with routines when life simply becomes 'too much', as flow turns into friction and stress mounts at work or at home? In the early years of the twenty-first century discussions about a new form of stress-related disease was very much in the forefront in Sweden, often called 'burnout syndrome', defined as a personal collapse caused by overwork and/or emotional overload. What interests us in this context is how people describe themselves (or are described by others) as cases of burnout and overload.

Our material consists of interviews with people who have lived through this kind of crisis situation and ended up on long-term sick-leave, trying to get back to a normal life (see Löfgren and Palm 2005). In the past, excess was not a problem for them. It was their pride that 'no' was not an answer. They were gluttons at work, stretching themselves thin, living an accelerating life that in retrospect often had a manic streak in it. Lars, who had built up a small electronic factory from scratch, described himself like this: 'Haven't been able to say no. I always thought: speed up and it will be OK. I could walk through the factory and make twenty decisions in two minutes. I felt in full control, it was almost compulsive: what the hell, I could make anything work!' People like Lars had never or rarely been on sick-leave before. As the stress mounted they felt irritable, had problems with sleep and woke up early thinking about everything that needed to be done. Work had invaded most of their life. The road to the breakdown was often long, a slowly growing overload. Many describe this phase of stress as a mounting insensitivity. You ignored the signals from the body and didn't listen to the warnings or admonitions from others until the crash landing occurred. It is often a dramatic change of scene that is described.

All of a sudden everyday life at work and at home became chaotic, just 'too much'. They found themselves sent home on long-term sick-leave. When Lars broke down he couldn't go near the factory; even the family became too much and he spent long periods alone in a summer cottage out in the woods, staring at the walls.

The flow of everyday life had turned into friction, order into chaos, and it became obvious how important the autopilot had been in dealing with work and home. Now you were at home on sick-leave with all the time in the world on your hands, but in a domestic world that also had become 'too much'. Many everyday routines became Herculean tasks. 'It could be a full day's work just to take a shower and wash my hair,' one woman said. You have to make decisions about even the most trivial acts that were earlier handled by autopilot: 'I remember staring at a flowerpot for hours, trying to make up my mind if I should water it or not.'

In the crash landing of burnout, old routines and habits, these technologies by which people cope with the myriad of tasks and decisions in everyday life, all of a sudden stop working. Life is out of step, out of sync, habits are drained of content, become meaningless or mysterious. Lars expressed it like this: 'It's damned hard to be on sick-leave, all of a sudden you're without routines and it was the routines that kept life running at work. It feels like the floor is pulled away from under you.'

A striking theme in the interviews is the constant return to questions of overload at home and in the office. The daily burden had been transformed into new kinds of stress, a body in constant pain or a state of sensory and social overexposure. The TV screen flickers too much, noises are too loud, smells are too strong. You want to retreat to the bedroom and draw the curtains and just lie in the dark.

In a life crisis like burnout, people often experienced a very dramatic change of pace. Before their collapse they had felt a manic satisfaction of having 'total flow', coordinating many tasks; now all of a sudden they had lost so many of the skills of keeping everyday life going. The body would not obey order, the autopilot had stalled and even minor tasks became huge projects. One thing that was lost was the old skill of multi-tasking (see Löfgren 2007). They had survived juggling their work and home life by being able to do many things at once.

In an autobiographical novel a freelance journalist, Felicia, describes her break-down into burnout. She remembers interviewing a female hotel manager who told her how she constantly developed her talent for multi-tasking. By buying a headset for her mobile she could vacuum her whole home while taking incoming enquiries from work. 'This is something for me,' Felicia thinks. But that was in the old days when she could combine any amount of work. Today it is no longer possible for her to eat pizza and watch television at the same time, cook food while talking on the phone, or sort out the dirty laundry while sitting on the toilet. 'Maybe I am becoming a man,' she thinks, 'I can only do one thing at a time' (Dahlgren 2005: 71).

Collective Collapse

There are, however, even more dramatic breakdowns of everyday rhythms and routines that face whole communities that go through a major crisis.

In her ethnographic study *War Within: Everyday Life in Sarajevo under Siege* the anthropologist Ivana Maček (2000) follows how the web of everyday routines collapsed as the city of Sarajevo became beleaguered during the Balkan wars. A new life of heavy bombardments and an ever-present fear of snipers drastically changed the rules of everyday life. All of a sudden the most basic routines of everyday life disappeared. A constant improvisation was needed to keep life going and the vulnerability of an everyday life that has been taken for granted emerged. The supplies of water and electricity became totally erratic; you had to spend a lot of time searching for a water supply and improvising new techniques for cooking and heating. Everyday routines like preparing a meal could become complicated tasks, calling for both innovation and patience. Can you make a small fire on the balcony? What would work as a water carrier?

If burnout is an example of a personal crisis, when all the old skills of routines suddenly seem to disappear, the Sarajevo example highlights other aspects of routines. For example, it illustrates how much ordinary routines create a seamless rhythm during the day. Now these normal rhythms were broken up by the erratic supply of basic amenities. Was there any water in the tap? When will the electricity come back? People had to devise new routines like sleeping with all the lamps in the bedroom turned on, so that you would wake up when electricity returned and could hasten out in the kitchen in the middle of the night to do the laundry or cook some food. By keeping the water tap on you learned to listen for sounds of water returning momentarily at the oddest hours.

Instead of the well-known habits and rhythms there was a constant improvisation and confrontation with unexpected situations, with no chance of long-term planning, no steady routines. 'If I have three children I will call them Electricity, Water and Gas,' a 10-year-old boy said. The new life was based upon a constant uncertainty, and this was a conscious strategy of the attackers. They were out to break routines and create chaos and thus get the civilians on their knees.

Another aspect of the Sarajevo ethnography concerns the ways in which routines that usually are taken for granted become elevated to almost sacred rituals in times of crisis. In Sarajevo the phrase 'to imitate life' became a common figure of speech that signalled a desire to keep some of the old and well-known routines and at least create an image of normal life. Even the most trivial routines acquired a new symbolic charge. People would do almost anything to be able to bake a loaf of bread or dare the snipers for a walk to a bakery. The smell of fresh bread turned into 'an oasis of normality'. Taking a hot bath or dressing up for a visit to a neighbourhood café turned into an event.

To sum up: private burnout and a society collapsing during warfare represent two different kinds of what the Swedish ethnologist Gösta Arvastson (2006) has called zero-making. What happens when old routines all of a sudden disappear and another everyday life has to be constructed from new conditions? What is it that gets lost? In Sarajevo it was demonstrated how much the routines of everyday life were based upon an often unnoticed infrastructure of amenities and resources. In burnout it was as if the skills of routines and multi-tasking just evaporated. The body refused to obey orders; the autopilot gave up.

In both cases, however, the crisis also created a new platform, a feeling that there was a possibility of building up an alternative existence. The breakdown of everyday routines does not only have to be paralysing, but also provides a chance to rethink and reorganize your life. Much that once was seen as given and absolutely necessary turns out to be possible to do away with or change into new routines.

Same Procedure as Last Time?

In our discussion of the cultural potentials of mundane routines we have looked at ways in which they are made and unmade. We have been interested in how they may sink into oblivion or taken-for-granted in ways that make them work as a seamless flow in everyday life or as unconscious reflexes.

There is also the transformation when routines all of sudden come up to the surface and demand attention, as in our examples of confrontations between different habits or times of crisis when the fabric of everyday habits collapses. We have mentioned make-up and other morning routines as culturally interesting cases of temporarily coordinating practices with different rhythms that sometimes are disturbed or disrupted. The loss of such self-evident routines – often connected to bodily functions, hygiene or eating and drinking – shows how necessary they are both for personal identity and for social organization. Their importance becomes clearer when we understand how they may give security, power and freedom in everyday matters.

It is easy to get stuck in the reassuring idea of a constantly repeated pattern. If we look at the transformations of making and unmaking, another more dynamic picture emerges. The times and rhythms of everyday life, at home and at work, can be analysed as a temporal order of material practices that are reproduced and rearranged.

By looking at the coordination and disruption of routines we have tried to approach the question of what shapes the temporal patterns of our lives. The evolution of daily, weekly and yearly calendars, in the disguise of ordinary, inconspicuous routines, is a fruitful arena for looking at the interplay between material, natural, social and emotional forces in everyday actions. In this chapter we have focused on two main themes. The first is the surprising complexity of everyday routines as temporal practices. One cannot be sure of what routines mean to different people in various situations. We have to observe behaviour or ask people to describe it and tell us about its importance. On the one hand the routines express a common need for predictability and security in social life. On the other hand when they produce feelings of entrapment – to feel captured by routines is a common experience – they are associated with a robot-like life.

The other theme is the art of multi-tasking. The ability to combine different tasks simultaneously – for example, driving the car, shaving, listening to the radio and having a conversation on the cell phone – is an acquired skill. Routines may create arenas for daydreaming or problem solving, as well as a chance to be both present and elsewhere at the same time. (A mode of being that others may find provocative.)

Our conclusion is therefore that it is important to look closer for traces of the subversive potential of routines. This aspect probably is not the first thing that comes to mind in connection to inconspicuous repetitive behaviour. But when you examine ordinary ways of everyday life, hour after hour, day after day, you may find that these seemingly repetitive acts in fact may produce small and successive changes, hardly perceived, but possibly important in the long run. What one sees as 'the same procedure as usual' does not have to be that repetitive at all. It may hide some surprising transformations, just as a trivial argument about morning routines may really be about something much grander.

References

Arvastson, G. (2006). Zero-making. In *Off the Edge: Experiments in Cultural Analayis*, eds O. Löfgren and R. Wilk. Copenhagen: Museum Tusculanum Press. (Also published 2007 in *Ethnologia Europaea* 35(1/2): 98–101.)

Bateson, G. (1973). *Steps to an Ecology of Mind.* New York: Ballantine.

Bourdieu, P. (1977). *Outline of a Theory of Practice.* Cambridge: Cambridge University Press.

Campbell, C. (1996). Detraditionalization, Character and the Limits to Agency. In *Detraditionalization: Critical Reflections on Authority and Identity*, eds P. Heelas, S. Lash and P. Morris. Oxford: Blackwell.

Certeau, M. de (1984). *The Practice of Everyday Life.* Berkeley, CA: University of California Press.

Dahlgren, E. (2005). *Det här är inte jag. Dokumentärroman.* Stockholm: Forum.

Ehn, B. and Löfgren, O. (2007). *När ingenting särskilt händer. Nya kulturanalyser.* Stockholm/Stehag: Brutus Östlings Bokförlag Symposion.

Ehn, B. and Löfgren, O. (in press). *The Secret World of Doing Nothing.* Berkeley, CA: University of California Press.

Elias, N. (1978) [1939]. *The Civilizing Process.* Oxford: Blackwell.

Highmore, B. (2002). *Everyday Life and Cultural Theory: An Introduction.* London: Routledge.

Highmore, B. (2004). Homework: Routine, Social Aesthetics and the Ambiguity of Everyday Life. *Cultural Studies* 18(2/3): 306–327.

Kaufmann, J.-C. (1997). *Le coeur á l'ouvrage. Théorie de l'action ménagère.* Paris: Nathan.

Kaufmann, J.-C. (2002). *Premier Matin. Comment naît une histoire d'amour.* Paris: Armand Colin.

Kaufmann, J.-C. (2006). *Casseroles, amour et crises. Ce que cuisiner veut dire.* Paris: Armand Colin.

Kjær, S.H. (2009). *Parforholdets laboratorium. Kulturelle forestillinger, kropsligheder og materialiteter.* (Diss.) Copenhagen: Museum Tusculanum Press.

Lindvall, K. (1983). Oförklarliga rus och moraliska rum. In *Korallrevet*, ed. K.-O. Arnstberg. Stockholm: Carlsson.

Löfgren, O. (2007). Excessive Living. *Culture and Organization* 13(2): 131–144.

Löfgren, O. and Palm, A.-M. (2005). Att kraschlanda i sjukskrivning. In *Att utmana stressen*, eds B. Jönsson and O. Löfgren. Lund: Studentlitteratur.

Maček, I. (2000). *War Within. Everyday Life in Sarajevo under Siege.* (Diss.) Uppsala: Acta Universitatis Upsaliensis.

Nippert-Eng, C. (1996). *Home and Work: Negotiating Boundaries through Everyday Life.* Chicago: University of Chicago Press.

Pink, S. (2004). *Home Truths: Gender, Domestic Objects and Everyday Life.* Oxford: Berg.

Sennett, R. (1998). *The Corrosion of Character: The Personal Consequences of Work in the New Capitalism.* New York: W.W. Norton.

Shove, E. (2003). *Comfort, Cleanliness and Convenience: The Social Organization of Normality.* Oxford: Berg.

Shove, E., Watson, M., Ingram, J. and Hand, M. (2007). *The Design of Everyday Life.* Oxford: Berg.

Section III
Rhythms, Patterns and Temporal
Cycles of Consumption

Calendars and Clocks

Cycles of Horticultural Commerce in Nineteenth-century America

Marina Moskowitz

Introduction

The Pulitzer Prize-winning essayist, editor and children's book author E.B. White (1899–1985) was, in a lesser-known avocation and in tandem with his wife Katherine, a gardener. In January 1952, writing as he often did for the 'Notes and Comments' section of the *New Yorker*, White explained the ritual many gardeners undertook each year at that time – his first trawl through the seed catalogues. Employing the first-person plural voice characteristic of the column, White recorded:

> Our first communication of the year 1952 was a card from a seed company, and this seemed a good omen. A new bush bean, rich in flavor. A new pickle, early, dark green, delicious. A new muskmelon, thick orange flesh of top quality. A new petunia, giant fringed, dwarfish. So starts the year on a note of planning and dreaming. The card went on to chide us – said no order had been received from us since 1949. That is a fantastic accusation; we virtually supported that seed house last year and the year before and the year before, back into the dim, infertile past. However, we don't expect seed companies to keep accurate records; the whole business is so wild, so riotous, so complex, it's no wonder they forget who their own best friends are. If there is any doubt on that score, though, we will gladly send the management a jar of our wife's green-tomato pickle from last summer's crop – dark green, spicy, delicious, costlier than pearls when you figure the overhead. (White 1990: 4–5)[1]

Unpacking White's evocative prose reveals a number of ways in which seed houses and gardeners traded on the natural cycles of planting. White shows the full fruition of a commercial exchange in seeds that developed over the course of the nineteenth century. Although seeds had been exchanged as gifts and traded informally for centuries, and were often highly prized, it was not until the nineteenth century that seeds were commodified on a large scale. One of the earliest businesses in the United States to employ mail-order sales, the seed trade relied on print culture to reach consumers. Trade catalogues and other ephemera served as calling cards to establish a commercial relationship and facilitate the exchange of horticultural knowledge. Like White's tongue-in-cheek offer to send his wife's green-tomato pickle, the language of the early commercial correspondence was often suffused with motifs of friendship and gift exchange. Keeping this market relationship going year after year was a way of inculcating and demonstrating brand loyalty; though White is humorously slighted that his regular trade has not been recognized, he is also eager to show his status as an annual customer to any in 'doubt'. To keep things interesting in these long-term market relationships, firms developed new commodities, 'novelties' such as the bean, melon and petunia that White describes.

White's mention of home-made relish also shows the cyclical quality of natural commodities and the uses to which they are put. The commodity of the seed is not an end in itself, as many consumer goods are, but rather implies the growth of some further natural object – flowers, produce, more seeds – which may be consumed by the grower, but which might also form the basis of additional exchange, whether commercial or affective. Not only might consumers (of seeds) become producers (of a variety of crops), but seed firms themselves acted as consumers, buying at least part of their stock to sell on. The seed trade was indeed as 'complex' as White states, though many a nineteenth-century proprietor would have taken umbrage at his suggestion that the firms were 'riotous' and disorganized. While obviously reliant upon the rhythms of nature, many seed firms as they developed in the nineteenth century tried to impose industrial time on agrarian practices (or at least they tried to present themselves as doing so), and might even encourage their consumers to do the same. For both purveyors and consumers of horticultural commodities in the nineteenth century, issues of time, calendars and routine behaviour were at the heart of their exchange. In an era when many consumer markets were expanding due to the increasing tempo of mechanized production, the seed trade reached a national market while still respecting, and even imprinting, an annual cycle of consumption.

Natural Commodities

Planting is a cyclical process. Left to their own devices, many plants eventually drop seeds onto the ground, some of which might take root, whether in the shadow of the original plant or carried elsewhere by wind, water runoff or birds and insects. A new plant might grow from this seed and start a new cycle. So how does it work when, instead of being left alone, the plant's seeds are harvested, stored, packaged, sold and planted elsewhere? What does it mean for a commodity to have its own life cycle?

The commodification of seeds takes the natural life cycle of plants and adapts it to new scales of time and space. The seed trade, in tandem with its consumers, allows each generation of plant to thrive in a different geographic location, on a schedule at least partially determined by the person who plants it. Humans cannot get too far away from a plant's life cycle (or at least they could not with nineteenth-century developments in botany); they can rush or retard growth, for example with the application or removal of heat or light sources, only within certain bounds. In the United States during the nineteenth century, horticultural practices were most frequently viewed as an annual cycle. Even in places (such as the extreme Southern states) where the climate might allow for multiple harvests of particular crops, individual plants needed their periods of renewal, or dispensed seeds for a next generation. The very categories in which plants were classified, and sold, recognizes this yearly sequence and its variations: annuals, perhaps the largest category of seeds sold, required yearly planting of new seeds; biennials required two years to reach fruition and produce seeds; and perennials could keep producing blooms or produce for more than two years without renewal by replanting.

From growing fields across the country, purveyors of seeds gathered what I believe to be the largest variety of products of any nineteenth-century business. The diversity of nature was augmented by the science of plant breeding to the point where each catalogue offered literally thousands of different products, or species and varieties of seeds. While the first years of the nineteenth century still offered botanists and plant hunters unexplored territory in North America, by the end of the century the American frontier famously had been declared 'closed' by the historian Frederick Jackson Turner. Plants were no longer as likely to be discovered by natural historians as created by plant breeders, often working in a commercial context. Publication of new species was still the right of those who developed and named the new strains, but was likely to come in commercial rather than scientific catalogues. This emphasis on hybrids unique to a given company was frequent in later nineteenth-century catalogues and continues to the present day.

White's description of the seed trade ephemera he received in January 1952 raises many of the qualities that were sought through plant breeding. With flowers, both purveyors and consumers looked for new colours or colour combinations; large, or double, blossoms; and quantity of blossoms per stem or plant. With produce, the desire for good colour, size and prolific nature continued, along with the shortest possible sowing to harvesting time. Prolific bearing on small plants was a particular boon for those growing to feed their family or sell their produce at market. Any quality deemed favourable in a plant might be the object of selection and breeding to ensure the continuation of that quality. Seed companies vied with one another to create, or purchase from creators, particular strains and varieties of vegetables that they believed would be attractive to growers; the new names for varieties often reflected the firm or breeder who developed them, so that even when sold by other companies, the seeds would provide advertising for a competitor.

Plant breeding had several effects on consumer behaviour in the seed trade. First, newly acquired strains and hybrids were part of the annual package that each catalogue offered to make one firm stand out from another. The 'novelties' for each year were often included in a separate section of seed catalogues, even printed on coloured paper to draw attention, suggesting the value of the work that botanists and breeders carried out each year, creating new strains for the consuming public. More importantly, 'new' seeds provided a reason for prospective consumers to purchase seeds: to grow plants they could not otherwise obtain and to continue growing them. Nineteenth-century botany did not appear to have as its aim the halting of the natural growth cycle that we find in today's 'terminator seeds'. Nonetheless, the common wisdom of the day taught that the seeds of hybrid plants were not productive of further generations of plants, at least not those reliably true to the original: for example, if a new strain was created by crossing two others, the seeds from the 'novelty' plant might revert to one of the 'parent' plants. Thus, in developing the unique qualities of hybrids, whether the deepest colour and largest blossom of flower or the earliest and most prolific bearer of fruit, seed companies were also ensuring that customers would return to them each year for a new supply of seeds. Ironically, 'heirloom' seeds, seen as an antidote to the intervention with the natural world according to human priorities, now serve as the 'novelties' in contemporary seed catalogues.

The hybrid 'novelties' that blossomed in late nineteenth-century horticulture were only the most obvious examples in the intervention of natural cycles at the core of the seed trade. For the seed industry to be successful, it needed to convince its consumers not to harvest seeds from their own gardens, but rather to buy seeds from the companies each year. Although debates about seed purchasing versus seed saving did appear, particularly in regard to grain seeds as evidenced in agricultural periodicals, the trade was largely successful in convincing many Americans to purchase their seeds. Using the mechanisms discussed above, ranging from the allure of specific plant material to the inculcation of seed purchasing as an annual routine, the trade persuaded gardeners to dispense with the final stage of the plants' life cycle. Instead, gardeners might rapidly deadhead flowers to encourage more blooms, or harvest all produce without letting part of their crop go to seed, preferring to devote the time and space available to them for a particular crop, rather than the means to continue growing that crop. Still, the persuasion of gardeners to purchase seeds was not as insidious an example of the push to consumption as it might initially appear, but was in part reflective of the new situations in which planting took place. For example, the rise in urban populations over the course of the nineteenth century led to a rise in market gardens, cottage kitchen gardens, leisure-time flower gardens and garden suburbs with vast lawns. The intensive planting methods of these urban and suburban settings simply would not have allowed for gardeners to reap true seeds without the natural crossing that occurs as a result of wind, birds and insects carrying the pollen of proximate plants.

So, does the phrase 'go to seed' indicate wastefulness or productivity? Of course, within the trade, allowing plants to go to seed was the requisite for productivity. But in order for seeds to be commodities, they had to be not only produced by one set of growers, but also discarded by another, who would then need to obtain them outside of their own gardens. Today, 'going to seed' tends to have a negative connotation denoting neglect and decay, stemming from the precedence that consumers grant to a plant's productive use as an object of sustenance, economy or even beauty, above its reproductive use as the starting point of a next generation of plants. This very small-scale form of 'planned obsolescence' sits directly at the intersection of the natural process of planting cycles and the means of altering and influencing those cycles to create objects for consumption. The commodification of horticulture shows a tension between being guided by nature and trying to intervene in its inherent patterns for commercial or other purposes. As horticultural life is cyclical, so the trade that grew up around it is cyclical too. Purveyors and consumers of seeds both abide by and negotiate the natural cycles of plants when establishing commercial routines.

Commercial Calendars

If plants themselves exhibited natural life cycles, people placed those cycles into units of time they could measure and record, often imprinting an annual calendar on the sequence of activities associated with growing plants. Many of the horticultural manuals written over the course of the nineteenth century drew their structure from the annual sequence of garden tasks, reinforcing a calendric approach to gardening. One of the earliest gardening advice books in the American context was Bernard M'Mahon's *The American Gardener's Calendar, adapted to the Climates and Seasons of the United States*, published by the author in 1806. The *American Gardener's Calendar*, which would continue to be published for fifty years through eleven editions, was the culmination of M'Mahon's career as a seed seller. M'Mahon was born c. 1775 in Ireland and immigrated to the United States in 1796. His background in Ireland and his reasons for leaving are not yet clear in the historical record, but he appears to have landed in Philadelphia with knowledge of both gardening and the printing trade. In 1801, M'Mahon worked for the printer William Duane, from whom Thomas Jefferson would later order his volume of the *Calendar*. He may also have worked for David Landreth, the proprietor of an extensive nursery and seed business in Philadelphia. By 1802, M'Mahon had established his own seed store; in that year or the next he issued a broadside catalogue of seeds with over 700 choices, and in 1804 he published a thirty-page seed list (Hatch 1993; *From Seed to Flower*, 1976). M'Mahon's store was a centre for the Philadelphia-based botanists and gardeners who legitimated his trade, and he supplied and maintained a correspondence with the best-known naturalist of his day, Thomas Jefferson (Betts 1944). As one of the earliest American seed sellers to reach a market beyond the geographic confines of his Philadelphia shop, and one of the first to employ print as a means of commodifying horticultural specimen, M'Mahon proves a good focal point for the consideration of routines in the American garden.

M'Mahon's text was one of many in the calendric form, with the text divided into twelve units, detailing the progression of garden tasks in each month of the year. The monthly schedule of horticultural advice was pragmatic: bounded enough to let novices know what they should be thinking about when, but loose enough to allow for local variations in soil conditions, temperature, rainfall and other factors that might affect planting and harvest. M'Mahon certainly drew on English precedents in gardening books, most notably the works of Philip Miller and Thomas Mawe (Hatch 1993). Though his horticultural advice may not have been unique, or even original, he did try to adapt it for the American climate, or, more accurately, climates – he drew distinctions between the three major sectors of the eastern seaboard, which he designated the southern, middle and eastern states. His prose was in the form of a direct address to the reader, setting out tasks and offering explanations for them. In the breadth of its assumed audience and its practical organization based on the calendar, M'Mahon's book echoed the traditional form of the almanac. However, he made sure to distinguish his own advice from folk wisdom regarding plants. He explained, 'I am not an advocate for sowing seeds on a particular day of the week, or month, nor in the full or wane of the moon, nor when the wind blows from the east, west, or any particular point of the compass; these ridiculous and superstitious notions, have been long since, deservedly, banished out of the well informed world' (M'Mahon 1806: 469). Instead, M'Mahon offered practical suggestions resting on botanical knowledge.

While it could be argued that all businesses benefited from developments in print technology over the course of the nineteenth century, there does seem to have been a special relationship between, or even overlap of, seed sellers and the printing trade. Like M'Mahon, several early American seed sellers were also trained as printers and published their own catalogues, while the larger seed companies that flourished in the late nineteenth century often included on-site printing works to produce their marketing materials. M'Mahon's distinction between a seed list to promote his business and a gardening manual to educate consumers was increasingly conflated as the nineteenth century progressed and the seed catalogue emerged as a genre combining commerce, instruction, entertainment and artistic merit. Even the ways in which information was presented in catalogues was usually routinized, with front matter about the company, horticultural instruction, different 'departments' or categories of seeds for sale, testimonial letters and illustrations, all in more or less the same order. These printed pieces had two main components, again themes we can trace from M'Mahon: instruction and inventory, which were themselves intertwined. Instruction ranged from botany to horticulture, even to design ideals. Catalogues and packages included Linnean nomenclature and some very rudimentary lessons in plant physiology. But the bulk of the instruction was in cultivation practices, and was often organized in calendric form similar to contemporary gardening manuals; some catalogues incorporated almanac pages into their seed lists and advice. It was of course in the company's best interest to offer these lessons, both to encourage gardeners to experiment with new plants they may not have been familiar with growing, and to ensure that they associated the company with successful seeds.

The burgeoning horticultural trades capitalized on the calendric nature of gardening practices. Seed catalogues not only contained information arranged in yearly cycles, but they themselves constituted an annual event. (Like the plants that formed the core of their merchandise, these catalogues were often even referred to as 'annuals', such as the Burpee Company's *Farm Annual*.) Though some larger firms that sold bulbs, roots, plants and trees in addition to seeds might issue two to four seasonal catalogues per year, January was the main event. To this day, the arrival of seed catalogues each January effectively brackets the winter holiday period and marks the start of truly looking ahead and planning for the year, at least for gardeners, or those who aspire to be gardeners. The January mailing of seed catalogues also encourages the gardener to think of the start of the calendar year as a useful start to the year's gardening, even if in many parts of the American market the ground is frozen solid. E.B. White's 'planning and dreaming' could also be considered New Year's resolutions.

This annual opportunity to enter consumers' homes and attract their eye with increasing numbers and quality of illustrations, designs for both ornamental and productive gardens, and of course recommendations of plant material provided a structure for the exchange of seeds. Consumers were encouraged to use the winter months as a time for planning, using the seed catalogue as a reference work; the occasional marginalia one finds today in extant nineteenth-century catalogues, as well as garden journals that detail what seeds were ordered from what catalogues, suggests that this advice was followed. I have seen seed catalogues that were used as colouring books, with the black and white illustrations providing outlines for hand painting, suggesting that the commercial object promoted very different rituals for different ages or members of the family perceived as a collective consumer.

Most of the catalogues started with some form of 'letter' from the seedsman to his 'friends', with headings such as 'Gossip with Customers' or 'A New Year's Gift'. James Vick and W. Atlee Burpee were the masters of this genre, which served to personalize a trade relationship conducted without face-to-face contact. These narratives couched commerce in the language of friendship, advice and gift giving. Seed companies recognized the important bond between seller and buyer in a trade where the commodity sold was difficult to judge or value before its use. As the Burpee Company wrote in their 1892 catalogue:

> The relations of the Planter to his trusted Seedsman are more intimate than those of the buyer and seller in any other line of business; with other goods the buyer can largely judge of the quality and value by the sample, while with seeds the purchase is altogether a matter of confidence. To merit and maintain this confidence is the constant aim of the conscientious Seedsman. (*Burpee's Farm Annual* 1892: 17)

Of course, firms strove to sell reliable and productive seeds as the first priority in 'maintaining this confidence'. But they also used the friendly counsel on the planning, sowing, tending and harvesting of fields, gardens, lawns and other planted landscapes to maintain a personal touch in what was an increasingly far-flung business. These marketing practices had both an abstract and specific aim: consumers first needed to be convinced that it was worth buying seeds year after year, and then convinced that they should buy them year after year from the same company.

The epistolary style of the company's address to the consumer through the seed catalogue invited a response. First, of course, came a response in the form of an order of seeds. But beyond the strict commercial exchange, the personal style of many catalogues suggested a person (or persona) behind the company, who would want to hear about the consumer's experience with those seeds, experience that was available only at the end of the growing season, whether at harvest time, or when considering purchases for the following year. This social convention, of writing what amounted to a 'thank you note' (even for items purchased rather than received as a gift), established a relationship that might then be continued in further correspondence. The forms of exchange between company and consumer – catalogues, letters, orders, all requested and sent on an annual basis – had the effect of encouraging brand loyalty in a trade that relied on a high volume of exchange. What we might now call a 'feedback loop' was created, not only between the company and consumers, but also, by printing customers' letters as testimonials, among the broad community of consumers.

The variety in the consumer base for seeds was used to advantage by the trade, which frequently published excerpts from customers' letters in catalogues, advertisements or other ephemera. The companies occasionally employed publicly recognizable names, such as the Rev. Henry Ward Beecher, whose endorsement graced several competitors' pages in the 1860s, or the author Anna Warner, whose 1866 letter to the Vick Company was accompanied by a short story, originally published in *Harper's Weekly*, which featured the company (*Spring Catalogue* 1868; *Vick's Illustrated Catalogue* 1867: iii; 1868: i). More often, however, the companies presented the experiences of ordinary customers, who shared the occasionally extraordinary moments of their lives. Testimonial letters were so effective in this broad and varied market because no particular status was needed to voice success; all parties could claim equal authority. The words of a well-established market gardener who relied on a given company's seeds for income were no more authoritative than the story of a self-described amateur gardener whose flowers were the envy of her neighbourhood. Having some sort of professional credential or expertise might lend credence to a testimonial, but *not* having this experience could equally well convince buyers that such results were attainable by anyone. As a letter from Rev. R.H. Waggoner of Hillsdale, Michigan, noted, 'The seeds I obtained from you gave great satisfaction. The marvel with all is that with the care, or more properly the neglect, they receive in a common garden they should come equal to your recommendation' (*Vick's Illustrated Catalogue* 1866: iv). Here, as in many of the letters, it is the status of the common gardener writing in appreciation that in fact becomes a valuable marketing tool.

For the consumers, writing these letters was a way of sharing horticultural success, in the many different arenas in which their practices took place. Letters recounted a range of rewards, such as neighbourhood acclaim for an abundant garden; prizes for a horticultural specimen deemed the best at county or state fairs; or financial gain from prolific crops with good market value. The model of a letter of gratitude to a company, whether for a specific gift or the general worth of the product purchased, provides a means of subsuming personal pride within the broader context of corporate praise; correspondents were also not above including complaints about a specific selection that did not grow as well as others. Thus, in their correspondence with seed houses, consumers took stock at the end of the growing season, effectively marking time on the horticultural calendar.

Horticultural Improvement

In the horticultural marketplace, the natural cycles of planting were augmented by cycles of commercial exchange. For both purveyors and consumers, the issue was not just one of dividing the calendar year into particular tasks, but learning how best to organize those tasks, to achieve their intertwined aims of, on the one hand, growing and selling seeds and, on the other, growing and harvesting crops from those seeds. Although at the heart of these pursuits were common agrarian acts of sowing seeds and tending plants, nineteenth-century horticulture played out against the backdrop of industrialization, bringing new approaches to the timing, ordering and sequencing of responsibilities.

As E.B. White stated a century after its maturation, the seed trade was 'complex'. When consumers selected a particular brand, they were not necessarily purchasing seeds directly from those responsible for growing them. The companies that sold seeds to the retail and wholesale market varied in how they themselves obtained the seeds they sold. Small firms might act solely as distributors, of seeds bought from other firms or from growers, while the larger firms did grow some of their own stock, while also buying from both American and European growers. No firms grew all the seeds they sold, as, in the words of the Burpee Company, 'this would be a physical impossibility' (*Burpee's Select List* 1889: 3). The world of the individual seed growers who supplied the retail firms was a highly localized and specialized business, differing from the state of agriculture at the time in its scale, choice of crops and modes of reaping, both crops and profits. While large-scale fields of grains were common economic endeavours by the nineteenth century, large-scale farming of vegetables, fruits and flowers did not take root until refrigerated transportation allowed for the movement of the crops, by train in the last quarter of the nineteenth century and in trucking not until the twentieth century. The seed growers, however, did plant such fields, harvesting not the produce but the seeds. Lines between producer and consumer blurred, as purveyors usually fell into both categories at once.

The seed trade took the seeds from their growing fields and added value to them by sorting, categorizing, storing, describing, packaging, mailing and offering advice through printed ephemera. This 'manufacturing' made seeds sold by firms more convenient, and perhaps even more valuable, than those saved by consumers from the previous year's plants. With these processes, natural produce was transformed into commercial products, and those products became associated with the firm that sold the commodity, even if that firm did not originally 'produce' or grow the seeds. We might consider these organizational processes the industrial influence of the seed trade, where industry implies a systematized and efficient approach to labour, usually towards an end product with a market value of some sort. The routines of these commercial forms of horticultural labour were linked to the routines of seasonal consumer activity. Unlike some commodities, which could be purchased and used at any time, seeds for the American market were generally purchased and planted in a narrow band of time in the late winter and early spring. The consumers' horticultural calendar determined the sequencing not only of the sourcing of seeds within the trade, but also such tasks as writing and printing the annual catalogue or working in the mailroom to open orders.

The purpose-built structures in which this processing and publicizing took place constituted the factories of seed 'production', along with the fields in which they were grown. In fact, many nineteenth-century seed companies promoted these sites of industry in their own ephemera. Promotional materials of the latter half of the nineteenth century frequently included engravings of these grand warehouse buildings. Trade catalogues might include several pages devoted to the different sectors of the interior workspaces, both graphically and verbally depicting the work that occurred within them – ranging from opening mail, sorting seeds, designing and printing marketing materials, packaging and mailing – as busy hives of work. The emphasis on these spaces of sorting, storing and sending, which mediated between the producers' and consumers' fields, showed the processes of distribution to be as significant to the development of the seed trade as those of growing. In 1867, the *American Agriculturalist* commended B.K. Bliss as a leader in the seed trade by writing, 'By liberal advertising, thorough system, and indefatigable attention to the details of his work, he has built up a business extending all over the United States, and demanding larger facilities' (*Spring Catalogue* 1868). The facilities in question, however, were not at the firm's growing fields in Springfield, Massachusetts, but rather their new warehouse building in New York City, through which all orders were handled. If the word 'industrial' suggests a highly organized or systematized form of work, it also connotes 'scale and scope' (to borrow from the business historian Alfred Chandler), in both production and potential markets. The urban warehouses of the seed trade symbolized in built form the breadth of the trade.

The seed trade placed this emphasis on the processing tasks that added value to the commodity of seeds because otherwise the modes of production of purveyor and consumer were hard to distinguish. In fact, it could be said that plants themselves 'produce' seeds, so the human role is one of tending and care. Many nineteenth-century industries developed mechanized production processes that, while replicating and replacing earlier craft-based work, could not themselves be replicated on a domestic scale or without significant capital investment. Seed growers, however, shared their work processes with the farmers and gardeners who would eventually buy their goods. Still, at least in the large firms, there was fluidity between work sites that brought aspects of one location to another. For example, the W. Atlee Burpee Company rotated employees between their Philadelphia warehouse and their growing and testing fields at Fordhook Farm a few miles outside of the city; stints on the farm would give the best training in identification and sorting to those in the warehouse, while an understanding of the processing would lead to increased systematizing of the Farm (*Burpee's Farm Annual* 1893: 1). The labour of the seed trade was indeed a hybrid of agricultural (or horticultural) and industrial practice.

In one important inversion of the rhythms of these sectors of work, the tasks within the urban warehouse work followed a seasonal calendar thought typical of agriculture while the presentation of the growing fields was in terms of rigid systems and clock-watching. Fordhook Farm was a popular site, certainly the best known of any seed farm in the United States in the last quarter of the nineteenth century, and was frequently profiled in agricultural and horticultural papers, as well as Burpee's own marketing materials. In one of the company's *Farm Annuals* the farm is described in terms that certainly call to mind industrial settings. The work at the farm

> could not be accomplished if it were not done systematically. And truly, this is the keynote of the great success attained here in high cultivation and development – system. Everything moves by clockwork, and everybody about the farm, from the manager to the boy in the fields, is regulated by the strictest of rules and observances. Every man know just what he has to do, and knows that no slipshod or incomplete work will be tolerated... It is hard to convey to the public any idea whatever of the enormous amount of work. (*Burpee's Farm Annual* 1896: 3)

Here, not just the calendar but also the clock sets the pace for horticultural work.

The emphasis on 'system' evident in Burpee's trade literature is perhaps not surprising, in a trade trying to avoid just the 'riotous' characterization that White placed on them a century later. But similar rhetoric reached consumers as well, in a variety of forms. A small genre of advice literature written in the form of novels emerged in the mid to late nineteenth century in the United States, using fictional characters and plot developments as an innovative form of prescriptive literature, often on matters of the home and garden. One practitioner of this genre, Charles

Barnard, wrote four such novels on various aspects of gardening for both home consumption and local markets. As an example, the book *Farming by Inches*, published in 1869, tells the story of a bookkeeper in an unnamed North American city with striking similarities to Boston. The clerk is in ill health and is advised by his doctor to get out to the country. As luck would have it, the very next day news arrives that a distant relative with no closer heirs has died, leaving the clerk a house and a few acres on the outskirts of a mill town. In due course, he and his wife decide to move there and try their hand at raising vegetable for markets in the town. In crafting the story of Robert and Harriet Nelson, which the last lines of the book state 'is a true story of actual experience', Barnard explains how the couple, with no background in tending the soil between them, learn to garden (Barnard 1869: 123).

Barnard's book echoes not only the description of Burpee's Fordhook Farm, but the agricultural reform movements of the late nineteenth century, through applying organizational ideas to small-scale gardening. At the start of the novel, the characters pledge, 'we resolved that all things should be conducted in the most systematic order. We would bring our methodical and mercantile ways of doing things into a business notoriously loose and inaccurate in its operation' (Barnard 1869: 20). Examples of organization usually considered hallmarks of the industrial era creep into their habits. In one instance, while doing the prosaic task of bundling radishes to prepare them for selling, Hattie asks if it would save time to divide the labour. They change the process so that their hired hand washes the radishes, Robert arranges the bundles and Hattie ties them; they work much more quickly as a result of this separation of tasks into constituent parts. In another scene, they wonder at the apparent leisure of a neighbouring farmer noting his 'utter indifference to the value of time' (Barnard 1869: 78). This passage raises the issue of task orientation and time orientation, the former usually associated with agricultural work and the latter with industrial work; the Nelsons slowly introduce the time orientation of their previous urban lives to their horticultural pursuits. To underscore this point, Barnard depicts the end of a day of preparing garden beds as coinciding with the sound of the factory whistle coming from the nearby mill town. Still, all the while, the Nelsons reject any kind of mechanized labour in the market garden, only in part because they are planting so intensively as not to leave any room for garden machinery. Barnard lauds the health benefits of outdoor, manual work, as well as of the literal fruits of their labour. He seems to advocate drawing on what he perceives to be the best components of the two prevalent economic and social systems.

The passages from Burpee's catalogue and Barnard's novel reveal varying attitudes towards time in relation to horticultural practice and, by extension, horticultural consumption. One of the differences between agrarian and industrial economies and cultures is the way labour is organized. Agricultural work is said to be 'task-orientated', in that there are a set of tasks to be carried out in the raising and tending of produce and livestock. Some of these tasks need to be performed daily and some seasonally; some tasks are affected by forces, such as weather or blight, beyond human control. So those engaged in agricultural work must organize their labour in effective ways, often adjusting as they go, to make sure the list of requisite tasks is completed. By contrast, much industrial work, especially in mechanized production, is 'time-orientated', with labour organized into specific, frequently repeated, tasks that are carried out for a certain period of time. These two approaches to the organization of time, one by nature, one by the clock, carry over from work to other facets of social and cultural life. For example, in the United States, the sports of baseball and (American) football developed in different ways, with the former played as long as it takes to complete a particular set of tasks, and the latter played for a specific amount of time, in which a set of tasks may be repeated any number of times.[2]

While these formulations certainly ring true in the starkest examples of agrarian and industrial labour and leisure, the case of horticultural work appears to bridge this divide. The hybrid nature of the business of supplying horticultural specimens and the varied ways in which consumers fit horticultural practice into their lives show a variety of approaches to time and the rhythms of tasks that, at least for the consumers, might be coded variously as work or leisure. For some consumers, horticulture might constitute their livelihood and they might approach their time in the garden as the main activity to fit other endeavours around; for others, gardening might be a hobby, something taken up as time allowed, whether regularly, for an hour a day, or really as a filler activity when space is freed up. Today, estate agents promote the ideal of the 'low-maintenance garden', to appeal to those who do not have much time to devote to tending plants; there has always been a broad spectrum in the ways in which horticultural consumers use their purchases.

In presenting itself as resident in the borderland between agriculture and industry, the seed trade recognized that its market was a hybrid as well. Consumers of seeds might plant grain, produce or flowers, for sustenance, economic livelihood, ornament or any combination thereof. Going as far back in the trade as Bernard M'Mahon, he cast a very broad net when it came to defining who the 'American Gardener' was in 1806. According to its extended title, the *Calendar* was 'a complete account of all the work necessary to be done in the Kitchen-Garden, Fruit-Garden, Orchard, Vineyard, Nursery, Pleasure-Ground, Flower-Garden, Green-House, Hot-House, and Forcing Frames' (M'Mahon 1806: iv). While the start of a demographic shift from rural to urban populations certainly did begin in the United States during the nineteenth century, that shift did not imply a decline in planting, but, rather, I think, a greater variety of markets. The variation in consumer profiles in the seed trade was reflected in the breadth of the commodities and in the varied approaches to horticultural pursuits.

Regardless of how horticultural tasks were carried out, they were linked to ideals of improvement, on a number of different scales – improvement of the soil, of the home plot and by extension of region or even nation. Regardless of the time they had to spend on horticultural practices, and the ways in which they organized that time, if gardeners sought to improve small parcels of land, their collective efforts would create a national landscape. Horticultural commodities seemed to have as much in common with mercantile goods as with agricultural produce, as both tastes and access to garden materials might be influenced by broad commercial contact. Horticulture, in all its many facets, provided a possible bridge between the Jeffersonian vision of a small-scale agricultural endeavour and the American System's support of larger scale commercial prospects. If Americans could see gardening as not only an artistic and scientific pursuit, but also an economic or commercial one, then improvement in the horticultural sense mirrored, rather than opposed, the cause of other 'internal improvements' that affected the composition of landscape on a national scale. Ultimately, improvement was another form of recording time, inscribing onto the landscape the changes between the 'dim, infertile past' and the abundance that was more readily possible as a result of horticultural commerce.

Notes

1. I would like to thank Elysa Engelman for bringing this essay to my attention.
2. For this formulation of different attitudes to time, I am indebted to the teachings of Jean–Christophe Agnew.

References

Barnard, C. (1869). *Farming by Inches.* Boston: n.p.

Betts, E.M., ed. (1944). *Thomas Jefferson's Garden Book, 1766–1824.* Philadelphia: American Philosophical Society.

Burpee's Farm Annual (1892). Philadelphia: W. Atlee Burpee and Co.

Burpee's Farm Annual (1893). Philadelphia: W. Atlee Burpee and Co.

Burpee's Farm Annual (1896). Philadelphia: W. Atlee Burpee and Co.

Burpee's Select List of Novelties and Specialties in Seeds (1889). Philadelphia: W. Atlee Burpee and Co.

From Seed to Flower: Philadelphia, 1681–1876: A Horticultural Point of View (1976). Philadelphia: Pennsylvania Horticultural Society.

Hatch, P. (1993). Bernard McMahon, Pioneer American Gardener. *Twinleaf.* n.p.: Thomas Jefferson Foundation

M'Mahon, B. (1806). *The American Gardener's Calendar, adapted to the Climates and Seasons of the United States.* Philadelphia: n.p.

Spring Catalogue and Amateur's Guide (1868). New York: B.K. Bliss and Son.

Vick's Illustrated Catalogue and Floral Guide (1866). Rochester, NY: James Vick.

Vick's Illustrated Catalogue and Floral Guide (1867). Rochester: James Vick.

Vick's Illustrated Catalogue and Floral Guide (1868). Rochester: James Vick.

White, E.B. (1990). Notes and Comments. In *E.B. White: Writings from the New Yorker, 1925–1976*, ed. R. Dale, New York: HarperCollins.

–8–

Fads, Fashions and 'Real' Innovations
Novelties and Social Change
Jukka Gronow

The Novelty of Fashion

A new fashion is by definition a novelty and, as such, is an invention. This is after all why fashion seduces its customers. Since fashion, at least in the fields of consumption with an institutionalized system of fashion like clothing, repeats itself in cycles, these novelties make their appearance at regular intervals. The best examples come naturally from the world of clothes with its eternally repeating cycles of new designs with broader or narrower, shorter or longer legs of trousers, bigger or smaller buttons, longer or shorter haircuts, blue or yellow colour tones, and so on. Fashion designs are often re-used or re-circulated but they never simply copy older models. Mostly, they make their reappearance in new contexts and in new combinations. Not even planned retro-fashions ('back to the 60s', for example)[1] simply repeat old ones. As any comparison with their older prototypes proves, the present fashion has always something new to offer. In order to be successful, any fashion must claim to be a novelty and, as such, a real invention.

Obviously, fashions can change rapidly or slowly. The normal cycles of the field of clothes fashion have been seasonal for the last hundred years or so but during the seventeenth century Parisian fashion – already the centre of European clothes culture – changed every seventh year (Mennell 1985). In clothing fashions, several uncoordinated cycles can operate at the same time. Fashions can be identified in many other areas of consumption and social life, too. Car models began to 'fluctuate' annually almost like clothes after the big American car producers successfully adopted the idea of continuous cycles in their marketing, an idea that was totally opposed to Ford's original idea of the extremely functional Model T which was there to stay (Löfgren 2006). The producers of many other consumer durables have, however, tried in vain to adopt the same planned obsolescence in their marketing. For some reason it does not seem to be as natural to market new refrigerators or freezers in the same way. Fashion cycles in naming children in Germany and the USA follow much longer, generational cycles (Gerhards 2003; Lieberson 2000).

Even though the same stylistic elements can repeat themselves or disappear without any trace from one cycle to another, once they are in fashion they become equally binding and compelling. Last year's models are totally out of fashion and look ridiculous on their bearers. The same fate, as we all know, awaits this season's fashion in the near future. The paradox of fashion is that, at the same time as it establishes its socially binding and pseudo-normative power over consumers as the only possible alternative at the moment, there is no rule – other than the fashion itself – which dictates what the present fashion should look like. There is no reason why legs of trousers should be long or short, broad or narrow. Following Georg Simmel (1902), one could claim that the decisive test of whether fashion cycles can operate in any one field of culture is to ask if things could just as well be otherwise. In other words, fashion is contingent; it constitutes a self-dynamic social process (Mayntz and Nedelmann 1987). The economic function of fashion is to make commodities prematurely obsolete and to accelerate the circulation of goods, but to fulfil this function any design is good enough, as long as it is new and succeeds in establishing itself as a fashion with its claim of exclusive validity. A particular fashion design does not have any other function. It could just as well be something else. Fashion offers us novelties for sake of the novelty.

This does not mean that 'anything goes' – what is fashionable at any one time is always quite exclusive and obliging. Despite trend-setters and their active efforts at marketing the next, or the next-next fashion, fashion itself retains a strong element of mystery. This does not mean that some fashionable novelties do not meet active and strong resistance. Not every consumer is willing to accept and adopt them. Such resistance against fashion can be of a dual nature. It can be directed either towards the whole institution of fashion, which can be experienced as external social coercion unnecessarily requiring us to comply with its power. Such resistance can be a sign of traditionalism and cultural inertia but can equally well be a result of an anti-consumerist consciousness. But resistance can also signal that a specific fashion design threatens some existing cultural or moral norms. Clear breaks with the traditions of clothing have often been connected with gender and generational rules of clothing. In post-war Europe many, for instance, experienced boys with long hair or girls in trousers as a serious threat to the traditional, established social order. In such cases, when appearing for the first time, a new fashion can make a real difference. Aesthetic taste has often had an ethical dimension (Gronow 1987). But once resistance has been broken and new habits have been established, a new fashion like the mini-skirt can peacefully join the available repertoire of fashion designs. It can circulate eternally as 'just' one more fashion.

From the point of view of the producer or seller of fashion, a new design is always genuinely innovative and is often a result of a tedious creative process, but fashion does not really make any difference in the world. Fashions are 'only' functional equivalents to one another (Meyersohn and Katz 1957: 595).

In sociological discussions of fashion inspired by Georg Simmel's classical contribution, fashion has been analysed mainly from the point of view of its social origins, functions and cultural meanings. According to Simmel (1902), fashion originated from the dual process of social distinction and identification. Even though its standards are rapidly changing, fleeting and ephemeral, fashion creates social order by offering guidelines to orientation in a rapidly changing world. It is a harmless way to learn how to cope with the rapid social and cultural change typical of the modern societies (cf. Lipovetsky 1994). Fashion is therefore a phenomenon of modernity *par excellence*, fleeting, changing and quite impossible to get a grip on. From the point of view of its wider cultural meaning, the particular contents of any particular fashion, as well as their process of production and distribution, are of less importance. Owing to its contingent nature, anything will, after all, do just as long as it is new – or is experienced as such.

Technical Inventions vs Social Innovations

Despite their seeming frivolity, fashions are real social and cultural inventions. No doubt, fashion designers and trend-setters work hard to create and invent the new 'revolutionary' models and designs to come. But they are no 'real' innovations. Despite the seemingly close resemblance between fashion and innovations as dynamics of cultural and social change, I have not found any studies which seriously and systematically reflect on the relation between these two extremely interesting and important social phenomena. As a matter of fact, the way that the great classic figure of innovation studies, Joseph Schumpeter, described innovation, it resembled 'Simmelian' fashion processes (Schumpeter 1911, 1939; also Kovács 2007). In Schumpeter's opinion, the 'raw material' of innovations, techno-scientific inventions, is on offer in large numbers. Chance alone seems to determine which will develop into real innovations. At any one time, only a few will end up as 'technical raw material' to an innovation. The transformation of an invention into an innovation and its further social diffusion follow a path similar to that of fashions: from just a few original inventors it will spread first to early and then to later adopters, and finally to those lagging, until it has penetrated the whole spectrum of a society or one or more of its sectors.

Schumpeter was mainly interested in this social process of innovation, in which, in his opinion, risk-taking entrepreneurs played a decisive role. The more technical and economic aspects of inventions were of less interest to him because only a small minority of inventions would ever develop into innovations, and, consequently, there was no lack of potential candidates. Inventions practically wait to be taken into use or turned into innovations by an active and innovative entrepreneur. The main obstacles to the innovative process in promoting socio-economic change and progress were not primarily of a technical or economic nature. The most demanding task a successful innovator-entrepreneur had to accomplish was to do the same thing expected from a fashion designer, that is, to seize an opportunity at the right time and to convince customers that they really need a particular invention. In doing so, an innovator might have to break the resistance of customers towards the invention. The extremely difficult job was to challenge and change traditions, habits and routines and thereby to open a way to a new path of social development. To accomplish all this, Schumpeter expected his innovator-entrepreneur to have almost heroic qualities. The resistance to innovations could include political, juridical and institutional limitations of all kinds and could be expressed in various ways, from harmless nonchalance, to strong disapproval and animosity, or even legal prohibitions.

The story of the shirt-pocket radio could serve as an 'ideal-typical' innovation process.[2] As Schiffer (1993) shows, technical solutions and models of a portable radio existed a long time before it became a marketable commodity. Even after the invention of the transistor in 1947 it took almost ten years before the shirt-pocket radio became a commercial success. This time lag was not the result solely of high prices or the inferior technical qualities of earlier models. When the local radio stations started broadcasting rock and roll music, American teenagers often defied their parents' strong disapproval to listen, and the shirt-pocket radio satisfied this new 'need'. Soon a new group of enthusiastic young customers were willing to experiment with totally new manners of listening to music.

Schiffer makes a useful addition to Schumpeter's theory of innovation by pointing out the important role of cultural imperatives:

> A cultural imperative is a product fervently believed by a group – its constituency – to be desirable and inevitable, merely awaiting technological means for its realization ... it is a fancy of a group, often a very small group, captivated by the vision. Members of the constituency are likely to believe that when the product is 'perfected' it will have popular appeal, but this belief may be little more than wishful thinking. (Schiffer 1993: 99)

This constituency of enthusiastic radio amateurs had existed decades before their cherished product found its broader customers and became an item of mass consumption. As Schiffer stressed, once the product has become commercialized, its possible successes and failures in the marketplace have nothing to do with the size or social character of its, often small, original constituency. The existence of such a constituency, resembling a hobby or art world (Becker 1982), is a necessary, but not a sufficient, condition for the emergence and survival of an invention (Schiffer 1993: 113).[3]

The Cultural Mediators in the Innovation Process

In many ways, this 'gap' between the original constituency, whether a group of enthusiastic amateurs, engineers or inventors, and the future wider group of buyers is what marketing and advertising departments try to fill in by offering ready-made models of life-styles and cultural practices that new products and services can fit into. For instance, in order to export Nordic walking sticks (Shove and Pantzar 2005), the company producing them has, very concretely, to export and make meaningful a totally new practice of walking with two sticks. When exported to other countries from Finland, the practice is radically transformed and effectively become quite another practice.

As Hennion et al. (1989) show, modern marketing and advertising are often as important a part of the process of product development as the scientific-technical laboratories and innovation centres of firms or universities. The gap between the producer and the seller, on the one hand, and the buyer or final customer, on the other hand, is not just a practical one. Their perspectives and the principles guiding their choices differ in principle (see Schulze 1992). Therefore, consumers have always played an active and creative part in the transformation of an invention into an innovation. Their role as co-innovators, however, has only recently received serious attention in innovation studies (McMeekin and Southerton 2007; cf. also Pantzar 1997). The consumer is as much the heroic innovator as the entrepreneur.

More often than not, innovations do not follow the original instructions for use suggested by their inventors or the entrepreneur who actively promotes them. Bell's telephone is already a classical example. He expected it to be used strictly for business and he could hardly imagine its use for pleasure and socializing. Today, by contrast, big corporations that actively promote and invest in new inventions try more systematically and extensively to integrate customers into an active role in the innovation process from the beginning (Kotro and Pantzar 2002: 39). On the other hand, an overwhelming majority of the novelties that reach the consumer goods market each year are more likely to be small variations or improvements on older products and therefore find a ready-made slot in the customary patterns of consumption. 'Big' innovations demanding drastic changes in the lives of their consumers are, after all, quite rare. Such revolutionary innovations do not appear on the market weekly or monthly and probably not even annually. It still makes sense to think of some important technical inventions, like automobiles, radios, TVs, refrigerators or the instruments of modern communication technology, as turning points or markers of historical periods in modern consumer society. It is, however, remarkable how different the time trajectories of many familiar items of home electronics and durables have been in different European countries (Tellis et al. 2003: 190). Quite often the original function of a new technical invention has been turned into its opposite, from 'toys' to 'instruments', from 'instruments' to 'pleasure' (Kotro and Pantzar 2002).

Fashion and Innovations

For Schumpeter, what distinguishes innovations from fashion cannot be found in the technical or economic nature or complexity of novelties – the scale is gradual – but in the nature of the social change they initiate and even presume. While a new fashionable design is relatively harmless or trivial, and it disappears from the social scene without trace almost at the very moment it has entered it, Schumpeterian innovations, as a rule, are here to stay. By their presence they make a real difference. This change can be smaller or bigger, more or less permanent, more or less encompassing, but it can always be identified. The mobile phone is an example which comes easily to mind. It is not just another fashionable model of the wired phone. On the contrary, it has dramatically changed our everyday habits of communication, creating totally new social practices. In many countries for example, the cell phone met resistance as an 'uncivilized' manner of communication. Now, in its turn, the cell phone has its own regular fashion cycles.

What, then, distinguishes a mere fashionable novelty *à la* Simmel from a genuinely innovative novelty *à la* Schumpeter? The technical or purely economic differences will not really do as an explanation. It is not reasonable to look for such differences in relative technical complexity or economic investments demanded. These could vary from case to case among innovations and fashions, even though one could empirically claim that the average Schumpeterian innovation would be more capital- and time-intensive than fashions. However, being an inventor of a new popular fashion or a first-comer among the competing firms in a fashion market can certainly make a big economic difference to the firms concerned. Similarly, the very emergence and establishment of the social system of fashion in any one field of consumption change its social character quite radically through the imperative of eternal change. The main distinction between these two novelties, fashion and innovation, is the real impact they have on people's social routines or habits and the extent to which they change social practices (see Warde 2005). Despite its novelty, a new fashion does not change any social habits. It leaves everything as it was. The idea of a more or less decisive and radical break with previous cultural traditions and social habits is, on the other hand, built into the very concept of a Schumpeterian innovation. Distinct from fashions, they can be compared to styles. As Ted Polhemus argued, 'a style isn't trendy... It's inherently conservative and traditional' (1994: 13). A new style is a 'real' social innovation which changes the lives of those involved.

New social and cultural practices are an essential part of innovation, but they can also 'invite' inventions and promote the transformation of inventions into innovations. McMeekin and Southerton (2007), in arguing for the important role of final consumption in the innovation process, emphasize that 'the process of appropriating goods and services into practices is itself innovative, and as social practices change, "spaces" (or demand, needs and wants) for new innovations emerge'. Kotro and Pantzar, speaking of the cultural landscape of a product, point out the importance of the new cultural meanings and interpretations related to a specific object (2002: 31).

Fads and Fashions

To clarify the difference between innovation and fashion clearer, it is useful to pay attention to a third social phenomenon in between these two, and equally typical of modern consumption. Despite the fact that fads are extremely important and quite common social phenomena, they have hardly been analysed sociologically. Meyersohn and Katz (1957) are an important exception. They did not, however, systematically distinguish between fashions and fads.[4] Fads are like fashions. They come and go, without any obvious reason and without leaving any deeper or more permanent traces in the community. They are like 'real' innovations in that they do not appear within a regular fashion cycle, like a new fashionable design. New fads are not the functional equivalents to any previous fads. As 'real' novelties they thus have to create themselves a social place of their own, and the habits, routines and new meanings attached to them.

Fads are typical among children and teenagers, who obviously have more need of simple and visible signs and symbols of common taste than adults do. Fads can be found in particular in various worlds of play and games. Good examples are hula hoops, yo-yos and the small collapsible metal scooters that made their sudden appearance about ten years ago. Fads seldom require great technical invention. Their prototypes are found as if ready-made. They can be modifications of some older products that have been around for a long time. This does not, as such, distinguish them form more 'serious' inventions. Even these can have existed among their own constituencies for a long time before being 'discovered' by entrepreneurs and the broader public. No great effort in the production process turns an invention into an innovation. Instead it is distinguished by its reception and integration into the social world of its users, even against their resistance.

Fads typically hit their customers like a storm and conquer them almost over-night. Suddenly, in my childhood, every kid in the neighbourhood had to swing a hula hoop or wear a self-illuminating Phantom ring. They could, even more than ordinary fashion, be understood as a typical crowd phenomenon. Often they are the only thing that unites otherwise totally disparate people whose fascination they have captured. Everyone has to have them, not just something similar but exactly the right make and model. After conquering the whole market they disappear as quickly as they appeared, just like fashions. Unlike fashion, however, they do not leave behind an empty place immediately to be filled up by another fashion. It can take a long time before another fad conquers the same group of consumers again. In some cases, they may turn into valuable and rare collectable items, or they remain cherished and hibernating among smaller groups, in which case they can become ordinary hobby objects. They can even make a comeback, but this renewed effort hardly ever manages to live up to the expectations created by their former glory. Some fads can even become a permanent part of the life of their consumers. This would turn them into real innovations.

Pure fads typically belong to the less serious spheres of social life, to children's worlds of play and game. Their capriciousness would therefore seem natural. But to characterize them simply as capricious or trivial does not explain anything. It is only another way of referring to their short life span and to the fact that they do not, as a rule, leave any permanent traces in human culture.

We can now better formulate what makes the difference between a fashion and a fad, on the one hand, and a 'real' innovation, on the other hand. As we have interpreted Schumpeter, the important thing in any process of innovation is the integration of a technical invention into a new social practice. First becoming part of its own practice makes an invention into an innovation. Whereas a fashion always remains embedded in the same old social practice, both fads and 'real' innovations have to find and establish new social and cultural practices. What separates a fad from a 'serious' or more long-lasting innovation is that a fad establishes only a very limited play-like social world of routines and practices of its own. As a rule, it leaves the world outside its limited scope untouched. Even though millions of children and even adults exercised enthusiastically with their hula hoops at the same time – its mastery took practice – and their diffusion assumed an almost epidemic scale, they did not change any other social practices or the cultural habits of their practitioners. They remained hobby items and their social and cultural extension was very limited. In contrast, a successful commercial innovation which will leave long-term effects behind it obviously has to penetrate and change wider social practices. According to Lehtonen, 'the higher the number of attachments and practices that are potentially connected with a technology and the better it fulfils the promise associated with it, the more likely a technology is to be seen as something "necessary"' (2003: 371). If, for instance, the mobile phone had remained just a wireless phone, or a toy to play with, it would not have revolutionized our culture to the present extent. Today the cell phone has multiple functions, with different degrees of importance to different social user groups, but everywhere it has clearly changed 'the path of development by breaking with former routines and habits' (2003: 371).

The Establishment of New Markets

There is, however, one principal problem in analysing inventions and their trans-formation into innovation from the point of view of their social and cultural evolution, as Schumpeter suggested. The firm can only observe, and is only concerned with the market and the market roles and performance of its close competitors. It does not have any direct access to information about the taste, habits and preferences of its consumers. (Market research tries to overcome this, but it is always faced with limitations on what it can observe. The information that guides a firm's actions is different from that of its customers.) From the point of view of a firm, the decisive criterion of an innovation or a 'real' novelty is whether or not it is a part of the same market segment as the old product, or if it has created a market of its own. There is no other way for the firm to know when it or its competitors have succeeded in producing a new product and not just a copy or a new version of an old one.

Following White's suggestion, we can treat markets as 'induced role structures' (White 1981a) or 'self-reproducing social structures among specific cliques of firms and other actors who evolve roles from observations of each other's behaviour' (White 1981b: 518). In any market the firms differ from one another as far as their production volumes and cost-structures are concerned, but, equally importantly, their products' 'taste structures' can also be ranked by quality. Aspers makes a distinction between a standard market and a status market in which the status orders between the firms in a market are relatively stable (2005: 19; 2007). The case of totally homogenous products (perfect competition), the quality of which does not differ, is quite exceptional. Normally any market consists of only a relatively small number of firms which have established and preserved their own product niches. They have relatively stable roles as producers of a particular good and their identities are based on their own and their competitors' mutual expectations. Almost tautologically, then, any novelty or improvement stays within one and the same market as long as the firms relate to its production costs and relative quality or status as competitors and take it into account in their strategic considerations. Once this is not the case, a new market has been established and a real innovation has been born.

The establishment of a separate market for mini-vans is probably the most significant development in the recent history of the motor vehicle industry. Analysing this example, Rosa et al. (1999: 70) argue that the emergence of a new market is equal to the stabilization of the usage of a new product category label, in this historical case the mini-van as distinct from station wagons, cars, trucks, and so on. The establishment of the separate mini-van market by old, established car firms was typically preceded by 'endogenous and exogenous disturbances' that 'give rise to novel experiences and perspectives on product usage and marketing' (1999: 67). Both the producers and the consumers gradually came to regard the mini-van as a category distinct from other kinds of cars in the wider market. Rosa et al. also offer an interesting example of the important role of the mass media as gate-keepers, as the 'institutional regulators' (cf. Hirsch 1972: 654), in this case mainly motor journalists, in creating new product labels, categories and thereby innovations. In the well-established fashion markets such regulators, like professional fashion journalists and critics, are firmly institutionalized.

Product differentiation can take place gradually, or a new product can break with its 'mother' market more abruptly, but the end result is really what counts. Many great and far-reaching innovations started out as gradual improvements or changes in an old product or service, through gradual product differentiation or the merging of two or more old products.[5] In this way novelties can presumably expect to face less resistance. Even a new fashion can undoubtedly start its life through product differentiation. In fact, only fads never result from 'natural' product development or differentiation. They are, by definition, one-time creations which establish a totally isolated and short-lived market of their own. In these markets the first-comers play a decisive role and the number of competing firms is usually very limited, at least in the beginning. On the other hand, if the costs of product development are low and imitation easy, the market is open for new potential competitors. As soon as the late-comers have grasped the opportunity, it is too late, since the fad is no longer growing in popularity and the market is soon so saturated as to become totally extinguished.

It is essential to White's analysis that a firm can only use a limited amount of information in judging its own and its competitors' positions in the market role structure. Firms observe each other. All the firms producing and selling related products or services form a group of partly overlapping clusters which are concentrated around the biggest firm in the market. The only firms that really matter are those which, according to some relatively limited criteria such as production technique, marketing and product quality, are regarded as rivals. (For an interesting empirical example in the Scottish knitwear industry, see Porac et al. 1995.) Since the firms usually have no direct information about their consumers' demands and tastes at their disposal, they reproduce their market positions – or create new ones – mainly by observing their closest competitors. A 'real' innovation is always equal to the emergence of a new role set for the cluster of firms and, thus, a new market emerges. When the car industry developed the new mini-van, the same actors could successfully coordinate the emergence of a new product and more or less reproduce and preserve their old relative positions in this new market.

Conclusion

I have claimed that among the consumers or users the criterion of a 'real' innovation depends on the degree to which its adoption and spread has broken old routines and habits and has succeeded in establishing new ones. As a rule, new product labels emerge in this process (cf. Meyersohn and Katz 1957). It would seem natural that these two sides of the coin – the firm and the customer – must somehow co-incide, mutually reinforce each other or, on the contrary, work against each other in individual cases. The Schumpeterian model of innovation presumes that the entrepreneur must play an active and even decisive role in the process of creating new practices and changing old ones in the use of his or her new product or service. Innovators need access to, and must be able to interfere in, the cultural habits and social practices of their potential customers. In order to succeed they would have to convince potential users of a new product that it is necessary and worthwhile, and they need to change their routines and habits, even when they actively resist. This is what firms try to do – with better or worse success – with their advertising, market research and marketing efforts. At times, they can be lucky enough to find a ready-made set of new practices awaiting their invention. Arvidsson pays attention to an important principle in brand management which could probably be applied more generally to innovation processes too: 'brand management works by enabling or empowering the freedom of consumers so that it is likely to evolve in particular directions' (2005: 244) In doing so, it can be just as important to resist certain uses as to invite others.

Again, this is not the case with fashion, even though the growth of fashion institutes which professionally create new designs in established markets makes this distinction less clear. But a new fashion does not radically have to change anything; 'all' the fashion designer has to do is to catch the right, fleeting, moment in order to introduce his or her own invention. They have to listen to the 'Zeitgeist' (Blumer 1969). Fads are, in this respect, more mysterious. What makes them so peculiar is the abruptness and totality of their transformation. New practices seem to appear from nothing and disappear again without any trace at all. It is hardly worthwhile to predict and plan them. Trend-setters are of little use in designing the next fad. All that the producer can do is to offer a large variety of items and hope that at least one of them becomes a success. As a consequence, in order to make ends meet or to make a profit, a firm operating in, for instance, book publishing or music producing has to cover the costs of eight or nine failures with the sales of one best-seller (Hirsch 1972).[6]

Producers and sellers, on the one hand, and customers, on the other hand, have their own principles and standards of quality to follow in making decisions, and these only overlap partially and temporarily (Gronow 2004). Therefore producers probe their way around, responding to the moves of their closest competitors or market leaders. Consumers choose from a bigger or smaller variety of alternatives offered on sale at any one time without any clear idea what would be most satisfying for them. In Schulze's (1992: 442–444) analyses of the modern (mass) consumer society of inner experiences, both sides, producers and consumers, come to favour small gradual changes. Producers offer new 'numbers' of old series, consumers stick to the familiar and safe and prefer more of the same with minor variations, making 'real' innovations which would radically challenge existing social and cultural practices exceptional and rare. Our everyday observations would seem to confirm such a conclusion. When looking at the great number and variety of commodities in the supermarkets or in home electronics, one often gets an impression of eternal repetition of sameness. Compared to the numerous new everyday items of consumption advertised regularly, which seem to increase exponentially, the emergence of 'real' innovations is very rare. Despite all the efforts and money put into product development and innovation, inventions which create new markets and constituencies of customers as well as new social practices or ways of life cannot occur daily or weekly. On the contrary, new fashions abound in most areas of popular consumption. Fashion cycles get more intensive. But they do not, after all, change the world that much. Fads also come and go, initially making a real difference, but then vanishing without leaving any traces in our culture except, perhaps, in our collective memory.

Notes

1. For a general history of fashion designs, see Steele (1997).
2. Cf. with the story of the, in many respects similar but somewhat later, commercial success of the Sony Walkman (Gay et al. 1997)
3. In their study on fads and fashions, Meyersohn and Katz (1957: 598) referred to urban bohemia as a cultural laboratory in which something new can be tried out. Similarly, fashion historians have paid attention to the various youth sub-cultures as creative milieus of experimenting with new designs and models. Schiffer's (1993) restricted constituencies, with their true believers in their own 'cultural imperative', in the desirability and need of a certain product, can play a similar role. What unites the urban bohemians, youth sub-cultures and constituencies of technical inventions is that all kinds of new ideas and products can be tried out in them without great harm for or impact on society at large.
4. More recently, Best (2006) analysed fads in social institutions like management, education and medicine.
5. It is an interesting question, which I am not able to take up in this chapter in any great detail, where such product differentiation due to technical improvements should be placed. In the case of the colour TV, for instance, it would be difficult to claim that this was a real innovation compared to its black and white predecessor since it hardly created any radically different, new cultural habits or routines. But quite early on it created a new market of its own, distinct from the market of the old black and white TVs.
6. As some researchers claim, internet marketing has changed this old rule. With diminishing sales expenses and greater access, sales statistics have extended to include an increasing range of lesser-selling products (the so-called 'long tail' phenomenon; see Anderson 2006; Falk 2007).

References

Andersson, C. (2006). *The Long Tail – Why the Future of Business is Selling Less of More*. New York: Hyperion.

Arvidsson, A. (2005). Brands: A Critical Perspective. *Journal of Consumer Culture* 5(2): 235–258.

Aspers, P. (2005). Status Markets and Standard Markets in the Global Garment Industry. Max-Planck-Institut für Gesellschaftsforschung, *Discussion papers* 05/10. Cologne.

Aspers, P. (2007). The Practice of Defining Markets: A Comment on Charles W.Smith. *Canadian Journal of Sociology/Cahiers Canadiens de sociologie* 32(4): 479–488.

Becker, H. (1982). *Art Worlds*. Berkeley, CA: University of California Press.

Best, J. (2006). *Flavor of the Month: Why Smart People Fall for Fads*. Berkeley, CA: University of California Press.

Blumer, H. (1969). Fashion: From Class Differentiation to Collective Selection. *The Sociological Quarterly* 30(1): 275–291.

Falk, A. (2007). The Dynamics of Supply and Demand in the Long Tail Economy: Consumer Empowerment as the Driver of Market Success. Master's thesis, Helsinki School of Economics, Department of Business Technology (unpublished).

Gay, P. du., Hall, S., Janes, L., Mackay, H. and Negus, K. (1997). *Doing Cultural Studies: The Story of the Sony Walkman*. London: Sage.

Gerhards, J. (2003). *Die Moderne und ihre Vornamen: Eine Einladung in die Kultursoziologie*. Wiesbaden: Westdeutscher Verlag.

Gronow, J. (1987). *The Sociology of Taste*. London and New York: Routledge.

Gronow, J. (2004). Standards of Taste and Varieties of Goodness: The Unpredictability of Modern Consumption. In *Qualities of Food*, eds M. Harvey, A. McMeekin and A. Warde. Manchester and New York: Manchester University Press.

Hennion, A., Méadel, C. and Bowker, G. (1989). The Artisans of Desire: The Mediation of Advertising between Product and Consumer. *Sociological Theory* 7(2): 191–209.

Hirsch, P.M. (1972). Processing Fads and Fashions: An Organization-Set Analysis of Cultural Industry Systems. *The American Journal of Sociology* 77(4): 639–659.

Kotro, T. and Pantzar, M. (2002). Product Development and Changing Cultural Landscapes: Is Our Future in 'Snowboarding'? *Design Issues* 18(2): 30–45.

Kovács, György (2007). Joseph A.Schumpeters's Theory of Social and Economic Evolution: A Reconstruction and Critique. *Commentationes scientiarum socialium* 70. Societas Scientiarum Fennica, Vammala.

Lehtonen, T.-K.(2003). The Domestication of New Technologies as a Set of Trials. *Journal of Consumer Culture* 3(3): 363–385.

Lieberson, S. (2000). *A Matter of Taste: How Names, Fashions and Culture Change*. New Haven, CT and London: Yale University Press.

Lipovetsky, G. (1994). *The Empire of Fashion: Dressing Modern Democracy*. Princeton, NJ: Princeton University Press.

Löfgren, O. (2006). Catwalking and Coolhunting. In *Magic, Culture and the New Economy*, eds O. Löfgren and R. Willim. Oxford: Berg.

McMeekin, A. and Southerton, D. (2007). Innovation and Final Consumption: Social Practices, Instituted Modes of Provision and Intermediation. CRIC Discussion Paper 79.

Mayntz, R. and Nedelmann, B. (1987). Eigendynamische Soziale Prozesse: Anmerkungen zu einem analytischen Paradugma. *Kölner Zeitschrift für Soziologie unf Sozialpsychologie* 39(4): 648–668.

Mennell, S. (1985). *All Manners of Food: Eating and Taste in England and France from the Middle Ages to the Present.* London and Oxford: Blackwell.

Meyersohn, R. and Katz, E. (1957). Notes on a Natural History of Fads. *The American Sociological Quarterly* 62(6): 594–601.

Pantzar, M. (1997). Domestication of Everyday Life Technology: Dynamic Views on the Social Histories of Artifacts. *Design Issues* 13(3): 52–65.

Polhemus, T. (1994). *Street Style: From Sidewalk to Catwalk.* Singapore: Thames & Hudson.

Porac, F., Thomas, H., Wilson, F., Patton, D. and Kanfer, A. (1995). Rivarly and the Industry Model of Scottish Knitwear Producers. *Administrative Science Quarterly* 40(2): 203–227.

Rosa, J.A., Porac, J.F., Runser-Spanjol, J. and Saxon, M.S. (1999). Sociocognitive Dynamics in a Product Market. *Journal of Marketing* (Special Issue) 63: 64–77.

Schiffer, M.B. (1993). Cultural Imperatives and Product Development: The Case of the Shirt-Pocket Radio. *Technology and Culture* 34(1): 98–113.

Schulze, G. (1992). *Die Erlebnisgesellschaft: Kultursoziologie der Gegenwart.* Frankfurt and New York: Campus.

Schumpeter, J.A. (1911). *Theorie der wirtschaftlichen Entwicklung.* Berlin: Duncker & Humblot.

Schumpeter, J.A. (1939). *The Business Cycles*, Vols 1–2. Philadelphia, PA: Porcupine Press.

Shove, E. and Pantzar, M. (2005). Consumers, Producers and Practices: Understanding the Invention and Reinvention of Nordic Walking. *Journal of Consumer Culture* 5(1): 43–64.

Simmel, G. (1902). Fashion. *International Quarterly* 10: 130–155.

Steele, V. (1997). *Fifty Years of Fashion: New Look to Now.* New Haven, CT and London: Yale University Press.

Tellis, G.J., Stremesch, S. and Yin, E. (2003). The International Takeoff of New Products: The Role of Economics, Culture and Country Innovativeness. *Marketing Science* 22(2): 188–208.

Warde, A. (2005). Consumption and Theories of Practice. *Journal of Consumer Culture* 7(5): 131–153.

White, H.C. (1981a). Production Markets as Induced Role Structures. *Sociological Methodology* 12: 1–57.

White, H.C. (1981b). Where Do Markets Come From?' *The American Journal of Sociology* 87(3): 517–547.

−9−

The Edge of Agency
Routines, Habits and Volition
Richard Wilk

Introduction

The community of dog walkers is rarefied and intangible. We do not know each other, but we meet and pass on sidewalks and in parks, our interactions focused on and mediated by our canine companions. We are generally dutiful, and though we are locked into the routines demanded by the needs of our pets, we are generally trying hard to enjoy the experience, even in the rain, late at night, and at times when we would rather be doing almost anything else. After all, we chose to have a dog in the first place … or did we? Archie the Dachshund was the answer to my daughter's forceful demands for a puppy, which she of course promised to take care of herself. The routine demands of feeding, watering, cleaning up, training and walking were not as much fun in reality as they were in her 12-year-old imagination. This kind of thing means pets are often on a strange boundary between choice and duty, desire and compulsion, and as such they provide an avenue for thinking about the degree to which routines are the products of our own volition, or patterns forced upon us by circumstance and the power of others.

Let me give another canine example of how complex the interplay between choice and compulsion can be. Taking Archie to the office with me every day turned out to be the solution to a problem of self-discipline. Once I sit down at my desk in the morning, the endless flow of short- and long-term tasks, the constant barrage of emails and phone calls, classes and appointments often consumes me to the extent that I grab a few bites at my desk at noontime so I can keep working through the day. Even going to the bathroom is an interruption of the flow. I know this is bad for me, physically and mentally – but I always have one more thing which needs to be done, and exercise, social time, breaks and stretching all keep slipping down the priority list. But a dog's bladder knows nothing of the urgent survey from the Dean's office and the stack of books which are overdue for review. When Archie has to go, I have to drop everything else and take him. And once outside, I get involved in the flow of the walk, the hunt for squirrels, meetings with other dogs and pleasant social time with other walkers. The dog's demands have become, for me, a kind of liberation from self-imposed drudgery, a means of jarring me out of one flow and into another.

This interplay between my own needs and those of the dog displays one of the most fundamental, yet also one of the most puzzling and poorly understood, paradoxes in the sociology of daily life: what is the relationship between choice and habit? Why do some routines give us a sense of freedom, and act as instruments of choice, while others seem to be so restrictive and keep us from making choices? Furthermore, why are some routines and habits voluntary and breakable, while others are compulsive and seem to drive us beyond our ability to control them?

This chapter is an exploration in the phenomenology of routines, with the goal of understanding better how daily life has come to feel for so many people like a heavy burden, a maze of relentless demands. Like O'Dell and Ehn & Löfgren in this volume, I am concerned with the subtle and often subjective differences between the routines which make life possible, and those which make living miserable. Is this a recent dilemma of the human condition, or is it something inherent in the way we perceive time and regulate our daily lives?

Routines and Modernity

Both Durkheim and Weber associated habitual and unthinking routinized behaviour with animals, and with primitive and traditional societies. Weber thought that uncivilized peoples had not yet developed the capacities for reflexive awareness and rationality characteristic of modern peoples. In this scheme it made perfect sense for anthropologists to focus their attention on 'ritual' as the major determining element of behaviour in pre-modern societies, since those peoples' lives were supposedly ruled by timeless prescriptive rhythms rather than rationality. Utilitarianism and rational choice theory, on the other hand, elevated the act of decision making to the core of human nature, and focus attention on modern societies where this form of rationality is supposedly given free play.

This equation of habit and routine with the world of animals and primitive people, and of choice and decision making with modernity, has the unfortunate effect of setting time's arrow on a course where the 'inevitable' future will see the complete elimination of ritual and habit, through the advancement of technology. Durkheim and Weber were reluctant modernists, but modernists nonetheless, and they were optimistic in their predictions about the growth in rational choice and transactional logic in social life. One of the great and enduring myths of modernization theory is that modernity 'liberates' humans from routine and enslavement to the forces of habit. The imagined future of modernization theory is life based entirely on improvisation, where every day is invented anew. This is a very odd utopia in many ways, for it is based on the assumption that people really do want to be liberated from 'dull' routine, that an endless flow of calculated choices is a way of life people would really *want*.

This realization lies behind new theories of time which argue that modernity brings with it a lack of freedom and increased time pressures which may have the appearance of rationality, but which are detrimental to society and the individual (e.g. Ritzer 1993). In *Rhythmanalysis* Henri Lefebvre argues that much of modernity is composed of mindless rhythmic routine, of a kind of external training he calls 'dressage', for which he uses examples like monasteries, schools and the military, which instil habits as a form of discipline. 'Liberty is born in a reserved space and time, sometimes wide, sometimes narrow; occasionally reduced by the results of dressage to an unoccupied lacuna' (2004: 43). In this, Lefebvre follows Durkheim, agreeing that liberty is found in a lack of routine; his quarrel is that modernity has not reduced the place for it in society. Instead the state and its institutions have stepped in to force us into a mindless pace of routine which occupies our daily lives and limits the space of freedom, turning the practice of autonomy into the *evasion* of routine, rather than self-discovery or exploration.

For Lefebvre and many others, the profusion of goods and advertising, as well as the sheer profusion of goods in consumer culture, are key elements in limiting freedom and creating the dull routine which characterizes modernity. In a similar turn, Simmel and Veblen long ago predicted that the rational thrust of modernity would get diverted into a forest of emotions and social games built around fashion and consumption. A host of other social critics, from Stuart Ewen (1976) to Benjamin Barber (2008), have elaborated on the critique that modern people have become slaves to their own shopping and spending, a kind of 'second serfdom' of luxury rather than agrarian squalor.

The growing literature on 'time drought' and the increasing pace of modernity raises the question of whether it is the *density* of events and crowding of experience into limited time which restricts freedom in modern times, or if instead it is the habitual and repetitious rhythm, the crushing boredom of routine which gives people the experience of time shortage. In other words, are we suffering from too much choice, or too little choice? Or is it possible that we could be suffering from both at the same time? This certainly would help explain Jalas's insightful comment that something about the pace and tempo of contemporary life allows boredom and busyness to coexist (2006: 42).

This cannot be the whole story, for it runs completely contrary to a well-developed and widespread popular perception that wealth and the choices of consumer culture in the marketplace are enjoyable, liberating and allow the full development of the human capacity for autonomous as well as social pleasure (see Maslow 1943, one of the most often-cited papers in social science). Certeau (1984) makes a strong argument for the way modern people make material culture choices in creative ways which undercut the efforts of advertisers and marketers to impose uniform categories. And the sociology of life-styles, sub-cultures and fashion communities is based on the idea that consumption enables people to craft new ways of life, forming cultures of choice around alternative life-styles (e.g. Featherstone 1991).

So, on one hand, we have a utilitarian narrative in which modernity liberates us from the drudgery of repetitive routines, and allows the free play of choice and rationality. On the other hand there is a romantic narrative which tells us just the opposite, that once we were free to live in nature, but that industrial society has trapped us into an ever-increasing pace of forced routine, that industrial lives are built around the careful choreography of simultaneous rhythms which exhaust and drain us.

One way theorists have tried to reconcile these conflicting stories is to posit two kinds of time, what Lefebvre (2004) calls the 'homogenous mechanical time' of industry and the 'rhythmic cycles' of nature and the cosmos. This is, of course, an echo of many other dichotomies of linear vs cyclic time, diachrony vs synchrony, structure vs history, hot vs cold, which try to express some fundamental difference between modern and pre-modern experiences of time, an enterprise which Gell convincingly argues is fundamentally flawed and doomed to failure (1992: 28–29). There are many more kinds and dimensions of time than can be captured by a single dichotomy or evolutionary generality.

Framing the question of routines and freedom in this way clearly is insufficient – the discourse of modernity with its associated dichotomies and oppositions pulls the argument towards extremes. How can we more productively think about alternatives to the dichotomy of freedom and bondage, the repetition of ritual and the open possibilities of improvisation? How could we effectively re-map the space of action without the extreme ideal types of free will and determinism?

Defining the Problem

Daily life would be extremely difficult if we did not have habits and routines. This becomes most clear when we move house, go through a disaster or undergo a life transition, and our routines and habits are disrupted. Suddenly we have to become mindful of little things, think through details which we normally take for granted, and which have become deeply embedded and encoded in our built environment and possessions. Bathing and brushing one's teeth, getting dressed in the morning, preparing a quick meal, all require conscious thought and coordination. This shows us how normal life is an intricate synchronized dance, and how complex it is to maintain our bodies, our intimate self, our families and social relationships, homes, pets, vehicles, finances, communications and health.

Even small disruptions can show us how important routines are in allowing everyday life to proceed. We spend hours trying to find our keys, wallets, simple things which should be in their normal places. For some people, the whole day can be spoiled by the lack of a single item in the habitual breakfast. In old age, as memory fails, the bodily habits ingrained in the geography of a familiar home may be the only thing which makes an autonomous daily life possible.

A functional approach tells us that routines accomplish many things in daily existence. By creating order they reduce the complexity of tasks and uncertainty, save time and energy, and reduce what economists call *transaction costs*. This in turn makes life feel more safe and secure, and makes our behaviour predictable both to ourselves and to others, a predictability which makes elaborate social interactions possible (Giddens 1986; Ilmonen 2001: 15–17). To a large extent, public social behaviour like crowds walking on sidewalks, moving in orderly ways in and out of doorways and driving safely on streets is dependent on unconsciously learned habits and routines of gaze, bodily movement, turn taking and coordination based on elaborate non-verbal cues and subtle gestures (Goffman, 1971; Hall 1966). The dividing line between routine and ritual is especially difficult to locate when these gestures, postures and behaviours become an unconscious element of everyday social behaviour.

One way to understand the continual attraction of simple models which oppose choice versus habit in social life is that they resonate with our daily experience as human beings (Jackson 1989). In other words, rather than being profound statements whose veracity is based on empirical research, they are general statements about human nature which correspond to the folk models we use to explain or rationalize our own behaviour and the behaviour of those around us (Wilk 1996).

Theories of agency and practice can be seen as attempts to deal with this contradiction between views of human beings as active decision makers involved in making rational choices, and humans as habitual crowd-followers of fashion, ritual, customs and routine (Ilmonen 2001). At a large scale, when we are thinking of societies and historical time scales, the interplay of structure and agency is easy to imagine. But as we move to the level of daily life, it is far too easy to lose sight of the micro-level processes through which people make and break routines and habits. Ilmonen points out that when it comes down to actual cases, Giddens 'sets aside routines, stresses the discursive side of the agent's consciousness and thus ends up closer to the idea of the voluntaristic, reflective agent which features in economic theory' (2001: 17).

How can we get closer to what we really mean by the process Giddens calls 'structuration', the interaction in daily life between the decisions and choices we make, and the structures which determine and limit our scope for decision and action? As Shove et al. (2007) point out, daily habits and routines are deeply encoded in every bit of material culture, in the spatial topography of home and work as well as the social codes which interest Giddens. But routines, which are structures of time, are another key component which, though often dependent upon or involving machines or objects, can also be entirely internal. They can best be studied phenomenologically, and there are questions we need to ask which reflect on the mysterious nature of routines themselves. For example, why do we sometimes experience routines and habits as functional, relaxing, comforting and time-saving, while at other times they are annoying, restrictive and even intolerable (see Löfgren 2007)? Why are some kinds of habits so easy to make and break, while others are hard to form, or hard to end? When are we in charge of our routines and when are they in charge of us, and is this a matter of objectivity, or purely an issue of subjectivity?

Some of these questions shade into the issue of addiction, which has a psychological and physiological dimension, and when we come to aversions and physical emotions like disgust a dividing line between the biological and cultural is almost purposefully obscured. In general, I would argue that any strict division between thoughtful conscious decision making and unconscious habitual behaviour is a sociological and historical artefact which has no particular relevance to understanding the reality of everyday life. As Halkier says, 'a sharp distinction between reflexive and routinized consumption practices is impossible to sustain in empirical analysis' (2001: 27). Real life occupies the space between thought and habit, in a more complex and textured, perhaps layered, wrapped or enfolded space area of partial consciousness. While Halkier conceptualizes this as an 'overlap' or as 'contingency', below I propose that this terrain is more complex and intricate, and we still need to explore it fully.

Subjective Experience – What Do Routines and Habits Feel Like?

The pace of a habit seems to carry me along, like a jostling crowd. I can see where I am going, but I cannot stop. There is a compulsion behind me, pushing. It is like gravity, easy to fall down the well, just following the stream, as if you are running in a set of grooves worn in the pavement through years of traffic.

I can push back. But it is like swimming upstream and sometimes it is exhausting. If I keep pressing against the habit, though, eventually the resistance starts to diminish. But some habits lie in wait, even after they appear to be broken. You think you have left them behind, but then you find yourself falling back into a familiar habit in a moment of stress, while your attention is somewhere else. Your body is performing the routine again before you know it, following an unwanted path without you, like riding a bicycle into an abyss.

I tried brushing my teeth holding the brush in my left hand instead of my right. The new action does not feel right the first few times. It has a nagging feeling, like a tooth with a chip in it, you cannot stop running your tongue over that spot. You have to keep doing it, until eventually the feeling of wrongness slowly fades away. It is more like you just forget to feel the wrongness one day – you are distracted by something else and your attention does not return. The next thing you know you are doing it without thinking about it. You forget to worry, and go on without thinking.

Getting a new habit going is climbing uphill at first, but you hope eventually you will get somewhere where you can relax and coast. It is like an investment in the future. The hard work you are doing in the present is a big distraction, but maybe once you get going it can become automatic and you won't have to think about it anymore. Your body will take over, and your mind can move on to other things.

Some habits are like old friends. I stroke and tug on my beard unconsciously when I am preoccupied or absorbed in a film. I know some people find that driving is relaxing because the habits and routines occupy enough of their mind to free their imagination, but driving does not work for me. The shower is where I can put my body on automatic: the soaping and lathering and wiping and drying create a bubble of inattention which works a kind of magic on my creative imagination. The ideas for this chapter emerged in the shower while my body was 'on automatic'. The rhythm of manual labour, digging in the garden, chopping weeds with a machete, has a similar meditative quality, far different from the 'flow' of total absorption in a task or meditation where the inner voice of consciousness is stilled and absorbed in the moment (Csíkszentmihályi 1996).

I do not doubt that others experience routine and habit very differently. In particular, many people report feeling less control and feel more at the mercy of the patterns of their lives. Yet in my research on food tastes and preferences I have not run into anyone who did not report at least a few instances where they were able to 'learn' to like something, to make something new into a taken-for-granted part of their daily life. Though most people seem much less aware of the process, most can also find an instance where they abandoned a habit and 'moved on' to something else.

An Analytical Approach

In an earlier paper I tried to develop a terminology for the way people turn desires into needs, making the things they want into essential aspects of their daily life, and then basic needs, requirements and expectations (Wilk 2001). Elizabeth Shove (2003) takes up a similar project in her investigation of the origin of daily bathing as a bodily practice in the UK, once a dangerous folly, then a luxury, and finally a necessity (see also Highmore 2004).

In my analytical approach, I divided the process of absorbing a new form of consumption into daily life into two parts: cultivation and naturalization. *Cultivation* refers to the processes which bring unconscious habits and routines forward into consciousness, reflection and discourse. To use Bourdieu's terminology (1977), cultivation brings things out of the *habitus* and into the realm of *praxis*. Cultivation can be active or passive, because we can actively initiate new routines, or we can have changes forced upon us. Conflicts between routines, for example, may push them forward because we have to figure out what gets priority.

Because so much of consumer society is a fine balancing act between fitting in and standing out, most people are exquisitely sensitive to the possibility that some of their personal routines or habits may be inadequate or offensive to others. 'Alarms' can easily be tripped that lead us reflexively to examine our grooming, eating, our dressing, walking, driving or other daily routines and habits to see if they have faltered, slacked or fallen out of fashion. We all need many moments when we pause to assess, 'Did we forget something today?' 'Did we fail to complete some routine?'

Cultivation is an essential part of any form of training or education, and it is also a component of many kinds of competitions and public displays that bring habitual forms of consumption forward into the public eye for examination and reflection. Advertising often challenges us to cultivate some habit or routine, to look at ourselves in the mirror or check the smell of our armpits, just like our parents and friends do when we are growing up.

And it is easy to see how a completely cultivated life would be impossible to live, because it would be entirely self-conscious and reflective, like being a celebrity on display all the time (without the resources of a professional celebrity). This is the kind of bewildering task faced by the 'burnout' victims studied by Löfgren and Palm (2005, also Löfgren 2006 and Ehn and Löfgren in this volume), people who have suddenly lost the ability to do things habitually. We have many defences which simply filter out and silence cultivating messages, keep them from impinging on our existing routines. What is the nature of these defences, and how do they work?

Naturalization describes the processes which push conscious practices back into the habitus, or keeps them from surfacing into consciousness in the first place. Many of our habits of life are so totally naturalized that we never even think of them: getting hungry and thirsty are seen as entirely natural processes which have no social component at all. Similarly, most people never think of comfort, cleanliness, beauty and other sensations as anything more than direct physical experiences, and engineers are quite willing to back them up with a whole raft of seemingly objective standards which tell us that whatever practices our culture has adopted are 'necessary' for our daily health, though historical analysis shows that these standards are constantly changing (Cooper 1998; Shove 2003).

People use many kinds of methods and tactics to make things routine or allow them to become so. I have made an initial distinction between the kind of naturalization which Bourdieu calls hexis, where alternatives never rise to consciousness, and that which he calls orthodoxy, where alternatives are actively repressed. I called the first *submersive* naturalization, meaning that the routine remains thoroughly submersed in the habitus. We cannot think of any alternative, for example, to washing our body in the shower with a bar of soap and a washcloth. That is what washing 'means'. It took a concerted effort on the part of the marketing industry to introduce an alternative liquid soap 'body wash'.

Repressive naturalization, on the other hand, includes the methods we use to *force* things into the background, both to keep a practice as a habit or routine after alternatives have challenged it, and to make something new into something routine and normal. An example of the first would be when I stay in a hotel and find that instead of soap, they have given me a tube of body wash for my shower. I quickly grab the face soap from the sink and take it to the shower, naturalizing my routine use of soap and rejecting the alternative of body wash. (See Figure 9.1 for a schematization of these processes.)

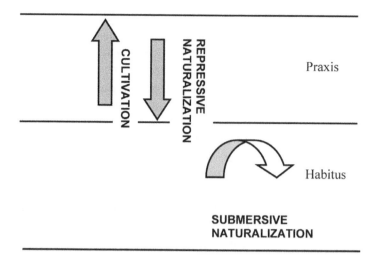

Figure 9.1 A simple model of the movement of practices in and out of conscious reflection (hexis) and everyday normality (habitus).

Every day we are faced with opportunities to naturalize something new. Children and pets are experts at this when they try to make an event into a precedent. Say we give a sweet as a reward for behaving well at dinner. The next evening the child says, 'Where is my after-dinner sweet?' A good deal of daily life is a struggle over what is going to enter the repertoire of routine, and there are tacit rules of repetition which govern how often things must be discussed before they can be done without discussion, how often things have to be repeated by agreement or with supervision before they can become an accepted part of shared daily routine.

Concluding Thoughts

My whole life I have had a deep aversion to hypodermic needles and injections, to the point of nausea, and I fell to the floor unconscious when I had to watch a doctor put a large needle into my wife's stomach for an amniocentesis. Three years ago I was prescribed a medicine which I have to inject twice a week. The very thought of doing so made me physically sick. The nurse who taught me how to give the injections broke the process down into a series of individual steps. First you squeeze air out of the syringe, then you open the alcohol swab, and so on. Turning the unimaginable act into a series of mundane easily learned activities broke down my resistance. Decomposing the routine in this way turns out to be an ancient technique of training, adapted well to complex technological operations like flying an aeroplane, where one begins with a 'checklist'. Once learned in bits and pieces, the whole routine is easy to assimilate, and after four or five injections, my phobia was gone.

There are some habits I resent terribly. When I was working for the US Embassy in Belize I had to get up every morning at 6 a.m. and dress especially for work in clothes much more formal than my usual; after six months my body was habituated to the routine so that even on the weekend I woke up at 6 a.m., and blue jeans and T shirts no longer felt like my normal clothes. There was a part of me that was happy to be awake and alert early in the day, in contrast to my slothful student days. But it felt like liberation when I finally quit and went back to the university, where I could sleep later and dress as I wanted. It took less than a week to lose the early waking habit. If I had enjoyed my routine and uniform, like long-time soldiers who love their jobs, would it have been much harder to return to my old clothes and late rising?

I have tried unsuccessfully to cultivate the habit of eating breakfast for many years. I know it would be better for my health if I could just get used to eating in the morning, but the idea of eating when I wake up usually makes me nauseated. Lefebvre and Régulier say it takes ten years to train your body to get hungry at regular mealtimes (1985: 191), and I have never had any external schedule or routine which forced me to eat breakfast at any particular time, in a hotel or an archaeological camp, for more than a few months at a stretch. I can get myself started eating break-fast, but the slightest interruption and I lose the habit almost immediately. But other habits are frighteningly easy to cultivate and extremely difficult to lose, like smoking cigarettes. And it is remarkable the degree to which the human body can get habituated to routines which are painful and unpleasant.

Can you have a habit of having habits? My college roommate Steven woke up at the same time every morning, ate the same thing for breakfast every day, went home for spaghetti dinner every Friday night, kept his desk meticulously organized and had his career carefully planned. My half of the room was a messy pile of clothes, and I had no schedule, no organization, no plan and no system. We managed to survive a year in a single room together only by drawing a diagonal line on the floor. He resisted my attempts to teach him to 'loosen up', and I subverted all of his efforts to organize my life. As far as I can tell from the last time I saw him, these have remained lifetime commitments, and he is happy as a very meticulous dentist.

This grey area between active and passive is complex and fascinating, for it is the space where we shift from being in control to being controlled. Repetition has a compelling power which we do not fully control; it relieves us of the burden of making the thousands of micro-decisions which would otherwise overwhelm us. We need to set priorities in the normal pace of life, and habits are our autonomous agents to handle trivia. They are also the chains which bind us and blind us. The rhythms of life both liberate us from constant worry, and keep us in constant bondage. These are not two separate kinds of experience, two kinds of time, as Lefebvre would have it. Instead they are two sides of the very same phenomenon.

Uncertainty about the degree to which we are in control of our own rituals, routines, rhythms and habits is itself a vital social resource, an instrument which enables human interaction. The structuring power of time gives us plausible deniability, allows us to step in and take responsibility, blame others for our own failings, give up all hope and wield invisible power.

On a larger scale, the grey area between structure and agency gives cultural change its paradoxical nature. On one hand, it seems to be the result of decisions and choices made by individuals; on the other hand, people seem to be following the dictates of fashion, patterns of habit common to society, and a kind of mentality which requires thorough precedent and familiarity before any action is taken.

I would suggest that the spaces between structure and agency also define a zone of comfort. The one extreme, where every moment is mapped out in advance and all of life becomes an endlessly repeated series of cycles of routines, defines what life in a prison or another total institution is all about. At the other extreme, life without any routines or regularity would be a chaotic mess of endless trivial choice. In between we can find some sort of compromise where we can engage with both consciousness and familiarity with ourselves, our companions and intimate others, our material surroundings and their various pressures and demands.

References

Barber, B.R. (2008). *Consumed: How Markets Corrupt Children, Infantilize Adults, and Swallow Citizens Whole*. New York: W.W. Norton.

Bourdieu, P. (1977). *Outline of a Theory of Practice*. Cambridge: Cambridge University Press.

Campbell, C. (1996). *The Myth of Social Action*. Cambridge: Cambridge University Press.

Certeau, M, de. (1984). *The Practice of Everyday Life*. Berkeley, CA: University of California Press.

Cooper, G. (1998). *Air-Conditioning America*. Baltimore, MD: Johns Hopkins University Press.

Csíkszentmihályi, M. (1996). *Creativity: Flow and the Psychology of Discovery and Invention*. New York: Harper Perennial.

Ewen, S. (1976). *Captains of Consciousness: Advertising and the Roots of Consumer Culture*. New York: McGraw-Hill.

Featherstone, M. (1991). *Consumer Culture and Postmodernism*. London: Sage.

Gell, A. (1992). *The Anthropology of Time*. Oxford: Berg.

Giddens, A. (1996). *The Constitution of Society: Outline of the Theory of Structuration*. Berkeley, CA: University of California Press.

Goffman, E. (1971). *Relations in Public: Microstudies of the Public Order*. New York: Basic Books.

Halkier, B. (2001). Routinization or Reflexivity? Consumers and Normative Claims for Environmental Consideration. In *Ordinary Consumption*, eds J. Gronow and A. Warde. London and New York: Routledge.

Hall, E.T. (1966). *The Hidden Dimension*. Garden City, NY: Doubleday.

Highmore, B. (2004). Homework: Routine, Social Aesthetics and the Ambiguity of Everyday Life. *Cultural Studies* 18(2/3): 306–327.

Ilmonen, K. (2001). Sociology, Consumption and Routine. In *Ordinary Consumption*, eds J. Gronow and A. Warde. London and New York: Routledge.

Jackson, M. (1989). *Paths toward a Clearing: Radical Empiricism and Ethnographic Inquiry*. Bloomington, IN: Indiana University Press.

Jalas, M. (2006). *Busy, Wise and Idle Time: A Study of the Temporalities of Consumption in the Environmental Debate*. Dissertation A-275. Helsinki: Helsinki School of Economics. Available at: http://hsepubl.lib.hse.fi/EN/diss/?cmd=show&dissid=306 (accessed 16 April 2009).

Lefebvre, H. (2004). *Rhythmanalysis: Space, Time and Everyday Life*. London: Continuum.

Lefebvre, H. and Régulier, C. (1985). The Rhythmanalytical Project. *Communications* 41: 191–199.

Löfgren, O. (2006). Wear and Tear. *Ethnologia Europaea* 35(1–2): 53–58.

Löfgren, O. (2007). Excessive Living. *Culture and Organization* 13(2): 131–144.

Löfgren, O. and Palm, A.-M. (2005). Att kraschlanda i sjukskrivning. In *Att utmana stressen*, eds , in B. Jönsson and O. Löfgren. Lund: Studentlitteratur.

Maslow, A.H. (1943). A Theory of Human Motivation. *Psychological Review* 50: 370–396.

Ritzer, G. (1993). *The McDonaldization of Society*. Newbury Park, CA: Pine Forge Press.

Shove, E. (2003). *Comfort, Cleanliness and Convenience: The Social Organization of Normality*. Oxford: Berg.

Shove, E., Watson, M., Hand, M. and Ingram, J. (2007). *The Design of Everyday Life*. Oxford: Berg.

Wilk, R. (1996). *Economies and Cultures: Foundations of Economic Anthropology*. Boulder, CO: Westview Press.

Wilk, R. (2001). Towards an Archaeology of Needs. In *Anthropological Perspectives on Technology*, ed. M. Schiffer. Albuquerque, NM: University of New Mexico Press.

Section IV
The Temporalities of Stuff

–10–

Buying Time
Daniel Miller

Introduction

One of the most curious aspects of the relationship between time and consumption is the circumstances under which we are able to, in some sense or other, buy time. When the busy rhythms and routines of our contemporary lives are such that we feel we don't have the time available to actually live out certain things we wish for, and decide instead to buy pre-packed time spent by somebody else, doing this living on our behalf, in the form of a commodity, off the shelf. This chapter examines two examples of this phenomenon of buying time, that of distressed jeans and the trade in antiques and flea markets. These case studies bring out a central paradox of the process of buying time which is the inherent tension between personalization and the impersonal. I conclude by attempting to explain this paradox through reference to Lévi-Strauss's image of rituals such as rhythms and routines as machines for the suppression of time.

Buying Denim Blue Jeans

Distressed blue jeans are an extraordinary phenomenon. The point about these jeans is that, in effect, someone somewhere is spending their time simulating the wearing out of your clothing, replicating the effect of you spending months or years wearing them. It is as though, on analogy with that common expression 'get a life', you could buy a period of your own lifetime off the shelf as represented by these apparently pre-worn jeans. Where once upon a time you had to be involved in heavy labour, or constant wearing, before the jeans reached a certain look, today you can buy all these effects ready-made. Indeed you can simulate life-styles, such as one based in manual work, or a highly adventurous life that might have resulted in these patterns of tearing and fraying, even if you never will or never have lived that kind of life.

It does seem rather bizarre that a textile should be sold as though it had already been worn, almost to death, before we even buy it. That workers in Turkey or Mexico should spend their time simulating these pre-worn effects as an integral part of what is sold to the consumer (on labour in the industry, see Bair and Gereffi 2001; Bair and Peters 2006; Tokatli 2007). Not surprisingly they don't actually wear these jeans to have this effect. Indeed the paradoxical nature of this process starts to open up as soon as we consider the reaction of a London consumer to the idea that a labourer in Mexico might have actual worked, sweated, ate, danced and lived years wearing this same pair of jeans. The consumer seems to want the illusion of themselves having worn the jeans. They clearly don't want a consciousness of vicarious wearing of those jeans by an actual other.

Instead industry has developed a wide range of techniques to simulate the effects of jeans having been worn. The very first distressed jeans were sold as stone-washed. The method of washing them with a large pile of pumice stones is still common today, though it is increasingly supplemented by cellulase enzymes, which are natural proteins that may used to obtain a stone-washed look. Apart from stone wash, one can opt for acid wash, moon wash, monkey wash, show wash, white wash and mud wash. Chemicals such as potassium permanganate are applied to shift the tinting. Resins may be used to set creases at particular places in the jeans. There is ozone fading or water jet fading. There are various forms of sandblasting, or handsanding, either on a flat surface or on dummies. Typical special effects including whiskering, that is, crease lines around the crotch, which can be produced with lasers, or by sandblasting, handsanding or abrasive rods. If one wants really fancy results, there are more elaborate methods. For example a laser beam can be passed through a shaped mask that comprises an aperture of the desired shape and is then deflected by a mirror to strike the textile substrate (Denim Academy n.d.; *ExpressTextile*, 20 March 2003)

One of the main effects that all of these methods are trying to copy is actually a fortuitous result of the nature of denim. Denim is a twill textile in which indigo-dyed warp threads are woven with white weft threads. The warp dominates the surface, which is why jeans appear blue on the outside and mainly white on the inside. As jeans are worn through, the underlying weft threads become more prominent, giving the characteristic worn effect. Clearly other forms of trousers might become well worn, but this would not be as evident because the warp and weft are of the same colour. So blue jeans lend themselves to the conspicuous display of being worn. But this would only account for one element, not the fraying, tearing and embroidering, and would not explain why we would want them to look worn in the first place.

As already noted, we do not wish to imagine an actual labourer wearing these jeans. We probably have no more desire to know about lasers, sandblasting and whiskering the crotch either. The clear preference is for all such processing to take place at some point entirely removed from our consciousness. To be conscious of how these effects were achieved would detract from the illusion that the effects are to be attributed to us, the wearer. This lack of consciousness and distancing from method is most acute when we confront evidence that this idea of other people living their lives for us sometimes becomes literally the case. One of the standard methods of distressing jeans is sandblasting. It is a technique that appears to remain quite common in small unregulated workshops in places such as Istanbul. Recently it has been found that young men who work in these conditions have been contracting silicosis (Akgun et al. 2005; Cimrin et al. 2006). In such cases someone really has given his life so that we are able to purchase our denim jeans with the illusion of spending some of our life in their wearing out. At a more general level, distressing of jeans is associated with high levels of pollution. For example, a report in the *Guardian* (17 August 2007, p. 25) called 'Distressed Denim Trend Costs Mexican Farmers the Earth' tells of the area of Tehuacan in Mexico, a place once famous for natural springs and health water but now heavily polluted.

> 'Jeans were born to be used by workers,' said a local activist, Martin Barrios, 'now they can cost thousands of dollars and are produced on the backs of exploitation and environmental destruction.' … Nearby factories were the problem – dozens of them, which are dedicated to doing to jeans in hours what used to take years of wear… The clean garments are left ready for sale, while in many factories the chemicals used to treat them are left to flow away in bright indigo waste.

Why is any of this happening? At least until recently, when some other genres of clothes seem to be getting in on the act, there were no other items of clothing that we would find in our retail stores which appear to have been speckled with bleach, torn at the knee, stained with rust, worn out with rubbing, ripped and frayed at several places and subject to a whole series of other destructive processes. If we saw signs of such abuse on any other clothing we possess, let alone intended to buy, we would ourselves become pretty distressed. The nature of the twill helps create the effect but does not of itself explain why jeans, which for a hundred years were sold without distressing, developed this unique other market.

One clue is that distressing goes alongside other forms of transformation. Blue jeans were a garment that at the same time that distressing processes were being developed also become subject to other forms of embroidered embellishments, ranging from sequins to flowers. These effects, too, have been commodified on analogy with distressing. If one goes to the main Levi's shop in San Francisco, one can order machine-made embroidery, adding sequins and other similar effects simply by conveying the style and form required. But standing in a Levi's shop in San Francisco, in particular, looking at embroidered flowers is an ideal circumstance to evoke a particular moment in the past, the time of the hippie.

The story can be told personally, in that I was of the generation whose behaviour is being copied by commercial distressing of pre-sold jeans. As a teenager I hitchhiked around rock concerts, wearing flares and flowered shirts (purple and adorned with beads, if you must know). I had blue denim jeans that were worn so much, in such rough conditions, and with so little attention to washing and care that after a while they became naturally abraded and frayed in just the manner that is simulated by commerce today. It was not that there was any fashion in the earliest stages for such extreme abuse of one's own clothes. The holes, the beer stains, the rips, the fraying, were the natural outcome of a specific life-style, combining lack of money to buy new clothes, independence from home and parental care, a sense of freedom, travel and general hippie personal irresponsibility where one just didn't care about such things. Stone washing of jeans followed rather naturally from the stoned state of the people who had been wearing them.

Campbell (1987) has noted the considerable significance of the hippie in the evolution of modern consumption. Although in retrospect we appear as of a particular style to which we conformed, for us as participants we believed that the 1960s and 1970s were the vanguard of an unprecedented feeling of personal freedom and experimentation that was a direct repudiation of the conformity of the 1950s and all previous periods. So although the deterioration of my jeans was merely a product of neglect, there was a strong sense that I was free to neglect them, that I didn't any more have to cut my hair, iron my trousers and reproduce in younger version the image of an older generation. This sense of the individual connected with the other major effect of this wearing through of fabric as it pertained to blue denim jeans. It was not simply that they were worn though, it was that in doing so they became intensely personal. A sense of the personal manifested itself in various ways. One is the quality of cotton to become extremely soft and comfortable after intense wearing. Another is that the jeans were wearing themselves to a very particular body – that they seemed over time to mould themselves to the way one walked, and lay down and carried oneself in the world. I can recall first learning about manufacturers suggesting that the first thing you should do when you purchased their jeans was to take a bath while still wearing them. This ideal of a shrink-to-fit processes enacted by the consumer was the intermediary stage before the development of commercial distressing. This individuality of fit was accentuated by the subsequent long periods of wearing, as you felt the creases, the pattern of wear, related to you as the specific wearer of the specific pair of jeans.

So denim jeans became the most personal, the most intimate item of clothing that anyone had yet experienced. The degree to which this could be the case was wonderfully exemplified in Hauser's paper (2004) on how the FBI could solve a robbery by identifying an individual through focusing upon the identifiable pattern of that person's interaction with a specific pair of denim jeans. Denim can also become a kind of embodied record of the particular movements and contours of the particular body, as noted by Candy (2005) using visual interviews and photography to locate characteristic patterns of wearing denim. Today there is a new equivalent to this sense of the self and the body in the growing (shrinking?) phenomenon of women and their skinny jeans. Many women have in their wardrobe the memento of the thinnest that their body ever became, as judged by the jeans size they were able to wear at that time. This image, popularized in an episode of *Sex and the City*, was found ethnographically by both myself and Sophie Woodward in our respective researches in London.

This personal relationship to jeans is clearly what commerce has attempted to replicate and then pre-empt through the phenomenon of distressing. Even if this is starting to spread to a few other garments, it clearly developed as a direct response to this unique relationship to denim. But this leads to a clear contradiction. My jeans were personal to my body because of the degree of time they spent on my body. Commercially distressed jeans are an artificial simulation of that process. Yes, you can probably artificially induce some of the softness that comes from constant wear, but not the way the jeans mould themselves to you in particular. Indeed the very sense of the commercial faking of this process seems to mitigate against the sense of the personal.

To understand what is going on, we need to situate the whole phenomenon of distressing within a wider appreciation of the special nature of blue denim jeans – a task which was recently undertaken by myself and Woodward in a paper we called 'A Manifesto for the Study of Denim' (Miller and Woodward 2007). This provides the academic argument for a larger Global Denim Project (www.ucl.ac.uk/global-denim-project). The paper argues for a consideration of distressing in the context or two other unique properties of denim. The first is the sheer global ubiquity. It is equally extraordinary that at a time when there is increasing choice in a post-fordist, competitive market that we should see something increasingly approaching half the world choosing only one particular textile to wear on their lower half, at any given time. This amounts almost to a global refusal of the dictates of fashion and capitalism, since although there are designer jeans, mostly it is a preference for the mundane and non-descript that dominates jean wearing. Secondly there is Woodward's work on women getting dressed in the morning in England (Woodward 2007), which shows that denim acts as a kind of foundational bedrock to the typical wardrobe. Woodward notes that very commonly women will start by trying one or two more adventurous items of clothing, and then find they don't have the confidence to select them on that particular day, and withdraw to the security of denim wearing. This in turn relates to a paper published in *Fashion Theory* by myself and Alison Clarke (Clarke and Miller 2002) which argues that it is this point of anxiety that should be central to the study of fashion, not the study of the industry.

So we have three extraordinary aspects of denim blue jeans, and it would be unreasonable to see them as merely coincidently in juxtaposition within this single garment. It is not just that denim turns out to have the capacity to be the most individualized and personal garment, but that it is simultaneously the exact opposite – the most global, ubiquitous and in effect anonymous garment that we possess. In short it manages within itself to encapsulate that well-worn phrase about the most local and the most global, and also to somehow address the core of the anxiety that exists in that relationship. Our manifesto paper argues that denim jeans are therefore one of the most profound forms of contemporary clothing, telling us a great deal about that same modernity that is the context for much of our more general discussion over the rhythms and routines of consumption. The degree to which distressed jeans matter is also evident in the strong feelings people have about them. Since June 2007, Woodward and I have been carrying out an ethnography of denim jeans consumption in three streets in North London. Already we have found that when people are talking about their jeans consumption, many consumers, especially older consumers, are adamant about the degree to which they would never, under any circumstances, wear distressed jeans, and have equally strong feelings about the circumstances under which other people also should not wear them, for example, at work.

The implication, as argued in our manifesto paper, is an evident need to acknowledge and account for denim jeans more in the tradition of a philosophy of practice than merely just as an item of apparel. There are many key philosophical issues raised, but for the purposes of a specific focus upon rhythms and routines of consumption the strongest conclusion from this discussion is the direct relationship between buying time, on the one hand, and then the establishment of an extreme polarity between personalization and impersonalization, on the other. If the key to distressing is the way it simulates the long-term personalization of jeans, as a means to negate the impersonality represented by denim's global ubiquity and homogenization, how is it that this can be achieved through a commercial, industrial and thoroughly anonymous process as represented by industrial distressing and with respect to the most anonymous and homogenizing garment we possess? Denim jeans possess an apparently oxymoronic quality linking the extremely personal and the extremely impersonal. When buying time, which of these are we buying into?

Buying the Patina of the Past

At this point I want to take this paradox back into the frame of anthropological reasoning by examining it in more general and comparative terms, starting with an entirely different social and cultural context and then exploring an opposition within a UK setting. The first case is drawn from a paper called 'Rituals of Death as a Context for Understanding Personal Property in Socialist Mongolia', by Caroline Humphrey (2002). This starts with one of the fundamental contradictions of materiality itself (Miller 2005), where objects are used to express the desire to transcend the material, here within a Buddhist context. When a person amongst the Buryat peoples whom Humphrey studied is close to death, certain treasured objects are taken away from them, to help them separate from desire and enter more smoothly into this other state. This is even more important after they have died since there is a category of material culture called refuge objects that the dead soul still desires and wishes to return to. An astrologer identifies these and they are either destroyed, given away or buried with the corpse. So one category of objects is considered too personal, too intimate for them to be inherited or even to survive.

At the same time Buryat people in general show a preference for things that have been worn as against new things. They like this patina of care to be attached to objects, but it should be a generic collective sense of the humanized object, not the hyper-personalization of these refuge objects. Humphrey suggests that these are more nuanced ideas of possible relationships between property and the person than those given by the legal bases of property in our society, or the extremes of Weiner's (1992) inalienable objects as things that can never be given away. The Buryat assume that merely looking after or caring for an object attaches a person to it and helps provide a transformational quality that allows it to grow, on analogy with caring after livestock. Overall Humphrey argues that when it comes to considering the dead, the Buryat aim for a balance between the degree of personalization and impersonalization that accrues from the temporality of association between a person and a thing. So it is not just in relation to ourselves and blue denim jeans that cultural normativity establishes through material culture a parameter based on the distinction between the personal and the impersonal quality of used objects, and within this polarity creates a point of preference. Rather it may be that this striving for balance and commensurability between these possibilities in the signification of material culture is rather common, though it will manifest itself quite differently in different social and cultural contexts.

For example, a paper by Gregson et al. (2000) provides an analogous instance closer to home. They examine the work of people in charity shops selling retro clothing: for example, dresses from the 1920s and 1930s. Their paper observes how the workers in these shops clean these clothes of evident stains. People will buy such clothes unwashed, but what they don't want to see are specific stains. In other words, just as amongst the Buryat, we want to wear something that has been given authenticity by its association with another person's life, but a generic other person, not someone as specific as represented by a particular stain.

My second comparative study comes from a strangely antagonistic dualism within our own attitudes to consumption. This dualism struck me as particularly acute when watching *Signs of the Times* – a television series about home decoration made by a documentary film maker trained in anthropology. One programme focused upon two groups of people, those who largely decorated their homes with reproduction furniture and those who prefer antiques. Needless to say each of these groups utterly despised the other.

The people who brought reproduction furniture saw this as a commitment to the high quality and style of the past. But they also tended to feel disgusted by the idea of having to sleep in a bed that someone else actually may have lived in, or, still worse, died in. They would see actual antiques as worn, possibly diseased, and in general rather revolting. As far as they are concerned their devotion to reproduction furniture grants them all the advantages of the past without any of these disadvantages. By contrast, those who buy actual antiques look quite disdainfully at people who buy reproduction, almost as though it was some version of stupidity, certainly vulgarity. They see these people as being in some sense fooled by fakes, and at least vicariously associating themselves with the inauthentic that cannot match the truth of an antique.

In general the people who buy antiques have higher status than those who buy reproduction – the former being associated with the arts, in which the original has always had to preserve itself from the mere copy. I suspect most academics would be on their side. My sense of this comes from my own experience as someone who generally prefers fake reproductions. My house is dominated by an 'oriental' carpet made in Belgium and purchased at John Lewis. As I would see it, both the European Renaissance and the Pre-Raphaelite could be regarded as reproduction styles, but actually the new context is a form of active reappropriation. If fakes and copies undermine the art market and its absurd prices, this seems entirely positive. But then some of my friends would see my taste as an affectation, either for the vulgar and philistine, or a desire for status by overtrumping style.

These matters are probably best argued over a drink. The point, though, is that in contemporary consumption we also often work with a contradictory and dualist relationship to time as represented in material culture, preferring to buy time in the sense of objects that were actually associated with past people rather than an appearance of the past. Most people privilege patina over veneer. One more step is required, however, to return this point to the overall focus of this volume, that is, our rhythms and routines of consumption. Fortuitously I was able to take this step recently when I was approached to facilitate a new research project. This is being carried out by Nicolette Makovicky, who had just finished a Ph.D. in my Department at UCL as research assistant to Gerry and Valerie Mars and Angela Burr. My task was to give a place for this project through our department under the title of 'A pilot study of interactions, interconnections and change in the antiques, car boot sale and collectable trades with special reference to income provision and the enhancement of social well-being among the retired and 50 and over unemployed'.

I suspect that in general people such as myself who tend to buy fakes and reproductions have not produced from this any particular rhythms or routines of consumption. Our purchases tend to be one-off and ad hoc, according to what we see as the needs of our home decorations. By contrast, the people who are the subject of this research project are responsible for one of the most concerted routines of contemporary consumption. Many of these people visit antique markets, or the various versions of flea markets and junk markets, with considerable frequency. One suspects that many of those who sell such items are hard to distinguish from the buyers, in that both parties seem to share a general sense of the amateur love of such things, and either of them might make the commitment to a weekly attendance at such events. Indeed in some of the more informal markets I see consumers who know the sellers well enough to spend an hour or two minding the stall while the seller takes time off to be a consumer. It is hard to think of many other aspects of consumption that therefore so fully confirm the sense of routine or rhythms of the consumption process as this highly regular commitment to being present often on a weekly basis,

This research project starts from the observation that there has developed in Britain a vast multi-million pound trade in various forms of antiques, junk and second-hand goods, often through more informal sites of provision such as flea markets and car boot sales (Gregson and Crewe 2003). On casual observation one can see that most of the people involved in this trade are 50 and over, and it seems particularly to attract those who are retired from regular work and can give themselves more fully to such activities.

This is clearly also an example of buying time, a trade in patina. These people circulate objects that have actually been used by some other person. One might have expected, then, that these objects would be possessed and treasured, respecting this patina of prior personalization on analogy with the heirloom. But actually this is not at all what we find. Instead the emphasis is rather on establishing routines of consumption. Those involved develop a very regular, often weekly ritual of trading, exchanging and collecting. The routines seem actually more important than the respect for the individuality of these objects, which are mostly gathered, traded, formed into collections, returned to the market, and so forth. This routine of exchange and consumption has the effect of making such objects almost trivial in their relative alienability and often transience of possession. The high-frequency circulation seems to cut against the idea that they are authentic to individual past lives and would be treated with appropriate respect as such.

Just as in the case of distressed blue jeans, these people seem to be buying time in the form of a material culture which seems to at first evoke a patina of its usage by other people. These objects also are worn, abraded, faded and signify their own prior lives. Yet just as with distressed jeans, this degree of personalization signifying their previous usage is instantly denied by its very opposite. They are actually highly alienated commodities that form a vast circuit of constant exchange which lends themselves to these particular routines and rhythms of consumption. As such they become tokens of a generic past rather than an individualizing past. As with the Buryat, they seem to work within a field established by these parameters of contrast, such that antiques and junk must be personal but not too personal.

Machines for the Suppression of Time

Having parked the question of why young people are involved in the purchase of distressed jeans, it is now joined by the question as to why older people are involved in the circulation of flea market goods. I want to suggest an explanation based on what is itself a well-worn classic of anthropological theorization with a patina of its own. In anthropology the concept of rhythm and repetition in time evokes the classic discussion by Lévi-Strauss on ritual and myth, as 'machines for the suppression of time'. In particular there is the opposition of Lévi-Strauss (1972) to Sartre's work on the dialectic of practical reason found in the last chapter of *The Savage Mind* called 'History and Dialectic', and which follows on from a previous chapter called 'Time Regained'. In brief, Sartre's love of history links him to his particular sense of the individual as a historical narrative leading to choices, to freedom and to death. Lévi-Strauss, by contrast, draws attention to the cyclical nature of repetitive time as another form of human experience that transcends and complements narrative time, with an emphasis on the endless and transcendent, the immortal qualities of mythic time. For Lévi-Strauss, forms of time that are constantly repeated, such as annual ceremonies or retold myths, are a means by which we deny the linear narrative sense of time that leads ultimately to death. This is why religions tend to proliferate rituals and routines of time as machines that suppress linear or narrative time.

This perspective lends itself to the second example of why an elderly segment of our population become increasingly involved in the purchase and sale of antiques and junk that is resonant of actual previous users. It explains why they should do so through markets that are frequented in regular and repetitive rhythm. As people age, the attraction of life as the narrative time of oneself leading inexorably to death may lose its attraction, while a more generic sense of material culture as an objectification of endless humanity in circulation becomes increasingly attractive. For this reason, some people become increasingly involved in an apparently commercial activity, but one that has little to do with making or spending money. Rather it is an activity devoted to the resurrection of objects that stand for particular lives and circulates them as generic lives. The result is to keep these fragments of past lives in ritualized circulation and increasingly to place oneself within this process. It is almost as though prior to one's own death, one gives oneself to a representation of immortality here enshrined by the endless circulation of junk and bits and pieces of lives. There is a new custom amongst environmentalists and also humanists to represent death itself as a kind of return of the disaggregated body to the endless circulation of atomic particles that make up the universe. I was recently at a humanist funeral which was full of such ideals. The junk market has rather pre-empted this conceptualization of a return to endless recirculation, but through an exploitation of mundane material culture.

This is why people who deal with antiques dislike the market in reproduction furniture, as not just fake, but something cold, anonymous and inhuman. Since there are no 'actual' past persons represented by reproduction objects, they simply don't work as an exemplification of this form of transformed temporality. Reproduction is not mythic, it doesn't act to suppress linear time. By contrast, in junk, actual lives are re-woven as fabric, which anonymizes but manages to make a comforting textile from the warp and weft of the threads of the dead.

If it accepted that this argument applies to the elderly and the circulation of antique junk, how does it apply to distressed blue jeans? After all, a clear pattern has already emerged in my current ethnography with Woodward, suggesting the dislike of older people for the wearing of distressed jeans, which they single out for disparagement. This should not surprise us if we reflect that distressed jeans are not actually used jeans. They are made to look like used jeans. They are really better viewed as reproduction jeans, veneer not patina. This makes them equivalent to the reproduction furniture these dealers define themselves in opposition to. If anything, they are worse than reproduction furniture, as the exemplification of dishonesty and inauthenticity. At least with reproduction furniture the owner is not claiming to have antiqued items that were actually used by someone else. Distressed jeans are doubly dishonest. Firstly they pretend to be used, when they are not, and worse still the purchaser lays claims to being responsible for wear, when the effect was actually achieved by someone else. Finally in the case of antiques or retro clothing, we do not assume that prior people deliberately spent their time living with objects in order to somehow 'add value' through this association with the person, as a result of which the objects could then be sold on. Most things become antique or retro by default rather than by design. Most people who bought things with the intention that they would one day become collector's items, such as first day of release stamps, are generally going to live to regret this investment, which rarely succeeds.

So there are clear contrasts between these two phenomena of buying time. Yet I would argue that understanding the junk/antique market as a machine for the suppression of time provides by analogy an explanation also for distressed blue denim jeans. As argued above, both are founded in the same paradoxical relation between the person and impersonal. In the case of blue denim jeans there is an equal threat of personal annihilation. But it is not that of death, but of consumers' increasing consciousness of the anonymity and massivity of global modernity. As argued above (and in Miller and Woodward 2007), the paradox of blue denim jeans is that they are simultaneously both the most personal and the most global and ubiquitous of all garments. There are few objects that so fully objectify the modern sense of global homogenization as blue denim jeans. Despite rather than because of the fashion industry, they have become the default conformity with what everyone else is wearing at the moment across almost the entire world. It is this property, as observed by Woodward and myself, which allows them to act to help alleviate the intense anxieties that people experience on an almost daily basis when dressing. The same garment brings this ultimate depersonalization into direct relation with the most intense personalization the majority of people ever experienced of a garment, a personalization that is signified in the techniques of distressing.

If flea markets are the circulation of everyman or everywoman of the past, then blue denim jeans are the circulation of the generic humanity of the present. This may well be a reason why the most expensive labels in the denim world today tend to have names such as 'citizens of humanity', 'seven for all mankind' or 'true religion'. I would think unwittingly these premium labels, which are all about adding value, evoke the place of jeans as something which links what otherwise might have seemed incommensurable, the extremes of the personal and the impersonal. In another paper I have shown that it is this process which has become foundational to the way we create value in the contemporary world (Miller 2008).

In conclusion, I have used as my title 'Buying Time', which phrase, when used colloquially, means that one is stalling, trying to fend of the inevitable progress of time, at least for a while. If my explanation of these two paradoxical forms of consumption is correct, then certain routines and rhythms of consumption are, in Lévi-Strauss's terms, precisely ways in which we try to hold a stance against our annihilation either by linear time or by the anonymity and massivity of modernity. We achieve this through a devotion to circulations of humanity either as the past or as the present. Distressed blue jeans for the youth and flea markets for the older generation are ways in which we try to resolve our sense of the profound gulf between the striving for personalization and individuality in life and our consciousness of the crushing anonymity of death and global ubiquity. In that case the phrase 'Buying Time', in its colloquial meaning as fending off time, would be entirely appropriate as a description of the phenomena I have tried to understand in this chapter.

References

Akgun, M., Gorguner, M., Meral, M., et al. (2005). Silicosis Caused by Sandblasting of Jeans in Turkey: A Report of Two Concomitant Cases. *Journal of Occupational Health* 47: 346–349.

Bair, J. and Gereffi, G. (2001). Local Clusters in Global Chains: The Causes and Consequences of Export Dynamism in Torreon's Blue Jeans Industry. *World Development* 29(11): 1885–1903.

Bair, J. and Peters, E. (2006). Global Commodity Chains and Endogamous Growth: Export Dynamism and Development in Honduras and Mexico. *World Development* 34(2): 203–221.

Campbell, C. (1987). *The Romantic Ethic and the Spirit of Modern Consumerism.* Oxford: Blackwell.

Candy, F.J. (2005). The Fabric of Society: An Investigation of the Emotional and Sensory Experience of Wearing Denim Clothing. *Sociological Research Online* 10(1) http://www.socresonline.org.uk/10/1/candy.html.

Cimrin, A., Sigsgaard, T. and Nemery, B. et al. (2006). Sandblasting Jeans Kills Young People. *European Respiratory Journal* 28(4): 885–886.

Clarke, A. and Miller, D. (2002). Fashion and Anxiety. *Fashion Theory* 6: 191–213.

Denim Academy (n.d.). *Rehber Kitaplar* (guide books). Faculty of Denim and Flat Applied Technology. Turkey.

Gregson N. and Crewe, L. (2003). *Second-Hand Cultures.* Oxford: Berg.

Gregson, N., Brooks, K. and Crewe, L. (2000). Narratives of the Body and Consumption in the Space of a Charity Shop. In *Commercial Cultures*, eds P. Jackson, M. Lowe, D. Miller and F. Mort. Oxford: Berg.

Hauser, K. (2004). A Garment in the Dock; or, How the FBI Illuminated the Prehistory of a Pair of Denim Jeans. *Journal of Material Culture* 9: 293–313.

Humphrey, C. (2002). Rituals of Death as a Context for Understanding Personal Property in Socialist Mongolia. *Journal of the Royal Anthropological Institute* 8(1): 65–87.

Lévi-Strauss, C. (1972). *The Savage Mind*. London: Weidenfeld and Nicolson

Miller, D. (2005). Introduction to *Materiality*, ed. D. Miller. Durham, NC: Duke University Press.

Miller, D. (2008). The Uses of Value. *Geoforum* 39: 1122–1132.

Miller, D. and Woodward, S. (2007). A Manifesto for the Study of Denim. *Social Anthropology* 15(3): 335–351.

Tokatli, N. (2007). Networks, Firms and Upgrading within the Blue-Jeans Industry: Evidence from Turkey. *Global Networks* 7(1): 51–68.

Weiner, A. (1992) *Inalienable Possessions*. Berkeley, CA: University of California Press.

Woodward, S. (2007). *Why Women Wear What They Wear*. Oxford: Berg.

Seasonal and Commercial Rhythms of Domestic Consumption

A Japanese Case Study

Inge Daniels

Introduction: Intermingling Rhythms of Consumption

[I]n contemporary Japan, changes of the seasons are related to cycles of consumption, and certain images – like those of mount Fuji and cherry blossoms – are used as a means of persuading people to buy things.

Moeran and Skov 1997: 189

In a seminal essay published in 1997, Moeran and Skov demonstrate that the Japanese advertising industry cleverly mixes and collapses key representations of the natural world to promote a diverse array of commodities. They argue that these advertisements challenge the existence of a unique Japanese perception of nature because seasonal 'images are made to symbolize as wide a variety of events and emotions as possible' (1997: 198). In this chapter, I will also examine the inter-relationship between seasonal and commercial cycles in contemporary Japan, but, unlike Moeran and Skov, my focus will be on domestic consumption practices. In the domestic arena the cyclical, natural rhythms of bodies, of days and nights, months and years, seasons and plants, intermingle with linear, social rhythms of work, child care, leisure and travel (Lefebvre 2004). Through an ethnographic investigation of contemporary Japanese urban homes, I aim to explore, firstly, how seasonal rhythms and commercial rhythms of commodities interact within this amalgamate of domestic rhythms, and, secondly, how this complex, ongoing dialogue both creates and marks time, and animates the Japanese home.

This chapter builds on multiple ethnographic encounters I had with Japan over the past ten years. However, the specific data presented were collected during multi-sited fieldwork in thirty urban homes in the Kansai area (Osaka, Kyoto, Kobe) between November 2002 and October 2003.[1] My research, firstly, complements a body of anthropological literature that investigates consumption in contemporary Japan (Clammer 1997; Moeran 1996). However, it differs from these previous studies in that, following recent trends in material culture research, it focuses on consumption practices in the domestic arena. Secondly, my study draws on a body of social research that discusses the temporality of everyday life inside the home. This literature has explored four main areas of study. These are: (1) the balance between home and work and the so-called urban 'time squeeze' (Jarvis 2005; Southerton 2003); (2) the changing aesthetic outlook of the home (Clarke 2002; Daniels 2001; Hecht 2001); (3) domestic processes of divestment and disposal and the ephemeral qualities of things (Daniels 2009; Gregson and Beale 2004; Marcoux 2001); and (4) the relationship between domestic spirituality and temporality (Uberoi 1999). My study will touch upon theme 2 and 3, but its main contribution lies in expanding on theme 4 by suggesting, firstly, that the mundane everyday might be at the base of the experience of transcendence (Daniels 2003), and, secondly, that commerce does not negate spirituality (Reader and Tanabe 1998).

Apart from ethnographic data, I will also draw on promotional leaflets (*chirashi*) that are produced by local businesses, ranging from high-quality department stores to local supermarkets and convenient stores, and are distributed by post on a weekly basis. Five people participating in my study agreed to collect these leaflets during one year from November 2002 until October 2003. Most *chirashi* advertise the latest food bargains, but they also promote a variety of other goods such as furniture, houses, Chinese medicine and gravestones. Whereas Moeran and Skov (1997) argue that the advertisements they studied, published in magazines or displayed on billboards nation-wide, did not reflect actual changes of seasons, my analysis of the collected leaflets reveals, by contrast, that local businesses cleverly synchronize their sales of specific goods with seasonal rhythms. The purchase of a number of raw foods such as bamboo shoots, mushrooms and oysters continues to be seasonal. However, in this chapter I am concerned with so-called 'festive commodities', food and decorations, used in domestic celebrations that are part of the yearly ritual cycle. These goods are advertised in weekly pamphlets, but they are also promoted in elaborate displays erected in commercial sites. The life cycles of these commodities and the rhythms of promotion and innovation are cleverly interwoven with the everyday rhythms of shopping.

A Uniquely Japanese Sense of Seasonality?

Anyone who spends a considerable amount of time in Japan will at some point be confronted with the statement that the Japanese have a unique, harmonious relationship with nature that comes to the fore in their sensibility to the four seasons. Throughout this chapter I aim to unpack and challenge many components at the base of this essentialist assumption. However, even the most sceptical of observers must admit that at first sight the Japanese seem to be more aware of – or at least more interested in – the changing rhythms of nature than other industrialized nations. The yearly excitement surrounding the first cherry tree blossoms is one highly visible example, but during my ethnography I observed more subtle manifestations of seasonal awareness. In all the urban homes studied, the arrival of seasonal foods such as water melons, mountain vegetables or mandarins, often gifts, caused real excitement and resulted in lively discussions about particular smells and tastes. Moreover, as temperatures rose, clothing, furniture and interior coverings associated with winter were exchanged for their summer counterparts; portable heaters and hot carpets were replaced by fans, rugs and blinds. Moreover, textile objects such as futons, sitting cushions and even slippers made of heavy, warm materials such as wool or felt were substituted for copies made in cotton, rattan or straw.

The Iwaiis' domestic interior stood out because of the exceptional attention paid to seasonal change. Unlike my urban participants, the Iwaiis, both in their mid-sixties, lived in a large house in small rural town in the south of Nara Prefecture. Mr Iwaii has a successful forestry business and Mrs Iwaii operates a kimono shop in the front of their home. This was the only home where at the start of June extensive seasonal changes were made to the Japanese-style rooms. Decorated paper sliding doors were replaced by doors made of rush, while tatami mats were covered with lighter rattan mats. Moreover, wooden sliding panels to keep out insects were inserted in the window frames, while bamboo or rattan blinds were attached to the outside of all the windows. Still, it was the display of seasonal goods on top of the shoe closet in the Iwaiis' spacious hallway that exposed the exceptional degree of Mrs Iwaii's seasonal awareness.

Mrs Iwaii called the items she displayed in her hallway 'seasonal things' (*kisetsu na mono*) because, in her words, 'well, according to the seasons, I make various changes. I place them in the hallway because they enable me to create a seasonal mood.' Mrs Iwaii has a large collection of seasonal things consisting largely of miniatures that she had brought home from frequent trips. Approximately every four weeks, she carefully selects a new item, and the seasonal effect is always completed with a fresh seasonal flower. In mid-June 2003 Mrs Iwaii replaced a miniature helmet, associated with virility and commonly displayed during the period leading up to Children's Day on 5 May in homes with male children, with an auspicious wooden *daruma* doll,[2] followed by a set of two insects made of rush, deemed appropriate for early summer, in turn replaced by a set of miniature deer, messengers of the deities linked with the famous Kasuga Taisha Shrine in Nara, and so forth, and so on.

The range of seasonal objects in Mrs Iwaii's possession as well as her commitment to make regular changes to the hallway display contrasted sharply with the attitude of my other urban participants. One example is Mrs Terayama, a part-time nurse in her late forties, who lives with her husband and teenage daughter in a small flat in the centre of Itami City. She displayed a mixture of things in her hallway: a group of four chubby, ceramic cats with their paws raised to invite luck, a group of ballet dancers made in origami place in a glass display box, which was a wedding present, and a figurine her husband brought home from a trip to China. On a scale of seasonal awareness, Mrs Terayama and Mrs Iwaii would be situated at opposite ends. Many of my other female participants, but particularly those over 45 years old, aspired to follow Mrs Iwaii's example. However, in practice, expressions of seasonality primarily consisted of replacing representations of zodiac animals once a year.

Seasonal Knowledge and the Traditional Arts

In her opinion, Mrs Iwaii gained her exceptional seasonal skills through working for many years alongside her mother-in-law in the family's kimono shop. Patterns, colours and the materials kimono are made of have to be in tune with the seasons, but also the particular occasion and the age (and the gender) of the wearer. In her extensive research about Japanese-style dress, Liza Dalby, an American anthropologist-cum-geisha, repeatedly discusses the complex relationship between kimono and the awareness of the seasons (Dalby 2001 [1993]). Seasonal kimono codes change almost monthly with the appearance of new plants and flowers, as the following list of appropriate motifs for each season illustrates: January–February: pine, plum, bamboo; March–April: cherry, butterflies, wisteria; May–June: iris, willow, birds; July–August: plovers, waves, shells; September–October: plumed grass, maple, chrysanthemum; November– December: bamboo in snow, pine needles and gingko (Dalby 2001 [1993]: 237). In post-war Japan, kimono ceased to be worn on an everyday basis, and this kind of knowledge has, therefore, become the prerequisite of professionals. The large body of advice literature as well as specialized magazines that target women who want to wear kimono illustrates this shift.

The fact that Mrs Iwaii is a keen student of the Japanese tea ceremony also contributes to her seasonal proficiency. The Iwaiis' house was the only one in my sample with a special room dedicated to the formal Japanese tea ceremony. In this ceremony seasonality based on performative knowledge (Moeran and Skov 1997: 199) is, firstly, demonstrated by the choice of the decorations placed in the decorative alcove, the focal point of the otherwise sparse Japanese-style room. Mrs Iwaii's tearoom was immaculate, and in June 2003 an ink painting of a blooming pomegranate tree decorated the scroll, while a lone iris was placed in a vase. A second way in which students of the tea ceremony can show seasonal proficiency is through their selection of traditional Japanese sweets served to guests. In her study of traditional sweet shops, the Japanese folklorist Oshima summarizes the yearly cycle of seasonal sweet ingredients as follows: January: narcissi or daffodils; February: plums; March: peaches; April: cherry blossoms; May: azaleas; September: balloon flowers or bell flowers; October: Japanese bush flowers; November: chrysanthemums (Oshima 2000: 71).

It should be clear by now that the production and selection of appropriate representations linked with seasonal change requires knowledge of and practical skills grounded in traditional Japanese aesthetics. Within this context it is interesting to refer to Ackermann's (1997) argument that the concept of the four seasons is used to visualize universal principles of cosmic order that should be obeyed in order to avoid calamities. Throughout Japanese history the ruling elite has drawn on these natural representations linked with correct social behaviour in order to establish their authority. Ackermann calls this phenomenon 'authoritarianism behind the veil of aesthetics' and singles out masters of the tea ceremony as well as presidents of large companies as those who continue to successfully exploit this ideology (1997: 40–42). Indeed, in contemporary Japan seasonality is also employed to create social distinctions. Indeed more than half the married women in my sample, all over 45 years old, had at some point in their lives practised the tea ceremony or another of the traditional Japanese arts such as calligraphy or flower arrangement.

The Annual Cycle of Events

Mrs Iwaii's hallway display consists of a sequence of images and objects that constitute the yearly cycle of seasonal change. The more ubiquitous displays of representations of zodiac animals, on the other hand, form part of a sequence of twelve years embedded within a larger sixty-year cycle of growth and decay. Both examples as well as the intricate series of seasonal motifs and changing natural patterns used in the production of Japanese sweets and kimono textiles, introduced earlier, are closely associated with cosmic principles of change and transformation at the base of East Asian thought, whereby specific phenomena are considered to be 'part of a sequence, these sequences in turn constituting the "backbone" of a traditional canon of images' (Ackermann 1997: 44). All these examples also reveal that the Japanese notion of seasonal change is far more complex than a simple awareness of the four seasons. In Japanese language literature the yearly cycle of change and transformation is commonly referred to as 'annual events' (*nenjû gyôji*).

In his seminal *Dictionary of Folklore*, Yanagita Kunio, the father of Japanese Folklore Studies, defines *nenjû gyôji* as 'festive days that annul pollution' through 'offerings made to the deities that are afterwards consumed among the community' (Yanagita 1951: 449). In other words, on specific days of the year a group of people, whether the household, the local community or the whole nation, would hold purification rituals to increase spiritual energy. Key Japanese folklorists such as Yanagita and Wakamori have equated these cycles of regeneration or reproduction, at the base of Japanese traditional cosmology, with the Durkheimian sacred (*hare*) versus profane (*ke*) model. However, more recently, Japanese anthropologists have questioned this approach by pointing out that *hare* and *ke*, and also the third concept of *kegare* (pollution), often left out of the discussion altogether, are 'inter-relative and supplementary' (Ito 1995: 126).

Ishikawa (2000) distinguishes between five different types of celebrations that constitute the yearly ritual cycle. These are: (1) events linked with the cycle of rice cultivation; (2) festivals to celebrate spirits and ancestors (New Year and Obon);

(3) the five auspicious days concerned with the celebration of life and reproduction grounded in Chinese Taoist ideas (9 January, 3 March, 5 May, 7 July, 9 September); (4) specific days to celebrate Shinto and Buddhist deities; and (5) rites of passage. However, during the last century these 'annual events' have changed dramatically. Firstly, the adoption of the Gregorian calendar in 1872 meant that the date for each ritual occurrence has become fixed and as a consequence many of the events no longer correspond to actual seasonal changes in nature. A second factor that had a far greater effect on people's perception of and involvement in 'annual events' was the progressive industrialization and urbanization of Japanese society throughout the twentieth century.

Before the Second World War more than 70 per cent of the population lived in rural farming communities consisting of extended families that operated as agricultural production units depending on mutual collaboration for their survival (Asahi Shinbun 2003). The whole community participated in 'annual events' that were organized around local shrines and temples. Moreover, knowledge about domestic ritual observances was passed on through the generations (Ogino 2000: 65). By contrast, the majority of Japanese born after the Second World War grew up in nuclear, (sub)urban families, commonly organized along strict gender roles. Women were housewives and mothers who stayed at home, while men were the main breadwinners who worked long hours as white-collar workers (*salariiman*) (Ishikawa 2000: 5).[3] Although community or neighbourhood networks continue to exist in both rural and urban areas, it is fair to say that for most urban Japanese school and work associations have become equally – if not more – important (Daniels 2008). As a result, ritual knowledge is no longer transferred through the extended family or the local community; the next section will focus on how commercial companies have managed to fill this gap.

Commodification of Ritual Practices

In his excellent ethnography of contemporary funeral services in urban Japan, Suzuki explores the effects of commodification on the ritual system. He pays attention to ritual processes of regeneration (*hare-ke-kegare*), discussed earlier, which he describes as 'a tricyclic circulation of an increase in vitality or energy and a depletion of energy'. *Hare*, the source of energy, can thus be interpreted as acting as a pump 'that eliminates *kegare* (enervated) and fortifies *ke* (normal spiritual energy)' (Suzuki 2000: 29). Suzuki reveals that in contemporary Japan, like in other industrialized societies, most people die in hospital. The removal of the process of dying from the home and, by extension, the decrease of funerals organized by the local community has had two main consequences. Firstly, everyday practical knowledge about funeral rituals has been largely lost and, secondly, community solidarity reiterated through these life cycle rituals has decreased. Professional funeral companies that offer assistance with the entire process have successfully filled the void. Their monopoly on ritual knowledge allowed these companies to obscure their profits, but new types of funeral practices have also resulted in new forms of dependency that are based on ties between individuals and occupational solidarity (Suzuki 2000: 217).

A second type of business that has been thriving as a result of post-war changes to the ritual system are companies involved in the production and publication of advice literature. A vast array of books and magazines feed the demand for information that used to be passed on in the community and in the home. A large percentage of this literature specializes in key life cycle events such as births, graduation ceremonies, weddings and funerals. Advice typically focuses on what clothes and accessories to wear, the way to behave 'properly' during the specific event, and the kinds of gifts to exchange. It is surprising that, by comparison, the advice literature surrounding 'annual events' is virtually non-existent. One reason for this might be that other businesses have successfully transferred this knowledge to the general public. Moeran and Skov, for example, mention that 'the Japanese advertising industry has paid particular attention to the celebration of annual "events", so that important points and stages in people's lives have come to be marked by increased and specialized forms of consumption' (1997: 199). Similarly, during my ethnography 'annual events' were linked with a range of products and advertised in magazines as well as on billboards and posters hung inside trains and buses. Local shops and supermarkets, the focus of this chapter, on the other hand, promoted and sold 'festive goods' for domestic celebrations of 'annual events'. The relationship between commerce and 'annual events' is not new in Japan, and records from the late eighteenth century, for example, mention special urban markets where rural sellers supplied materials and ingredients necessary for ritual events (Ogino 2000). In contemporary Japan, local businesses are suppliers of seasonal goods, which are generally accompanied by written explanations that elucidate the origin of the 'annual event' concerned as well as their 'proper' use. By consuming these commodities in the home, anyone can participate in and reap the benefits of 'annual events'.

During my ethnography it became clear that Ishikawa's classification of 'annual events', introduced earlier, needed to be updated for the twenty-first century (Toyama 2000). Local festivals linked with agriculture continue to be organized at religious institutions throughout Japan. However, most agricultural feasts held in urban areas have either become difficult to sustain remnants of past practices or widely advertised tourist attractions, and for my urban informants this category of 'annual events' had very little resonance. Special deities days, celebrated at community shrines or temples, continue to attract large local audiences. However, those actively involved were primarily elderly informants, especially those who co-habited with their children and acted as representatives of their extended family. By comparison, auspicious '*sekku*' days in which young people are central, such as the Girls Festival (3 March), Boys Day (5 May) and Tanabata (7 July) are far more popular. Moreover, among rites of passage, those that focus on children, such as the Seven-Five-Three festival (when boys of 5 and girls of 7 and 3 visit religious institutions) or school graduation ceremonies, are widely celebrated. Both are rare occasions for children to wear traditional dress. The continuous pull of these latter two types of events is also linked with the fact that children learn about and actively engage in activities surrounding these festive occasions in school. Their popularity provides further evidence for my earlier claim that social relationships surrounding children and schools carry more weight than local community ties. Moreover, the main target audience of newly created 'annual events' such as Christmas and Valentine's Day, which I will return to below, is also children and youth.

Finally, commemorations of ancestors continue to be important 'annual events' in contemporary Japan. These celebrations held twice-yearly during the New Year and Bon (mid-August) period are particularly pertinent for my discussion as their main focus is the home. Until the end of the nineteenth century it used to be common for the extended family to return to the house of the main family branch on both occasions to pay respect to the ancestors enshrined in domestic Buddhist altars. However, as a result of a campaign to create State Shinto under the Meiji government (1868–1912), New Year became associated with Shinto and auspiciousness, while Bon celebrations were linked with Buddhism and death (Rupp 2003: 106–107). In 2003, New Year was celebrated by all those participating in my study, while only half my informants commemorated their ancestors during the Obon period. Statistics confirm these findings (Ishii 1994: 24–25) and I have therefore chosen to explore the relationship between commercial and domestic rhythms of consumption during festive periods by focusing on the New Year's celebrations. The focus will be on two 'festive goods' that were widely advertised in the leaflets during the weeks leading up to New Year 2003, namely decorations and food.

New Year's Celebrations and Product Innovation

New Year is a key period in the Japanese ritual cycle of regeneration, when a series of purification rituals are performed in order to rid oneself of last year's misfortune (Daniels 2003). Among participants in my study the feeling of starting the year anew was most strongly associated with carefully attending to any outstanding business.[4] Moreover, in the days leading up to the New Year the house needs to be thoroughly cleaned. The fact that cleaning products are heavily advertised during this period attests to this. However, my data also suggest that the importance of the special New Year's house cleaning ritual (*ôsôji*) has somewhat diminished because of the regularity of everyday domestic cleaning routines. Still, the fact that in many homes husbands and children were drawn into the New Year's cleaning also sets it apart from more mundane routines (Ishii 1994: 48).

Decorations: Hybrid Ropes

Once the house is clean and last year's business had been dealt with, New Year's decorations, which temporally transfer the home into a sacred space, are put up. A typical New Year's decoration is the sacred rope or *shimenawa*. These are straw ropes (*nawa*) decorated with paper festoons (*shime*) and an orange-type fruit that are used to demarcate sacred space (Figure 11.1).

Figure 11.1 A sacred rope placed over a sign that advertises a number of businesses situated on the ground floor of an apartment block in the centre of Kyoto during January 2003.

Except for the four students in my sample, all other participants hung a *shimenawa* outside their home during the New Year's period. Half of these ropes were hybrid objects: half Christmas wreath, half sacred rope. Decorations for the New Year advertised in the pamphlets included pine arrangements and sacred ropes, but most prominent were the hybrid New Year's Wreaths (Figure 11.2).

The hybrids come in a large variety of sizes and styles, ranging from models to hang outside the house to miniatures that can be attached to car windows or even bicycles. The pamphlets stress the convenience of these kinds of 'festive goods' because they can be left outside throughout the Christmas and New Year's period (Hashidate 2002: 48). However, Mrs Terayama, who hung a hybrid rope outside the door of her flat in Itami City, offered another explanation for their increased usage. She explained that their housing association had forbidden 'traditional' ropes because the straw and grains attracts birds. Whatever the case, one important factor

Figure 11.2 Advertisement for New Year's decorations; a variety of hybrid wreaths are depicted on the left and at the bottom of the page.

to take into consideration is that sacred straw ropes place a burden on the inhabitants of the home concerned because they belong to a category of objects that need to be ritually disposed of at religious institutions at the end of the New Year (around 7 January) in order to avoid calamities. By contrast, many informants saw no ill in using the same hybrid New Year's wreath during consecutive years.

The example of the straw rope demonstrates that certain cultural forms may become obsolete, while others are replaced with new products that fit in better with people's changing social and economic circumstances. In turn these forms might be replaced by yet others that might consequently be invented anew or disappear altogether. The market both responds to and plays an active role in this incessant process of obliteration and innovation.

Food: Auspicious Rice Cakes

The main New Year's decoration inside the homes studied was the so-called *kagami-mochi* (mirror-rice cake) display which consists of two large pounded rice cakes of different sizes placed on top of each other and a number of decorative elements with auspicious qualities. The rice cake display, a typical New Year's offering, is generally placed on top of auspicious plants such as seaweed and fern leaves, while paper festoons are draped across, and the display is topped off with a mandarin-type fruit. The various auspicious ingredients vary according to regional as well as household preferences (Matsushita 1991). In the Kuwaharas' home in Itami City, for example, the *kagami-mochi* was placed on top of a large piece of dried seaweed and further decorated with a chestnut, a dried persimmon and a clay bell in the shape of a sheep, the zodiac animal celebrated in 2003 (Figure 11.3). The whole display sits

Figure 11.3 A decorated mirror-rice cake on display in the Kuwaharas' decorative alcove on 1 January 2003.

on a special tray made of white cedar wood that is also used to make offerings to the deities at temples and shrines. In the home these offerings are placed either on the god shelf or, more commonly, in the decorative alcove, as was the case in the Kuwaharas' home.

At the end of the New Year's period (around 7 January) the pounded rice cakes have to be broken up and shared among either the community (when offered at religious institutions) or family members (in the home). As Yanagita (1951) highlighted in his definition of annual events, the sharing of food offerings is a key element of Japanese rituals of regeneration. Inside the Kuwaharas' home some pieces of the *kagami-mochi* were warmed up and eaten with soya sauce; others were integrated either in soups or in other everyday dishes. Some pieces were wrapped in foil and taken home by Mrs Kuwahara's unmarried sister; others were given to an elderly neighbour who lives on her own. The fact that these offerings need to be consumed completely is rather problematic in contemporary Japan because family size continues to shrink, single-person households are on the increase, and neighbourhood networks through which surplus food was formerly shared have become weakened (Daniels in press). Moreover, even the larger families in my sample told me that they were not that keen about having to eat *mochi* for a considerable time after the New Year. While, some of the younger mothers, meanwhile, complained that their children did not like their taste or their texture.

Despite these changes, *kagami-mochi* continue to be popular. During the last week of December 2002 large quantities were sold in a variety of sizes in department shops, supermarkets and local stores in the Kansai region. However, a particular *kagami-mochi* produced by the Sato Company, advertised in all leaflets collected, demonstrates how Japanese businesses actively create new 'festive products' in tune with changing consumer practices. Although at first glance this product looked identical to the offering I described above, it actually is a plastic replica. The genius of the product lies in the fact it is sold with a smaller edible rice cake that can be placed inside the mock-up. This enables consumers to display an elaborate offering without actually having to eat the large rice cakes. The price varies according to the size of the real rice cake inside: the smallest cake weighs only 132 gramme and costs 498 yen (about £2.50), while the largest 1980 gramme cake sells for 3.888 yen (about £18). An additional design feature is that the product is wrapped in a large box that can be transformed into the shape of a traditional serving tray for offerings, while additional pieces of paper can be draped over the box in order to re-create some of the auspicious elements of the original display.

Commercial Rhythms of Domestic Consumption

> [S]easonal change forms a rhythm which is continually articulated and actively staged on the market, rather than one to which the market merely responds.
>
> Moeran and Skov 1997: 199

The above discussion about the Japanese New Year discloses how Japanese businesses have adapted to social and economic factors that have had a major effect on the yearly ritual cycle. However, the examples also demonstrate that the market actively articulates and stages seasonal consumption rhythms. This is evident in the creation of innovative products but also in the fact that businesses have been the driving force behind the invention of a number of new 'annual events'. Famous examples are Christmas and Valentine's Day, so-called 'Western' traditions that were re-invented by Japanese sweet companies. In Japan Christmas is associated with giving presents to small children, but even more so with love and romance between unmarried couples (see Moeran and Skov 1993). Christmas Day 2002 was spend by those in my sample in their late teens and twenties with boy/girlfriends, while families, many of whom had decorated the entrance to their home with a Christmas wreath, celebrated with consuming a *Christmas Keiki*, a strawberry sponge cake covered with whipped cream. Kimura reveals that these cakes were first produced by the Japanese sweet company Fujiya during the 1910s, but their consumption only became widespread during the 1960s (Kimura 2001: 104–140).

Another type of 'festive food' invented during the 1970s by Japanese companies producing Western-style sweets are Valentine's Day chocolates (Ito 1995: 113–114). At first 'love chocolates' were given by women to men they were potentially interested in, but soon they turned into what most of my female informants dismissively called 'obligation chocolates'. In other words, women ranging from Office Ladies to female students felt obliged to give chocolates to men in positions of power whom they were indebted to. On Valentine's Day 2003, some women in my sample bought 'obligation chocolates', but many decided to make their own batch at home. The ubiquity of shop displays promoting key ingredients to make chocolates during the first two weeks of February highlights the popularity of this new practice. Some home-made chocolates were given to a special person, but most were consumed with the whole family at home.

The changing practices surrounding Valentine's chocolates illustrate how consumers might actively appropriate and transform 'annual events'. Some aspects might become obsolete, while others might be (re)produced in different forms. Many new 'festive foods' such as cakes or chocolates resemble 'traditional' food offerings because they can be easily employed in the creation of domestic sociality either by dividing them up or because they already consist of a number of parts. However, the durability of old and new types of festive foods differs significantly. Christmas cakes covered with whipped cream and chocolates perish relatively quickly, while foods such as pounded rice cakes remain edible for a very long time. Preservation enabled women to take a deserved break from cooking during the festive period when shops were closed.

Conclusion

In previous studies, I have challenged the assumption that commercialization negates spiritual power by arguing that the commodification of Japanese religious forms enables democratic access as well as personal interaction with the Divine in the home (Daniels 2003). In this chapter, I have expanded on this argument by demonstrating how commerce might actually be an active force in facilitating but also invigorating a variety of spiritual practices. My ethnography reveals that in contemporary Japan the spiritual continues to be part of all domains of life.[5] In times of need, most Japanese visit temples and shrines to ask deities for assistance, whether to recover from illness, pass exams or become prosperous in business.

Moreover, most of my informants, of all ages, were aware that in order to avoid calamities they needed to engage in ritual practices at specific times of their life cycle, but also at particular times of the year during so-called 'annual events'. In this chapter I have focused on the latter types of celebrations, which are linked with a 'native' notion of seasonality.

Although the scale and intensity of the ritual calendar in contemporary Japan might be surprising to non-Japanese, participants in this study, like most Japanese, were aware that in order to have a happy, fulfilled life it is necessary to regularly create and re-create connections with other human as well as non-human entities. Importantly, although the New Year is celebrated by all, the number of other 'annual events' in which a particular family might actively participate depends on their specific circumstances. For those without deceased in their immediate family group, and more and more those without children, the annual cycle of events is far less dense. The overall decrease in family size, the scarcity of informal networks through which food and other goods can be redistributed, and, more broadly, the occurrence of blockages in the disposal of festive goods has also resulted in a decline in opportunities for social and spiritual sociality at the base of the ritual system of regeneration. Still, this chapter also hints at the development of innovative practices that enable new forms of sociality. The market plays a key role in this process.

The focus of 'annual events' used to be on invigorating the local neighbourhood, but as school and work networks have gained in significance in peoples' everyday lives, practices that celebrate the welfare of children, the celebration of intimate family life inside the home and business prosperity (Ito 1995) have taken centre-stage. Ritual knowledge pertaining to specific 'annual events', once transferred through local communities and the extended families within, is now primarily managed by commercial businesses such as funeral and wedding companies as well as producers and distributors of advice literature. Moreover, through resourceful commodity promotion and innovation, local businesses have been able not only to adapt to and align themselves with, but also successfully to steer domestic rhythms of consumption. In the home the life cycles of commodities become closely connected with the embodied temporal and spatial rhythms of the inhabitants, whose biographies are thought to be directly influenced by larger cosmological principles.

Notes

1. The majority of dwellings studied were inhabited by families, but the sample also includes university students, recently married couples and elderly people living alone. Like some 90 per cent of the country's population (Taira 1993: 169), all considered themselves to belong to an undifferentiated Japanese middle class. However, in Japan, as elsewhere, social distinctions are constructed around consumption. This research was made possible thanks to the generous support

of the Japanese Society for the Promotion of Science and the British Academy. Special thanks goes to my Japanese mentor Prof. Senda Minoru and all those who opened up their homes for me, but especially the family Kagemori, Kadonaga, Kuwahara, Matsui, Nakao, Nishiki, Sakai and Takahashi.

2. *Daruma* are hollow, round wish dolls with no arms or legs, modeled after Bodhidharma, the founder and first patriarch of Zen.
3. Of the fifteen married women over 45 years old in my sample, eight became full-time housewives when they married, while only three continued to work throughout their married lives. The eight married women in their thirties and early forties who participated in my study continued to work after they married. In both cases, Japanese men continue to be largely absent in the home and are unlikely to share any domestic shores or play a role in childrearing
4. This included sending seasonal gifts to people one was indebted to as well as literally paying off credit card debts.
5. The Japanese religious landscape is diverse, but I am primarily concerned with the amalgamation of Shinto and sectarian Buddhism grounded in practice.

References

Ackermann, P. (1997). The Four Seasons: One of Japanese Culture's Most Central Concepts. In *Japanese Images of Nature*, eds A. Kalland and P. Asquith. Richmond, Surrey: Curzon.

Asahi Shinbun (2003). *The Japan Almanac*. Tokyo: Asahi Shibunsha.

Clammer, J. (1997). *Contemporary Urban Japan: A Sociology of Consumption*. Oxford: Blackwell.

Clarke, A. (2002). Taste Wars and Design Dilemmas: Aesthetic Practice in the Home. In *Contemporary Art in the Home*, ed. C. Painter. Oxford: Berg.

Dalby, L. (2001) [1993]. *Kimono: Fashioning Culture*. London: Vintage Random House.

Daniels, I. (2001). The 'Untidy' Japanese House. In *Home Possessions*, ed. D. Miller. Oxford: Berg.

Daniels, I. (2003). Scooping, Raking, Beckoning Luck: Luck, Agency and the Interdependence of People and Things in Japan. *Journal of the Royal Anthropological Institute* 9: 619–638.

Daniels, I. (2008). Japanese Homes Inside Out. *Home Cultures* 5(2): 115–140.

Daniels, I. (2009). The 'Social Death' of Japanese Gifts: Surplus and Value in Contemporary Japan. *Journal of Material Culture* 14(3).

Daniels, I. (in press). *The Japanese House: Material Culture in the Modern Home*. Oxford: Berg.

Gregson, N. and Beale, V. (2004). Wardrobe Matter: The Sorting, Displacement and Circulation of Women's Clothing. *Geoforum* 35: 689–700.

Hashidate, M. (2002). Mono kara miru nenjû gyôji – sono 2 (The Material Culture of Annual Events – vol. 2). *Shizuokaken Minzokugakushi* 23: 48–58.

Hecht, A. (2001). Home Sweet Home. In *Home Possessions*, ed. D. Miller. Oxford: Berg.

Ishii, K. (1994). *Toshi no nenjû gyôji* (Urban Annual Events). Tokyo: Shunkasha

Ishikawa, J. (2000). Nenjû gyôji oboegaki (Annual Events – A Note). *Shizuokaken Minzokugakushi* 21: 1–7.

Ito, M. (1995). *Zôyokôkan no jinruigaku* (An Anthropology of Gift Exchange). Tokyo: Chikuma.

Jarvis, H. (2005). Moving to London Time. *Time and Society* 14: 133–154.

Kimura, J. (2001). *Kôchikushugi no shôhiron* (The Structuring Principles of Consumption).Tokyo: Chikura Shobo.

Lefebvre, H. (2004). *Rhythmanalysis: Space, Time and Everyday Life*. London: Continuum.

Marcoux, J. (2001).The 'Casser Maison' Ritual. *Journal of Material Culture* 6: 213–235.

Matsushita, S. (1991). *Iwai no shokubunka* (Festive Food Culture). Tokyo: Bijutsu Sensho.

Moeran, B. (1996). *A Japanese Advertising Agency: An Anthropology of Media and Markets*. Richmond, Surrey: Curzon.

Moeran, B. and Skov, L. (1993). Cinderella Christmas: Kitsch, Consumerism, and Youth in Japan. In *Unwrapping Christmas*, ed. D. Miller. Oxford: Clarendon Press.

Moeran, B. and Skov, L. (1997). Mount Fuji and the Cherry Blossoms: A View from Afar. In *Japanese Images of Nature*, eds A. Kalland and P. Asquith. Richmond, Surrey: Curzon.

Ogino, A. 2000. Kattesuzukeru nenjû gyôji to sono zendankai shudan (Annual Events before Commercialization). *Shizuokaken Minzokugakushi* 21: 57–70.

Oshima, B. (2000). Wagashiya to nenjû gyôji (Annual Events and Japanese Sweet Shops). *Shizuokaken Minzokugakushi* 21: 70–72.

Reader, I. and Tanabe, G. (1998). *Practically Religious: Worldly Benefits and the Common Religion of Japan*. Honolulu: University of Hawai'i Press.

Rupp, K. (2003). *Gift-giving in Japan*. Stanford: Stanford University Press.

Southerton, D. (2003). Squeezing Time. *Time and Society* 12: 5–25.

Suzuki, H. (2000).*The Price of Death: The Funeral Industry in Contemporary Japan*. Stanford: Stanford University Press

Taira, K. (1993). Dialectics of Economic Growth, National Power, and Distributive Struggles. In *Postwar Japan as History*, ed. A. Gordon. Berkeley, CA: University of California Press.

Toyama, S. (2000). Nenjû gyôji no ima (Annual Events Today). *Shizuokaken Minzokugakushi* 21: 7–28.

Uberoi, P. (1999). Times Past: Gender and the Nation in Calendar Art. *Indian Horizons* 46–47: 24–39.

Yanagita, K. (1951). *Minzokugaku Jiten* (Dictionary of Folklore). Tokyo: Tokyodo.

–12–

Special and Ordinary Times
Tea in Motion
Güliz Ger and *Olga Kravets*

Introduction

A group of students accompanied us on a trip to Mardin, a historical city they had never seen before, and had a long day visiting numerous historical sites and climbing uphill. While taken by the beauty of the architecture and the scenery, everyone was reaching total fatigue, getting cold and wet on this rainy day and still trying to stick to a tight tour schedule. Suddenly, the tour guide appeared with a tray full of freshly brewed hot tea in small tulip-shaped glasses. All the faces shined, smiles appeared, hands wrapped around the glasses warmed and tired bodies were reinvigorated. A trip to an extraordinary place had turned into ordinary tourist fatigue in the course of six hours and the mundane tea returned the magic in a second.

Even while on vacation, we count and calculate time. The special weekend to the ancient city of Mardin in Mesopotamia, an escape from routine class schedules, turned into a series of intentions, plans and to-do lists queued on a time line that we tried to follow despite the rain, the mud and the hills. By timing our activities and rushing, trying to keep to a schedule, we converted this special weekend time into a relatively ordinary one. Then we rediscovered a special time, a magical time while drinking tea and watching Mesopotamia stretching below us from the mountain top. In this case, the mundane tea interrupted the ordinary fast-paced life of that special day. The tea had not been planned; it was the spur-of-the moment thoughtfulness and hospitality of the guide. By drinking tea, we experienced a special time, purposeful, valid and enjoyable in and of itself, as well as feeling re-energized for the remaining activities of the day.

How can a mundane practice such as tea drinking engender a special time and itself become an object of such a time? In this chapter we discuss how tea drinking objects and practices in Turkey bring us into particular relationships with time and how ordinary and special times are made and facilitated by tea drinking. We consider how the introduction of various objects of convenience changes the temporality of the tea drinking practice. We explore the micro-practices, routines and material implements of making and serving tea, as well as the material aspects of the tea itself. Through interviews and observations, we interrogate how materials in different contexts call upon particular sensibilities. We aim to understand how materials, idea(l)s and competences afford and/or impede different temporalities – ordinary and special times – in the tea drinking practice. In Turkey, tea used to be and sometimes still is drunk continuously 'like water' or even 'instead of water', and unlike the popular imagery of the Japanese or the British tea ceremony, it is an informal activity. It is this quality of being continuous or the *untemporality* of the 'traditional' tea drinking practice that we argue is critical in understanding how forms of convenience introduce changes into this practice.

A special time can be defined or marked by extraordinariness, ceremonial rituals, magic and enchantment (Durkheim 1995 [1912]; Gronow and Warde 2001; Kozinets 2001), slowness as opposed to fastness (Petrini 2003), a process of warming (Ger 2005), a healing power (Belk et al. 1989) or an orientation to leisure, pleasure and contemplation (Petrini 2003; Stevens et al. 2003). Special times seem as if separate from the ordinary, largely taken-for-granted, therefore barely noticeable time. They are distinguished from ordinary times through particular discourses, sensibilities and objects. Objects not only serve as symbolic marks of particular times, but also bring us into particular relationships with time. Consider objects such as handmade laces that serve to warm the cold present of modern electronics (Ger 2005) or background music that 'moves' time-stilled boredom into a time of joy (Anderson 2004). In this way objects partake in the process of making ordinary and special times. Notably, unlike Durkheimian special time, which is objectified with extraordinary things and rituals, we argue that special times can also be objectified with mundane consumption, as in slow food, slow tea, hobbies, watching favourite sports games, reading a magazine, playing cards, lighting a cigarette, drinking alcoholic beverages, listening to music, watching television or doing Tai Chi (e.g. Jalas 2006 and in this volume; Nowotny 1994; Petrini 2003; Slater in this volume; Stevens et al. 2003).

Tea Culture in Turkey: Untemporality and Unspatiality

Turkey is more known for its coffee than tea. Yet, Turkish people drink more tea than coffee. Fifty-two per cent of their non-alcoholic beverage consumption is tea. Turkey tops the charts in per capita tea consumption (2.5 kg compared to the UK's 2.1 kg in 2004).This high rate is due to the availability of places to consume tea, social practices and norms, and domestic production along the Black Sea coast. Turkey is the second largest tea market in the world (after India), with a total tea volume of about 180,000 tonnes in 2004. Indeed, tea is served anytime – for breakfast, before and after meals – and everywhere – offices, hospitals, buses, trains, cafés, restaurants and homes. In the streets, one can see a *çaycı* (tea-waiter) making his continuous tea delivery rounds, carrying tea-filled tulip-shaped glasses on saucers with tiny teaspoons and cubes of sugar on a silver platter that hangs from silver chains. In airports, representations of such 'Turkish tea' welcome international guests, who may well be served teabag teas in mugs in the upscale establishments of the airport (see Figure 12.1). In many workplaces, there is often a person whose official duty is to make hot tea available to employees at all times. In many homes, a *çaydanlık* (double teapot) is continuously boiling, so that some steaming hot tea is ready all the time. Our informants noted that tea drinking is 'a natural part of daily life', 'any time is a good time for tea' and 'you can get tea everywhere, in all places'.

Figure 12.1 Billboard advertising of a mobile operator at Istanbul Airport.

Tea drinking became an integral part of Turkish life and culture relatively recently. While some had for centuries enjoyed teas imported from China and India, the masses took to tea in the 1930s, when tea was cheaper than imported coffee and provided a drink that was safer than water in many areas. Tea production began in 1924 and grew soon after 1937 when the first tea factory was established by the young Republic, in its pursuit of economic self-sufficiency. Today, Turkey is the world's fifth largest producer of tea, behind India, China, Kenya and Sri Lanka. Over 200,000 families and 300 factories are involved in the cultivation of tea.

Since tea's mass adoption, tea drinking became a significant part of daily life, with particular ways of making and drinking black tea and certain cultural ways of thinking about and relating to it. Traditionally, in Turkey, tea is prepared in a samovar-style double teapot (*çaydanlık*), where loose tea leaves are put into a small kettle placed on the top of a larger kettle with boiling water. In North-eastern Turkey, and in the best tea houses (*çayhane*) across the country, tea is prepared in a samovar. It is common to mix different teas (including different brands of teas) in order to create a unique blend. The ability to make a wonderfully flavourful tea is a matter of pride. The type of top kettle to be used (porcelain is believed to be the best. and metal, especially aluminum, the worst), the type of water to be used, the time to preheat the kettle and the time of brewing and standing are among the numerous criteria related to the making of 'proper' tea. After brewing, steeped tea from the small top kettle is poured into the glass and then diluted with water from the bottom kettle to the desired strength. This method allows each person to drink the tea as they desire it: strong and steeped, or light with lots of water added. Serious tea drinkers take their tea *koyu* (dark and strong). There is a belief that the further east one goes in Turkey, the darker the colour – *tavşankanı* (rabbit's blood) – preferred. The dark tea colour is also associated with toughness, whereas the light-coloured tea is referred to as *paşa çayl*, suggesting that such tea is only for a pampered or a frail person (a sissy) or a child. The serious drinker takes her/his tea black: Turks rarely add milk to their tea, but sometimes a slice of lemon may be preferred. Generally, two small sugar cubes will accompany tea served in public. It is customary to have a few rounds of tea at a time.

The tea glass is so important in daily life it is used as a measurement in recipes. The glass is called *ince belli* (thin-waisted) after the ideal female body shape (see Figure 12.1). The tiny tulip-shaped glass has to be held by the rim to save one's fingertips from burning. Fingers wrapped around the *ince belli* provide warmth in the winter and the hot tea is said to balance the body temperature in the summer. The clear glass allows the drinker to appreciate the ruby colour and the radiance of the tea that some poems refer to. Many poems and folk songs make allusions to the colour, sensuality and sociality of tea:

> Your lips are red,
> Like the tea from Rize.
>
> (section from an anonymous folk song,
> http://www.biriz.biz/cay/kultur/turkcaykul.htm)

> The nightingale is immersed in the troubles of love,
> Pour the tea, in the colour of the rose,
> In the gathering of wise men,
> Fill the glasses, and fill again.
>
> (section from a Sufi hymn,
> http://www.biriz.biz/cay/kultur/turkcaykul.htm)

Phrases such as *çay keyfi* (pleasure of tea) refer to the sensual pleasures of tea drinking. The sensuality emphasized includes the ruby colour of the tea, the shape of the glass, the embracing hold of the hand on the thin waist of the glass, the warmth in your hands, especially on a cold day, the curving steam rising from the *ince belli*, the melody of sipping and the teaspoons clinking, as well as the taste and the smell.

Çay keyfi refers to the coziness, homeliness and relaxing comfort of the home as well. In many Turkish homes where the homemaker is a housewife, a teapot is put on the stove in the morning before breakfast and is continuously boiling, with water being added periodically to the bottom kettle and new tea leaves to the top kettle, until the family retires for the night. If the homemaker is a working woman, then the tea is continuously boiling after dinner. The conventional presence of the boiling teapot indicates that tea drinking is an ongoing, almost a background, activity; tea is consumed during breakfast and before or after any meal, while working and resting, talking and meditating, watching TV and playing backgammon, or entertaining guests. To our informants, the sound of the kettle on the stove is the definition of the home and the rhythm of family life. Tea is offered to a guest casually (at times, without asking first) as a sign of hospitality, whereas coffee is considered to be more ceremonious. At home or at the office, it is considered rude to refuse the tea offered and a refusal of the tea is taken as a refusal of the hospitality of the host. Thus, tea is a nearly indispensable part of any gathering or meeting in Turkey.

Tea is a beverage that is consumed either privately or publicly, in tea houses (*çayhane*) and tea gardens (*çaybahçesi*) or when receiving guests at home. An introductory guide to Turkish culture says: 'It is hard to imagine breakfasts, social gatherings, business meetings, negotiations for carpets in the Grand Bazaar, or ferry rides across the Bosphorus without the presence of tea. With tea servers in streets, shopping malls, and parks shouting, 'çay!' (chai) the beverage is always within shouting distance. It is fundamental to Turkish social life...' (http://www. turkishculture.org). Indeed, tea houses and gardens have been the preferred social hub where people meet, exchange news and gossip. Gaining popularity in the 1950s, tea gardens became sites for social outings of extended families. One informant recalled that his

> whole family (about fifteen people) would go to a tea garden, order a samovar to the table, regulate its heat to keep tea boiling hot and chat for hours. The kids would play with the pebbles or chase each other, while adults would talk, play backgammon or cards. Occasionally, you could buy *simit* [thin bagel-shaped pastry] there or sunflower seeds, but generally it was just tea, lots of tea for three–four hours.

Unlike the serene Japanese tea garden, Turkish tea gardens are bustling with social activity, with kids running around, music playing and lively chit-chatting, people coming and going, and, of course, the ongoing clinking of tiny teaspoons in the tea glasses. At the tea garden or at home, tea is a democratic social lubricant. Anyone can afford it and serve it to guests. While telling us their experiences with tea, most informants recall sitting together and having a cozy time with friends or having a pleasant evening with family over rounds of tea. Many practices of sociality such as playing backgammon or cards or simple *sohbet* (relaxed, friendly, enjoyable conversation or chatting) are also accompanied by tea.

Such a homely and socially and sensually loaded drink is perhaps surprising to see at business meetings, where it is prominently partaken. At the workplace, tea disrupts the institutionalized rhythms and injects a dose of warm sociality into industrial environments. Consider the continuously boiling electric pot at a departmental meeting or tea served at the beginning of an interview or a meeting by a tea server employed solely for that purpose. Turks do not stop for a tea break; rather a boiling teapot is often placed in a meeting room, so participants can enjoy fresh hot tea, refilling their glasses whenever and as much as they want. The association of tea with sociality and hospitality makes tea a welcome disruption to work times and spaces. And such fleeting enactments carry the spirit of sociality on a regular basis. Yet, the disruption becomes routinized itself. Now carpet shops automatically offer tea as part of the sales process and most meetings at the workplace start with tea. Even though tea service has become a norm and a routine in the workplace, it is still seen as a marker of sociality and hospitality and is missed if not offered.

We have heard it said that Turkish tea is timeless. Tea is such an integral part of Turkish culture that it appears to have 'come from very, very long, history, it comes from maybe Asian Turks...' Many informants speculate that it will not disappear because tea drinking fits the Turkish culture: it implicates cherished idea(l)s of hospitality, sharing and togetherness. Indeed, the word 'natural' was a leitmotif in our informants' comments, as they talked about tea being a 'a matter of routine' and of 'having a cozy time being and chatting with others'. That ethos of timelessness is reinforced through tea's omnipresent visibility: in one informant's words, 'You can always see tea in Turkey, everywhere, you can see it ... everywhere! In shops, people are ordering tea, in restaurants, after dinner ... also at ... places where you can't imagine you would get tea. For example, people offer tea while you wait at a repair shop or gas station.' In turn, timelessness and the omnipresent visibility are reified through the particular materiality of tea: the imaginary of one colour (ruby-red), one taste (slightly tangy, perhaps similar to strong English breakfast tea), one shape (tulip-shaped glasses). Even the billboard advertising of a mobile operator welcoming tourists at an airport reinforces such imaginary in the way it represents the country tourists are arriving at by the symbolism of tea being served in tulip-shaped tea glasses on a silver tray that hangs from silver chains (Figure 12.1). Consistent with Schatzki's notion of 'timespace' (in this volume) the untemporality of tea goes hand in hand with its unspatiality.

Changes in the Implements of Turkish Tea Culture

The first teabag in Turkey was brought by Unilever. Lipton, which entered the market in 1984, has now captured 15% of the tea market. Çay-Kur, the state-affiliated enterprise that evolved from the first tea factory in Turkey and enjoyed a monopoly until 1984, when tea processing and packaging were opened to private enterprises, has 65% market share. After Lipton, numerous Turkish firms also introduced their teabags. Loose tea has recently been losing share to teabags, which showed a 34% growth (versus 24% for loose tea) in retail sales between 1997 and 2004. Now teabags constitute 5–10% of the tea market. The head of the tea industry association says that '[i]n the developed countries 85% of tea consumed is in the form of tea bags. Since Turkey is a developing country, that's what will eventually happen in Turkey too. Tea bags are an inevitable result of technological development' (http://www.reyon.net/roportaj_ayrinti.aspx?intvw_id=29)

Teabags were among the first material objects of convenience to be introduced and, as the above quote indicates, became a marker of progress in Turkey (cf. Shove 2003). In the late 1980s and early 1990s fashionable cafés and restaurants served only teabags in cups and mugs and one would be hard pressed to find tea brewed in a *çaydanlık* in the high street. Moreover, industrial-size tea machines made their appearance in hotels and offices, along with foam and plastic cups. However, the new millennium saw the introduction of larger tulip-shaped glasses, the reintroduction of 'traditional' saucers, electric double pots and electric samovars, and the return of brewed tea to those same trendy cafés and restaurants. Now most cafes have two items on their menus: *demli çay* (brewed tea) served in *ince belli* glasses and *çay* (tea) served in cups or mugs. The latter, the normalized tea, is the teabag, that comes in numerous kinds of black, green, herbal and fruit teas.

With the introduction of teabags, a large variety of stovetop and electric teapots, tea glasses and saucers appeared in stores, cafés and homes (see *http: //www.tasarim. itu.edu.tr/images/genova/genova_2.jpg* for examples). Appliance firms produced electronic versions of the double teapot, which they claim provides the perfect tea. In turn, for those who don't want to give up their *çaydanlık*, electric or stovetop, Lipton introduced large teabags to fit it. Teapots evolved from a uniquely shaped metal or the bottom kettle metal with a porcelain top kettle to a large variety of forms, designs, patterns, and materials. There also used to be a single-sized tea glass, but the 1990s saw a larger tulip-shaped glass, which increased in size again in 2005 and appeared in a variety of designs. The large ones (holding more tea, and some with handles, like a mug) mark fashion, novelty and modernity. These new bigger but still *ince belli* (thin-waisted) glasses are referred to with the names of the Turkish female pop singers – Sibel Can or Ajda – perhaps implying at once modernity and Turkishness. The tea plates also follow fashion: from metal and plain glass to contemporary designs to all kinds of retro designs, reminiscent of rustic rural or Ottoman patterns. So, now designers practise their trade on decorated and multicoloured kettles and on contemporary and reinvented glasses and saucers.

In recent years, the wide availability of electric teapots and teabags has produced some interesting changes in the tea drinking practice in Turkey. We argue that what engenders such changes is not solely new materials and the discourses around their use (cf. Shove and Pantzar 2005), but also the temporalities implicated in these materials.

From Untemporality to the Choices of Tea Time: Temporality and Spatiality of Tea

As teabags made an entry and conventional tea implements underwent some changes, in size, design and increased variety, tea making and drinking practices diversified. Rather than the one colour, one taste, one size brewed tea, tea drinking suddenly became riddled with choice, and consequently individual decisions could be made regarding brewed versus teabag, type of flavour, amount and time. There even is a decision to be made whether to drink tea or not. As one informant explained, because an electric teapot boils water fast, there is no need for continuous boiling, but then the tea is 'not already there', so she finds herself not drinking tea as much but opting for something already there, such as Coke or juice. Then, there is a decision to be made about the kind of tea. To be sure, for brewed tea there are also decisions to be made about kinds of tea to mix for a perfect blend for everybody to enjoy. In contrast, the decisions related to teabags are based on individual preferences and, potentially, for each cup. Also, there is a decision about how much tea to have. If one is to have only one cup, one takes a teabag; if one feels like a lengthy 'tea drinking session', one makes a kettle of brewed tea and refills one's tiny glasses periodically. Thus, the tea drinking practice associated with the use of new and old tea drinking materials has evolved into a choice-based, individualized activity.

The presence of such choices brings to the fore a reflexivity regarding the purposes for tea drinking across different times. In this manner, tea drinking comes to mark different times and designates time periods. For our informants, in the morning tea drinking is a wake-up time, whereas tea after meals is a digestion time. Tea while running errands or shopping is 'a stop–revive–survive' time; similarly, when travelling 'a tea break' means a time to refresh. Consumed during studying or working, tea helps concentration, whereas tea after work helps to unwind. The tea served at the beginning of the meeting is both the icebreaker and the invitation to get on with the business, whereas complementary after-meal tea in restaurants signals the bill time. Tea on a Sunday afternoon creates a pleasurable time: served to company, it creates a warm social time of hospitality, or to oneself, relaxing me-time which is not to be interrupted by anyone, including one's children. Even at business meetings tea marks a time for hospitality. During travel or work, it can also generate a resting time. Furthermore, an offer of tea signals the expected duration of an encounter: at a meeting, it means 'I have 15–20 minutes for you', whereas at a repair shop it might signal a wait of 15 minutes. Then, at a carpet shop, it is an indispensable part of selling as carpets are shown and stories told about meanings of patterns, the wools and the silks, how they were made and where. The time period designated by tea is not fixed. For example, in the words of one informant, if visitors indicate that '"[they] are coming for tea" … it is like saying "we will stay for a couple of hours and leave at a reasonable time"'.

These tea times are composed in and through sets of materials, idea(l)s and ways of doing. That is, tea makes a particular time not by itself but rather in concert with a wider relational field, including breakfast or snack foods, notions about the proper sequence of meals and events, conceptions of appropriate conduct during certain times of the day, long-haul travelling, idea(l)s of hospitality, work and leisure. Tea drinking gets incorporated into the routines of daily life through re-occurrence, for example 'for every breakfast' or 'when studying'. Tea drinking clearly partakes in the temporal rhythm of daily life, be it a part of a habit or a more reflexive choice. Moreover, some of the tea times call for brewed tea, others for teabags: we observe a hybrid, intentional and habitual use of the old and the new tea materials. Tea drinking as an enactor of daily rhythms is a variegated amalgamation of the new and the old.

What is perhaps more interesting than the hybridized choices of the new and the old is the (cor)responding idea(l)s. The presence of options engenders the necessity to articulate and legitimize the emergent decision, be it brewed tea or a flavoured teabag. We find that such articulations relate to the idea(l)s of either modernity or sensual/aesthetic and social pleasures. Teabags and electric teapots are usually associated with modernity – efficiency ('time-saving' and 'only one cup'), progress ('technological innovation'), Western novelties and individualism and choice ('only one cup' and 'can choose which tea you want'). When discussing the grounds for adopting teabags and electric teapots, not unexpectedly people cite speed, convenience and efficiency. For example, an informant said that her family purchased an electric *çaydanlık* because 'it was a new machine and easy to use', but then she added, 'we don't normally use it … only when we have lots of guests', when her mother brings it into the living room to serve tea quickly. Even those people who see teabag tea as tasteless admit that this type of tea could be an option for work time and in circumstances of time constraint. As one person put it, since it takes little time and effort, 'you can have it as you put your shoes on'. In addition, the teabag is not only quick but it is also clean and efficient; ironically, therefore, the teabag frees us of the burden of the mundane (cleaning), but then itself turns into the mundane ('you can have it as you put your shoes on'). Time is precious in today's world, so the instant and the quick are seen as both necessary and fashionable. Such is the sentiment adopted and propagated by Çay-Kur's teabag advertising – 'For everyone who believes time is money.'

The other idea(l) is sensual/aesthetic and social pleasures. As a counterpoint to the multiplicity of tea choices, there emerges the discourse of tea time, which flows smoothly, pleasantly and peacefully. Here, tea time is not a resource allocated for a particular purpose, rather it is 'made with anticipation' and sensual and 'tasteful enjoyment' of life itself. For example, one informant noted that 'despite all the hassle of waiting for it to boil and adding water', she prefers a stovetop kettle to an electric one, because 'the sound of the boiling teapot is homely'. Drinking of 'traditional' tea – brewed tea of ruby colour in an *ince belli* (thin-waisted) glass – has come to be regarded as a distinctly sensual aesthetic experience, animated by the magical sound of the *çaydanlık* boiling, the smell of a personalized blend of tea leaves, radiating colour, the warmth of the glass in one's hand, holding the glass from its waist, and the sound the tiny teaspoon makes over the glass when stirring. All of these and more culminate in the sensual and affective *keyif* (pleasure) of tea drinking.

The care in preparation and consumption are consonant with the calm attendance to the tea and its pleasures. The informants pointed out that tea drinking requires time because one has to savour the taste of tea and enjoy the melody of tea sipping. That is, there is a pleasure in tea drinking that is incompatible with rushing, so 'no time – no tea', as one informant put it. All of these pleasures are about experiencing tea in slow-motion: if you drink tea 'as you put your shoes on', you will not notice or discern any of the above. In contrast to the unnoticeable ordinary, the special is when time is noticed and claimed. Then, slow tea drinking is perhaps partaking in the performing of a particular time. Moreover, morality is implicated in the performance of time: whereas a fast flow is valued for efficiency, a slow flow is valued for leisurely pleasures.

Taste is, of course, a critical sensory facet. The common understanding is that freshly brewed tea tastes better. Those who brew it in their *çaydanlık* emphasize the colour and the flavour they obtain, ways of brewing the best tea, and display an aura of higher morality and aesthetics than the bag people. For example, one self-acclaimed connoisseur never adds more water to the top kettle that has the tea leaves, and when the water runs out she throws those leaves away and puts in new leaves for the next, 'fresh', round of tea, almost every thirty minutes. This informant complained about her neighbour that she is a sloppy person since she keeps on adding water to the top kettle throughout a Sunday afternoon. Teabag tea is called *sallama çay*, which is a *double entendre*, referring to shaking or swinging as well as something done without much care or attention. Indeed, in contrast to the teabag tea, which, as one person put it, 'borders on laziness and practicality', the preparation of the brewed 'fresh' tea involves some effort, art and know-how. For example, 'fresh tea' is not just-made tea but the tea brewed in the small top kettle for the right amount of time. As an informant pointed out, 'one has to know when the right time is'. This, in turn, involves know-how in terms of mixing different types and quantities of tea leaves to produce a perfect blend full-flavoured tea.

The idea(l) of social pleasures entails cozy togetherness. Tea is frequently associated with getting together with friends and family and having a good time. Prepared with care and 'in anticipation of joy', tea is regarded as part and parcel of an experience of serenity and informal warmth. When served to guests, it objectifies sociality and hospitality. The above informant, whose mother uses an electric teapot, emphasized that they use it only when they have 'lots of guests', and legitimized their reliance on the efficiency of technology with domestic hospitality. More significantly, social time with friends and family, 'cozy togetherness' and hospitality are envisaged to be central aspects of Turkish culture; and tea is regarded as a 'natural' part of such occasions. Our informants linked *sohbet* (informal conversation and chatting) with *keyif* (pleasure): the imagined and lived joys of tea entail sociality and cozy homeliness as much as sensual aesthetics.

Materiality is very much part of these sensual and social pleasures. The material constituents such as the glass with its shape and texture, the liquid with its hotness and colour, the kettle and the spoon with the sounds they make, and the particular blend of tea leaves with their smell and taste inaugurate particular senses as well as sociality and hospitality. They also (re)present tea drinking as a sensual experience. The materials do more than just activate the senses in the actual moment of consumption: tea drinkers encounter a quasi-corporeal dimension of the materiality of tea – an aesthetic and affective side. Embodying senses, emotions and knowledge, the materials and the qualities of those materials articulate various cultural ideal(s), such as comfort, virtue, friendship and efficiency.

In sum, in the face of the rapid cultural transformation in Turkey, the once mundane *çay* becomes the special *demli çay*. The new tea implements and the changes in practices, along with underlying discourses of modernity, prompted a fracturing and splitting of the tea drinking practice. The arrival and adoption of the new demarcated brewed tea drinking as special, with associated discourses of leisurely sensory and social pleasures, apart from the ordinary and the taken-for-granted activity. The convenient tea drinking materials turned an untemporal, mundane and background activity into a temporal, involved and dedicated one. Teabags and electric pots signify tea drinking as fast, efficient and instrumental, in contrast to the *demli çay*, which is slow, messy and something for leisurely pleasure. Informants said that although they use teabags at work, they generally prefer *demli çay* in their leisure time. Having *demli çay* is associated with time that is not structured and hurried, when one can enjoy a carefree, friendly conversation with family and friends, a casual game of backgammon or unhasty people watching. Made in a slow-boiling double teapot, it almost literally serves to warm the cold new modern present, making it safe and liveable (see Ger 2005). Further, when juxtaposed with the novel mugs, plastic cups, teabags and electric kettles, the well-worn tulip-shaped tea glasses, loose tea and *çaydanlık* came to articulate and objectify that slowness, that special time, distinguishing it from the fast, normal and new time. Then, the cultural meanings associated with tea drinking practice in Turkey, such as hospitality, sociality and sensual aesthetics, become emphasized anew through the use of the conventional implements as opposed to the new ones. For some, *demli çay* is the blood of social life, an affirmation of a culture being left behind, and as such it bears a sense of nostalgia. But, generally, *demli çay* drinking is about participating positively in Turkish culture, performing it and re-actualizing present-day Turkishness through a reliably familiar activity, which is made special through the interaction of new and old objects and doings as people negotiate the new in relation to the commonplace, moving back and forth between the two as they go about their daily lives. Thus, commonplace objects when set against new alternatives can potentially gradually become extraordinary artefacts, actualizing and materializing slow and special times. Furthermore, untemporality can become special temporality as people oscillate between various temporal logics, culminating in a continuing cycle of ways of doing, which reflect idea(l)s and moralities.

Hence, a mundane practice such as tea drinking can become special when new materials along with the associated discourses of modern convenience encounter and defamiliarize a taken-for-granted practice. When there are choices, decisions to be made, the old ordinary also generates its legitimizing discourse: sensory aesthetics, hospitality, sociality – the morality of slow time. Moreover, a reflexive taking of time marks a particular break as special and sets it apart. However, the distinction between the temporalities of ordinary and special is contingent at best. These times are dialogic and constantly interrupt each other. Special times, along with their accompanying objects, punctuate and exist within and in relation to the linear flow of fast time; they sustain it by making it liveable. While both the transient Carnival and the transcendental Christmas are special times, the interaction between the two is akin to the oscillation between the special and ordinary tea times in Turkey (Miller 1994). The interplay and the movement between the ordinary and special times are more imperative than the specifics of any one of them.

Tea drinking practices in Turkey reveal some interesting insights. We see that, in addition to new things and new doings being framed by their relation to the old (Shove in this volume), old things and doings are also framed by their relation to the new. As the new is framed as the modern, clean and efficient, the old gets to be framed as the slow, experiential and special, in turn making the new rather ordinary. What was unseen, always there, and mute now becomes marked, elected and vocal, hence special. While the new makes the old visible, the old refracts through the new in multiple ways (electric double kettles, different designs of glasses) and thereby becomes visible. While the new marks and frames the old, the natural, the normal, the old marks and frames the new. Our study of tea practices in Turkey makes us realize that 'what does the old do?' is a question as important as 'what does the new do?'

Secondly, we suggest that convenience technologies change the organization of time, but in multiple directions rather than one. Shove (2003) argues that convenience technologies have contributed to a flexible organization of time. For example, washing moved from 'laundry days' to fragmented moments of loading and unloading washing machines and thus disrupted collective rhythms. In the case of the convenient teabags, the reverse happens: tea drinking moves from any time to designated times that are consistent with the collective rhythms of leisure and work times.

Finally, akin to Eliade's (1957) observation that profane time made sacred time possible and vice versa, we find that ordered in time tea drinking associated with teabags turned a common way of tea drinking in Turkey into a special activity, set apart in time. Perhaps, here 'the divine' is the Turkish culture, its values such as sociality and hospitality, its artefacts such as the *ince belli*, and its institutions such as the family. Furthermore, it is 'largely the history of the devaluations and the revaluations which make up the process of the expression of the sacred' (Eliade 1957: 25). In this case, the role of the material objects in 'the devaluations and the revaluations', thus in producing special and ordinary times, is of particular interest. It is the interaction of the new and the old tea drinking materials, discourses around their use, and associated time and ways of doing that afforded rediscovering and re-evaluating the now-special times in the formerly mundane.

While consumers enjoy diverse choices in tea drinking, there is a different story at the political economy level. Lipton has been selling loose leaf tea with the package label 'Rize tea, Turkish tea from the Black Sea', in addition to their popular teabags. Recently Coca Cola bought 50% of Dogadan (literally, 'from nature'), a herbal teabag manufacturer. Reportedly, Coca Cola will invest $40 million in this business. After the acquisition, the firm started producing loose leaf black tea and advertising it as 'nature comes to you'. With Coca Cola's financial muscle, there are new factories at the Black Sea region and a very intensive advertising campaign. The television advertising depicts bright green leaves flying in from recognizably Karadeniz tea plantations to a very urban high-rise skyline, then into several open kitchen-living room areas. The *ince belli* and *çaydanlık* on the stove are as prominent as the people, young and old, drinking tea while laughing, talking and having a good time. We wonder if Lipton and Coke will eventually drive out various local firms and dominate the tea market within which tea moves, along with the movement between ordinary and special times.

References

Anderson, B. (2004). Time-stilled Space-slowed: How Boredom Matters. *Geoforum* 35: 739–754.

Belk, R.W, Wallendorf, M. and Sherry, J.F. (1989). The Sacred and the Profane in Consumer Behavior: Theodicy on the Odyssey. *Journal of Consumer Research* 16(2): 1–21.

Durkheim, É. (1995) [1912]. *The Elementary Forms of Religious Life*. New York: Free Press.

Eliade, M. (1957). *The Sacred and the Profane: The Nature of Religion*. New York: Harcourt.

Ger, G. (2005). Warming: Making the New Familiar and Moral. *Ethnologia Europea: Journal of European Ethnology* 35(1/2): 19–22.

Gronow, J. and Warde, A. (2001). *Ordinary Consumption*. London: Routledge.

Jalas, M. (2006). Making Time: The Art of Loving Wooden Boats. *Time & Society* 15(2/3): 343–363.

Kozinets, R. (2001). Utopian Enterprise: Articulating the Meanings of *Star Trek*'s Culture of Consumption. *Journal of Consumer Research* 28(2): 67–68.

Miller, D. (1994). *Modernity: An Ethnographic Approach.* Oxford: Berg.

Nowotny, H. (1994). *Time: The Modern and Postmodern Experience.* Cambridge: Polity.

Petrini, C. (2003). *Slow Food: The Case for Taste.* New York: Columbia University Press.

Shove, E. (2003). *Comfort, Cleanliness and Convenience: The Social Organization of Normality.* Oxford: Berg.

Shove, E. and Pantzar M. (2005). 'Consumers, Producers and Practices: Understanding the Invention and Reinvention of Nordic Walking. *Journal of Consumer Culture* 5(1): 43–64.

Stevens, L., Maclaren, P. and Brown, S. (2003). *Red* Time is Me Time. *Journal of Advertising* 32(1): 35–45.

–13–

Making Time
Reciprocal Object Relations and the Self-legitimizing Time of Wooden Boating
Mikko Jalas

Introduction

This chapter develops and substantiates the argument that material, stuff and objects have temporalities. In particular, I want to explore the idea that such temporalities are not located in or properties of the material itself, but rather that the temporality of stuff is a relational phenomenon situated in between human actors and the material world. I will argue that human action around materials and objects results in reciprocal relations. With this notion of reciprocity I aim to capture the dual role of materials in configuring human temporalities. On the one hand, materials and objects constitute media through which humans articulate and enact different aspects of temporalities such as pace, rhythm and changing temporal horizons. On the other hand, reciprocity implies that materials and objects are indeed able to configure time, establish horizons and reproduce rhythms.

Wooden boating represents a good case with which to illustrate reciprocal object relations through which the practitioners of wooden boating anchor themselves in the material world. This world is populated with wooden vessels of various kinds that appear to be unique, priceless and entitled to good care. Equally, the boating fabric includes visual representations and narrative boat-histories. While some of these objects are officially labelled and registered as instances of maritime heritage, other boats spell out their unique position in more subtle ways. This world of boating also includes the dedicated human practitioners who strive to excel in the skills of maintaining and using such boats. Moreover, humans also figure as dedicated stewards who assume responsibilities and duties towards the material world. Wooden boating is hence a constellation of physical material, cultural meanings and human agents that is, as a whole, able to convince and capture practitioners, absorb human labour, demonstrate skill and craftsmanship, and request various resources such as dedicated time and money.

Wooden boating affords different temporalities and entails multiple ways of establishing them. This chapter, which approaches wooden boating as a practice, explores the notion that there might be a self-referential and autotelic time of wooden boating. During such time, the question of how to do wooden boating overwhelms everything else. In other words, the chapter describes a timeless time of humans working *with* wooden boats and the moral, aesthetic and practical understandings of wooden boats that permeate this self-referential temporality.

Before continuing to the world of varnish, dust and decay, let me first establish some leeway for writing, and a particular bearing on wooden boating. The focus of this chapter is in the meshing of the individual human subject with the external world in ways that allow that rationalities are multiple, context-specific and weaker than we might be comfortable with or than we might wish politically. In the same vein, the meshing also brings about context-specific temporalities instead of a universalizing idea that time is a money-like resource. Such theorizing is a conceptual tool for seeing the world differently, radicalizing social thought and opening up new political spaces. As such, the most relevant question for such an analysis is not how accurately, universally or objectively one is able to describe the mutual constitution of humans and the material world. Rather, it is evident that writings on object relations reach a point and take forms that are alien to everyday life. The job of describing how people *live and act with objects, and feel, understand and appreciate them* therefore represents a research task that involves a deliberate reinterpretation of everyday life.

Such accounts frequently deal with elusive phenomena that easily fall apart and vanish once spoken aloud or written down. They also encounter resistance, because they challenge and ridicule dominant rationalities and expose the fragmentation of individual reasoning. In this chapter I will put forward a few such fragile moments of wooden boating. Apart from being hard to seize, the phenomenon is also apparently marginal from the point of view of mass consumption. However, it is my understanding that the obscure ways in which wooden boats establish and carry meanings, organize time and capture people may represent a pattern that is more common than one might at first suppose.

The Emergence of Wooden Boating

Wooden boating is a distinct yet versatile phenomenon, which includes a variety of old objects, new materials, skills of performing wooden boating, images of boats and boating as well the cultural processes of reading and writing the meanings and the 'text' of the practice. The type of objects and the practices and relations that appear in wooden boating are bound to vary from one context to the next. The following excerpts are based on a study of the phenomenon in Finland in the late twentieth century (see Jalas 2005, 2006a), in which I have documented the re-emergence of wood as a boat-building material following the rapid introduction of fibre-glass as the dominant material for constructing leisure boats. The other relevant parallel process has been the aestheticization of a fleet of vintage yachts and the respective valorization of their owners.

All these practices share a common ground. By the end of the 1970s the gradual substitution of fibre-glass had virtually abolished wood as a material for boat-building. On the basis of data from annual sales catalogues, one could argue that this situation has not changed: wooden boats remain outside the mainstream commercial catalogues. However, since the 1970s there has been an increase in the number of active sites for performing wooden boating: magazines, fairs, associations, races, web-pages and blogs are all 'locations' in which boats, owners and crews meet and enact wooden boating. New practices have evolved around the old boats, old designs and, in general, around wood as a distinctive material.

Despite this shared background, the Finnish case is itself fragmented. The various genres of wooden boating revolve around wooden vessels of different age and type. There are those who sail replicas of vernacular boats or attempt to catch the mood of the Vikings on the sea, there are those who restore and embellish the forgotten glory of vintage yachts, and yet those who seek to produce modern designs using modern materials of wooden boat-building. The genres link with diverse developments in other geographical areas: whereas the Swedish fleet of vintage boats has long been envied and admired in Finland, the modernization of boat-building with epoxy resins make use of techniques and practices of the northeast United States.

Wooden boating draws on particular ideas and skills. Hence, the practices of wooden boating include (the learning of) cognitive and practical skills of maintaining boats in boatyards and of using them on water. Equally, they include the skills of representing boats on web-sites, speaking and writing about them, and strolling around specialist exhibitions and fairs. The variety of orientations or genres and the degree of exposure, involvement and skill create a mosaic of unique ways of doing wooden boating.

Vernacular Replicas as Reconstructed History

Vernacular traditions form the basis of one particular and prevalent way of doing wooden boating in Finland. The first association dedicated to wooden boating was set up in the late 1960s to document and reconstruct small vernacular models of fishing boats. Since then, numerous new associations have been established, and vernacular replicas now fill the order books of many contemporary boat-builders. This activity is most obviously about remaking history (Laurier 1998). The boats are replicated in detail, and modern materials such as Dacron cloth for sails and epoxy resins for gluing are frequently excluded. At local events these vessels are matched with humans who clothe and decorate themselves in keeping with their boats. Tar, cotton for sails, linen for the seams and ornamented wool for the clothing make much of this practice.

However, these gatherings do not only consist of the materials and designs of a particular age. Actually using the boats calls for much more detailed replication. On the minute level, tacking moves and manoeuvres with these clumsy vernacular hulls and rigs differ from those of modern yachting. Furthermore, special events imitate or reconstruct particular routes like the mail-carriage between Finland and Sweden, the summer journeys for following stocks of Baltic herring, or journeys to and from markets and cities. The enacting of particular uses and of particular routes results in apparent authenticity.

Vintage Glamour

Aestheticized racing yachts represent another class of objects around which many practitioners orbit and perform acts of wooden boating. This genre builds on the glamour of sailing as a sport and on the celebrities who feature in the narrative of boat histories. Story-telling, aesthetic judgement and visually representing boats are key skills in this field. What results is a view that the core objects of this practice are unique, priceless and prestigious. Accordingly, boat-classes such as the International Rule boats and the square-metre boats receive much publicity, despite the fact that they are now few in number.

Races are the sites in which these boats perform their role in staging human passion to compete and excel. Ironically, the priceless objects are exposed to the hardship of racing: collisions, stress and strain. The racing context implies a merger between outdated and new technology. In the time of their design, commissioning and building, these boats involved and required the most advanced designs and best available technology. In the same vein, their life as competitive boats on the race course was short. This genre of wooden boating now merges dated technological advances with new innovations. Hence, boats with old-fashioned hulls receive modern rigs, and are operated and trimmed with the aid of advanced carbon-fibre technologies of Spectra and Dynema. The combination of dated high-tech and contemporary high-tech presents endless very concrete problems for the practitioners. These may be solved by simple statements like 'above the deck everything is modern but below the deck we aim for originality'. Responding to these and similar dilemmas also calls for and enables one to practise and demonstrate the more sophisticated skills of a restoration professional. As a boat-owner and a museum-chief explains: 'Converting a canvas deck to a teak deck is perhaps a matter of maintenance. But is it a good enough reason to alter the weight balance and radically change the overall appearance of the yacht? The pious yacht-owner of course chooses to stay with the original solution' (Nordlund, 2004, translation from Swedish by the author).

The race yachts warp and condense time in another sense as well. These vintage boats cut through decades not only in terms of technological advances, but also in terms of social reality. It is very common for boat-owners to collect and publish the list of previous owners, and to catalogue the races and other gatherings in which the boat has been involved. Such boat-histories connect present and previous owners of the same yachts. While this is for many just a matter of documenting the history of the boat, it is also one particular way through which boats gather momentum and establish themselves as distinctive and special. For example, the sixtieth-anniversary publication of a 6 metre yacht called *Maybe IV* written in the early twenty-first century elaborates in detail on the acquaintances of the person who commissioned the boat in pre-Second World War Scandinavia, thereby establishing the uniqueness of this particular vessel and its owners.

The Epoxy Bonds

Modernized wooden boating constitutes a third significant genre of wooden boating. Starting from the 1970s in the United States and in the early 1990s in Finland, it became commonplace to argue that modern materials and designs could re-establish the competitiveness of wood as a boat-building material. In Finland, these claims led wooden boats to be included in technology policy, and to the renewal and in many cases to the establishment of educational institutes for wooden boat-building both at vocational and at polytechnic level. Such institutions imported knowledge from the United States to Finland through the mobility and extended visits of staff in both directions. The results of this exchange were many. Composite structures of wood, fibre-glass and epoxy resins were the concrete outcomes of these efforts. Such outcomes blurred the boundary between fibre-glass and wood. Wooden boats could, when desired, be made to imitate the appearance of those made from fibre-glass. In addition, aspects like those of convenience and ease of maintenance have also begun to converge. In establishing a new discourse of modern boat-building, it was essential to argue that wooden boats are distinct *and* that they can nonetheless match fibre-glass in terms of convenience and maintenance.

Each of these genres could, of course, be divided into further categories. Yet these three selected types revolve around a handful of essential differences and distinguishing features. The vernacular boats draw on nostalgia, on the deliberate inconvenience of the objects, on the roughness of finishes, and on the presumed character of the working sailors whose style is imitated. On the other hand, the vintage fleet revolves around notions of elegance. The skills of appreciating and representing these boats as aesthetically superior objects are at the core of this practice. These boats consequently serve to construct and articulate social distinctions. Whereas the replication of vernacular boats is frequently driven by interests in maintaining the diversity of traditional boat-building skills, the practices of vintage yachting focus on particular objects *per se*, and on their qualities as priceless embodiments of very specific skills. Finally, the modernization of wooden boat-building represents a subtle attempt to merge craft production with capitalistic interests and to exploit the image of wooden boats as one-off hand-crafted items. Unlike forms associated with replicas and the vintage yachts, modernized wooden boat-building is positioned in direct relation to the mass-manufacturing of fibre-glass boats, and with comparable qualities like those of price and convenience.

The Workings of Wooden Boating – Skills, Sensations and Obligations

Regardless of the genre or orientation of doing wooden boating, these practices require investments of time and money, skills on the part of the practitioners, and committed institutional constituencies such as schools of boat-building, associations and publishers of dedicated books and magazines. This observation, and the very simple question of why people engage in wooden boating, begs for a nuanced answer; one may wonder how wooden boats are useful and reasonable, or how they 'make sense'.

Practitioners have multiple and elaborate ways of reasoning wooden boating. One needs to appreciate the ways that boats appear unique, beautiful and prestigious. One needs to account for fun and for the ability of boats to evoke craft sensibilities and feelings of locality. Equally, one needs to understand the story-telling and the workings of patina within wooden boating. In short, while recognizing that wooden boating is a culturally thick social activity in which the people involved invest various resources of time and money, it is relevant to ask that how it is that boats are able to require these resources and convince the humans actors to play along.

In the following section I consider three ways in which boats collect resources and capture human practitioners. Firstly, I will reflect on the accumulation of skills as a practical explanation of how it is that boat-owners face an always extending list of things-to-do and of how engagement with their boats becomes ever more complicated and resource-intensive. I then consider emotions as a second sphere of interaction between boats and practitioners. Here I highlight the ways that boats are able to evoke emotions in those who build, own, use and care for them. Finally, I consider the emergence of the boat as an entity that has moral rights and that places obligations on those with whom it interacts. This last possibility arises, in part, out of practical, emotional and aesthetic understandings of boats. Yet, it appears as a distinct and particularly strong outcome of mutual exchange between the boats and practitioners.

The Skills of Wooden Boating

Wooden boating is rich in details that can be discussed, learned and disputed. As such, the accumulation of relevant skills is vital. The knowledge that boaters acquire and the skills they develop encompass different aspects of boating. Some concern maintenance while others relate to using the boat on the water. I concentrate here on the former. In caring for a wooden boat, one encounters and accumulates knowledge of how boats were traditionally built, and of contemporary techniques both of building and of renovation. One develops knowledge of different raw materials – wood, screws, cloth or chemicals – and of their availability, suitability and use. One learns to judge whether suggested methods and materials are appropriate – to tell whether it is acceptable to, for example, colour your varnish, or to use epoxy resins to strengthen the seams of a hull from the 1930s. Judging also involves the naming of deviations and problems of quality such as the 'orange-skin' finish in varnishing.

However, simply knowing about wooden boating does not make the boater a capable practitioner. Crucially, boaters develop practical, bodily capabilities of performing wooden boating. To establish a glossy and evenly varnished surface or to fit in a piece of new wood are highly demanding practical tasks that require the training of the body. For planing, carving or cutting, this bodily learning entails sturdy hands and a tight grip,but the touch of the paint-brush is different. Varnish requires a correct sequence of application on different surfaces, and a human arm accustomed to the controlled dipping and applying of liquid in unhurried rounds of thousands. In sum, skills imply an increased ability to plan, perform and judge the acts of wooden boating.

The accumulation of such knowledge and bodily skill establishes boaters as parts of a network of things, skills and images. For, example a male practitioner 'V' states in an interview that: 'There is nothing better than to be out with a boat, which is in good condition and which one has thoroughly renovated oneself ... of course the best would be to have built the whole boat oneself.' 'V' is thus a carrier of specific skills and has an identity that only becomes available once relevant objects and evaluative criteria are also present. His statement echoes ideas of 'good condition', of 'renovation', and an appreciation of boat-building as a craft. The complex that is formed by boats, and by relevant skills and understandings is strong enough to force 'V' to undertake hundred-kilometre journeys to acquire materials, draw on his friends and spend his holidays, unwillingly, repairing his boat.

Boat Sensations

Writing on car cultures, Mimi Sheller argues that feelings about driving provide insight into the relation between humans and the material objects of driving. She argues that such feelings merge aesthetic appreciation and kinaesthetic sensing of the object. In her words, 'an emotional agent is a relational entity that instantiates particular aesthetic orientations and kinaesthetic dispositions toward driving. Movement and being moved together produce feelings of being in the car, for the car and with the car' (Sheller 2004: 222).

So it is with boats. 'V's experience already hints at the way that boats are not only worked on, but also approached and appreciated emotionally and sensually. But how do boats bring these experiences about? What are the mechanisms by which wooden boats evoke strong feelings? What is the agency of boats when they intrigue us, and capture and move us emotionally?

One obvious answer is that wooden boats have been collectively established as altogether superior in terms of aesthetic and tacit qualities. After fibre-glass became a dominant boat-building material in the late 1960s, it did not take long for boating discourse to suggest that the *aesthetic qualities* of wooden boats were quite simply distinctive. Wooden boats still enjoy such a distinguished position and receive ongoing support so that this status is maintained. Architects and industrial designers frequently practise wooden boating, and articulate its aesthetics in ways that make use of their professional skills. In such cases, wooden boating benefits from the design expertise of those who do it while at the same time providing materials for aesthetic play.

Aesthetic delineations and categorizations like 'clinker-built hulls are ugly, but carvel-built hulls are beautiful' represent feelings about boats. Contemporary practices also celebrate the tactile properties of wood and of wooden boating. As Skogström spells out, 'the smell of wood, the looks and the warmness and the sounds of water touching it, emphasize the joy of building and owning wooden boats' (1994: 47, translation from Finnish by the author). It is thus not only the boats themselves, but the very activity of wooden boating, and the feeling in the boat, that have been given an aesthetic quality. Furthermore, boats in general, like the cars in Sheller's account, open up and offer kinaesthetic experiences: acceleration, the sensation of cutting smoothly and repeatedly through waves on a tack on open sea, the rolling sea and creeping sea-sickness. Likewise, boats establish their own soundscape of engines, howling wind and tight ropes, and of the hull squeaking and resonating under heavy stress. Moving, roaring and shivering things appear especially good at evoking feelings, and wooden boats are no exception.

Given such experiential and sensational qualities, it is no wonder that owners become attached to their boats, firmly tapping them after harbouring from a rough ride and turning back to give them a last quick look from a distance. It is also no wonder that ex-boat-owners frequently cry when parting for good and handing the boat over to a new and, they hope, good home.

The infrastructure of wooden boating reflects these intimate relations. As unique objects, boats, almost always, and often also by law, have names compared with the plain registration numbers of cars. On the other hand, the beauty contests of wooden boats are set up to both establish and evaluate their distinctive qualities. Personification is present also on the internet. For example, the web-pages for wooden boats under the auspices of the city of Kotka (a middle-size Finnish coastal town) initially adopted a rhetoric of pet-care: the site called the 'The Clinic of Wooden Boats' featured a 'Doctor of Wooden Boats' who disseminated expertise and suggested treatment for particular problems. Wooden boating is thick with various verbal and practical ways of treating the objects as worthy of good care. In the next section I explore the meaning of naming and personalization in greater detail.

How do intimate relations develop? Novelties such as new cars are subject to aesthetic judgements of look and feel, and, as Campbell (1987) suggests, sensory relationships with objects may involve elaborate dreaming, often strongest when not (yet) possessing the objects in question. One could thus argue that practices like wooden boating recruit practitioners by means of particularly vivid and tempting images. However, once captured, practising is self-reinforcing. Intimacy may not be a result of a sensory encounter, but might rather stem from continuous engagement. For example, Ilmonen (2004) suggests that we gradually develop attachment towards our possessions. This may take place through increasing personalization of the object, or as the marks and memories of past occasions (and uses) accumulate (McCracken 1988). Equally, it may be the result of acquiring relevant skills.

Objects that bear marks of social history and human engagement can be significant in other ways as well. For example, Ahuvia (2005) describes a category of 'loved objects' which includes collections, gifts and inherited family objects. Family belongings appear important to us because they remind us of other important people, establish links between people and bring together senses of community. On the other hand, the patina of objects represents continued human effort on the part of other, often more distant actors. One can push these ideas further and identify situations in which objects come to be valuable, unique and special in their own right, as the persons involved become more distant and less particular.

Obligations, Duties and the Stewardship of Wooden Boats

Solidarity with and dutifulness towards objects implies a particular kind of emotional and moral link between the object-world and human practitioners. Boats provide a vivid illustration of such co-determination. Wooden boating includes processes through which boats enter the category of heritage. Once established as such, they are able to argue for rights and call for human stewards. This is one example of how objects in general manage to convey and place requirements on human practitioners. There are others. If boats are regarded as family members, pets or even persons, they may also have rights regardless of whether they are registered as national heritage or not. In all such cases, the humans involved identify duties and moral obligations to boats. In considering these relations I start by commenting on the more objective qualities of uniqueness and right-claiming, and then return to the mystic and spiritual ways that boats are made alive.

Some sections and tons of the material of wooden boating are regarded as unique parts of common maritime heritage due to their rarity or status as being representative of a wider class of objects, and are protected like nationally important buildings. In 1994 in Finland, the National Board of Antiquities established a register of existing large historical vessels and a fund for their restoration. These national efforts paralleled an international focus on maritime history. The first European Maritime Heritage Conference was held in 1992 and the fourth congress issued the so-called 'Barcelona Charter' in 2002, which 'set out a Code of Good Practice for owners and operators of traditional vessels along the lines of the Athens Charter drafted by architects and museum technicians in 1931 (as amended in Venice in 1964) to give guidance on the restoration of historic monuments' (http://www. heritageafloat.org.uk/Barcelona.htm). Even if the scope of the charter is limited, and the text hardly known among boat-owners, popular magazines and books on wooden boating rephrase and broaden the overall argument: the owners of wooden boats are in the trusted position of taking care of a unique and priceless fleet of boats and of reproducing a pool of related skills.

Kopytoff (1986) argues for a cultural biographical approach in which appreciation of material objects depends upon knowledge of their history and lifecourse. The owners of wooden boats reflect and exemplify this argument in their efforts to collect various facts about the history of the boat: the names of previous owners and where they lived. They also weave in more emotional details of hazards at sea, war-time destinies or periods of forgotten glory. Once such a history has been told, each object becomes singular regardless of its official heritage value or the number of celebrities involved.

These person-like qualities of uniqueness are further supported by mysticism and animism. Experienced builders are celebrated as specially gifted master craftsmen who create, carve and force boats out of difficult, living material. They are, typically, men who (are claimed to) have a deep understanding of wood material, trees and nature as a whole, often handed down from father to son. It is not only that they posses such skills. The frequent use of emotional language – boats are reported to have been built with *love* – suggests that designers, builders and dedicated owners convey their life forces to the boats they make.

It comes, then, as no surprise that boats are often thought to be alive. Ownership is described as a relationship or form of companionship; like pets, boats are thought to deserve good and constant maintenance and, at point of sale, dedicated new owners. Boats are described as carrying the features of their designers (Whynott 1999) and owners. And to take such animism further, boats are thought to be able to sense their environment, to tell if a big or a small wave is about to hit, and to murmur to each other during long dark winters in the boatshed (Whynott 1999). On her website, *Silene*, a 6-metre yacht, bursts into being:

> Independent of any race success my old hull has always been taken good care of. A few years ago I had all my keel bolts checked and re-zinced, my wooden keel was inspected, found healthy and impregnated, and I got a new rudder, lighter than before. Four boards on each side of my under-water planking were replaced and a number of spars were

also repaired. Every year my bilge has been impregnated with a sweetest natural linseed oil and all varnished parts have been looked after, not forgetting my dear rig and sails. Sometimes I truly feel that I am getting younger year after year. I hope, however, that I can keep my classic beauty. (http:/www.6mr.fi/DAS/yachts/981119-125927.html)

Such screenplays written for the drama of wooden boating bring boats to the fore and stage owners in the background as responsible care-takers of boats which are both unique and personified. The owners of *Silene* thus construct a duty for themselves, a moral location, as well as a location in the material world. However, it is not only the boat as an assembly of boards, bolts and spars which is capable of playing the role of *Silene* and of placing compelling demands on the owners. In addition, taken-for-granted ways of appreciating boats and maintaining them properly – the shared practice of wooden boating – constitute an essential scenery and a stage on which this drama unfolds.

Scripting the Times of Wooden Boating

In this chapter I argue that human understandings of time, that is, temporalities, depend on, reflect and partly stem from the material world. Such notions of mutual constitution or co-determination bear on the tradition of science and technology studies. In this tradition Law (1992, cited in Ilmonen 2004), for example, points out that humans have preferences in how to use and interact with goods, but that this is reciprocal. Goods, too, have preferences, in the form of inscribed modes of use. Goods thus tell us how to approach them and what to do with them. Accordingly, temporalities can be regarded as particular scripts. However, the notion of reciprocal object relations implies that scripting is an ongoing process. Scripts are not located solely in goods or in the material infrastructure. In the case of wooden boats this is very obvious. Racing boats that were initially designed to be short-lived experiments and tool-like vernacular boats are now being restored and renovated in ways never anticipated, let alone scripted, by their designers or builders.

As we have seen, the accumulation of skills is one dynamic feature of material interaction. Accumulations of skill can result in an ever-closer relationship to (or unity with) specific objects. Equally, inscribed ways of practising may be so demanding as to exclude novices. On both counts, the skilled practitioner *understands* the object and has attuned his/her body-mind to it in the course of learning the trade.

Considering the skilled actions of a co-determined practitioner provides one way to think about the autotelic time of human action (Szerszynski 2002). For the sake of simplicity, one can contrast two extremes: 'economic man', who has the will and the ability to constantly optimize time use, and the skilled human being, or a body-mind (Reckwitz 2002), who is accustomed to use particular tools for pre-given purposes with an 'objectively' and materially given rhythm. In the latter case, the particular context of, for example, wooden boating establishes tasks such as 'the impregnation of the hull with linen oil', which is to be done at fifteen year intervals and to last for at least twenty-four hours per each treatment. In this case time is strongly configured by the practice and precludes ongoing efforts to optimize and economize one's use of time.

Intimate and aesthetic relations with boats appear to constitute slightly different time, the legitimacy of which stems from the sensory aspects of wooden boating. Might such time be called slow? Or is it rather a playful coexistence with the neat material of wooden boating? As a third understanding, I would suggest a body-aesthetics of wooden boating in which the proper rhythm and pace of sanding, sawing, masking and painting reflects the human body, in contrast to the rhythms of external pace-keepers such as curing and fixing times.

Finally, the time of the dedicated and dutiful stewards of wooden boats is quite specifically but also rather differently organized. In this context, boats are not material for aesthetic play but figure instead as part of a common heritage entitled to receive good care and maintenance. Hence, they call for disciplined and skilled actors. Committed stewards may be well informed about the history of a particular boat, and understand it emotionally as well as in terms of a more objective language of heritage. Providing such practitioners have relevant skills, they face a growing list of things-to-do. In identifying this temporality I offer a partial explanation for one especially puzzling phenomenon: the practitioners of wooden boating experience extreme stress and pressure in pursuing the cherished goals of replicating an un-hurried past or of materializing and realizing specific forms of aesthetic play. This is a temporality that I have previously called localized busyness (Jalas 2006b).

Discussion: Reflections on Object Relations

In this chapter I have maintained and substantiated the argument that the physical world, including materials and objects, is intertwined with human temporalities. Such temporalities can be thought of as scripts that guide human action, establish particular rights and ways of acting and preclude others. However, the case of wooden boating clearly shows that scripts are not inherent in the physical material but are, rather, continuously rewritten on that material. For example boats built as short-lived tools or racing experiments are now treated as priceless parts of common heritage. Rather than carrying pre-given scripts, objects such as wooden boats represent physical matter with which humans can play, on which they can demonstrate skills and by which they can be carried away.

This description of boat-relations and boating moments positions them as a form of addiction, involving compulsive behaviour and loss of control and agency on the part of the human participant. However, one can also argue that such processes are much better controlled than this account suggests. Allowing, imagining, cultivating and communicating romantic sensibilities regarding the agency and spirit of objects serves obvious purposes of social distinction and, on the other hand, it seems to provide a means of resisting a dominantly instrumental orientation.

Firstly, practices like wooden boating provide an arena in which social distinctions are reproduced and enacted. As a reflexive novice notices: 'After sailing a week with a wooden boat, I understood wooden boating. Just because of the boat, everyone was looking at us when we entered harbours. We didn't have to have a big and fancy boat to attract attention' (U, female). Instead of mere possession, this distinctive display and identity construction revolves around skills and understandings of ways of using and being with the objects. On the other hand, wooden boaters seek to articulate identities and mutual relationships with objects in ways that counter forms of capitalistic power. For committed practitioners of wooden boating in Finland, the skilled performances, the tactile object relations and the roles of stewardship compensate for many of the ills of their working life. Equally, 'strong' objects that are placed high in the moral order of things contribute to understandings of 'community' and sense of a location in an increasingly global world. Yet the stress, the rolling demands and the lengthy lists of things-to-do that the boat-owners encounter reveal that the relatively powerful position of the wooden boat is a double-edged sword. While dedicated practitioners may be able to establish a sense of a community and tackle existential questions, they most often fail in trying to resist harriedness as a phenomenon of modern capitalist society.

To conclude, the temporalities that arise from reciprocal relations and actions around physical objects involve uncertainty and emergent qualities; they are not something that humans write with a firm hand and clear mind. Social distinction may be an unintended result of enthusiastic history-writing on a particular boat; the traditions evoked through replication may reflect modern anxieties on a pre-conscious bodily level; really working with your hands really does feel different compared to merely pushing paper around, and the smell of tar is inviting. What is also evident is that if wooden boats indeed play their role so well that practitioners and the publics around them are captured, convinced and moved, it important to recognize that boats themselves rewrite the temporalities of human action and that they make time.

References

Ahuvia, A. (2005). Beyond the Extended Self: Loved Objects and Consumers' Identity Narratives. *Journal of Consumer Research* 32: 171–184.

Campbell, C. (1987). *The Romantic Ethic and the Spirit of Modern Consumerism.* Oxford: Blackwell.

Ilmonen, K. (2004). The Use and Commitment to Goods. *Journal of Consumer Culture* 4(1): 27–50.

Jalas, M. (2005). The Art of Loving Wooden Boats. In *Manufacturing Leisure: Innovations in Happiness, Well-being and Fun*, eds M. Pantzar and E. Shove. Helsinki: National Consumer Research Centre. Available at: http://www.ncrc. fi/files/4717/2005_01_publications_manufacturingleisure.pdf (accessed 24 April 2009).

Jalas, M. (2006a). Making Time: The Art of Loving Wooden Boats. *Time & Society* 15(2/3): 343–363.

Jalas, M. (2006b). *Busy, Wise and Idle Time: A Study of the Temporalities of Consumption in the Environmental Debate*. Dissertation A-275. Helsinki: Helsinki School of Economics. Available at: http://hsepubl.lib.hse.fi/EN/diss/ ?cmd=show&dissid=306 (accessed 16 April 2009).

Kopytoff, I. (1986). The Cultural Biography of Things: Commoditization as a Process. In *The Social Life of Things: Commodities in Cultural Perspective*, ed. A. Appadurai. Cambridge: Cambridge University Press.

Laurier, E. (1998). Replication and Restoration: Ways of Making Maritime History. *Journal of Material Culture* 3(1): 21–50.

Law, J. (1992). Notes on the Theory of Actor Network: Ordering, Strategy, and Heterogeneity. *Systems Practice* 5(1): 379–393.

McCracken, G. (1988*). Culture and Consumption: New Approaches to the Symbolic Character of Consumer Goods and Activities*. Bloomington and Indianapolis: Indiana University Press.

Nordlund, I. (2004). *Båtälskare* (Boat Enthusiast – in Swedish). Available at: http:// www.int5m.fi/historia/ivar/ (accessed 24 April 2009).

Reckwitz, A. (2002). Toward a Theory of Social Practices: A Development in Culturalist Theorizing. *European Journal of Social Theory* 5(2): 243–263.

Sheller, M. (2004). Automotive Emotions: Feeling the Car. *Theory, Culture and Society* 21(4/5): 221–242.

Skogström, L. (1994). *Puuveneveistäjien koulutus ja alan kehittäminen* (The Education in and the Development of Professional Wooden Boat-Building – in Finnish). Kehittyvä ammatillinen koulutus 1. Helsinki.

Szerszynski, B. (2002). Wild Times and Domestic Times: The Temporalities of Environmental Lifestyles and Politics. *Landscape and Urban Planning* 61(2–4): 181–191.

Whynott, D. (1999). *A Unit of Water, a Unit of Time: Joel White's Last Boat*. New York: Washington Square Press.

−14−

The Ethics of Routine
Consciousness, Tedium and Value
Don Slater

Introduction

This chapter opens up a slightly different analytical level: the 'ethical framing of routine'. We need to look not only at empirically occurring routines, but also at the normative or ethical framing of the very notion of 'routine', '*the* routine' (or the mundane, the habitual, the taken-for-granted), 'being routine', 'routinization'. Notions like 'routine' and its cognates are labels that accord particular social status and value to forms of action and practice, and that strategically stabilize them in specific ways. This is true in two senses. Firstly, to label a structure of action 'routine' is always already a value judgement or ethical framing. As we will explore in a first example (the hobby), the idea of 'routines' occupies a conventional role in many Western moral cosmologies: routine distinguishes unthinking conformist 'behaviour' from critically conscious and ruptural 'action'.

But beyond the question of moral judgement, I want to press a second, stronger claim, that the ethical framing of 'routine' is central to the different ways in which routines are themselves constructed and then related to other practices. In this sense, discourses on routine should be considered as performative, and processes of routinization (whether successful or resisted) centrally involve participants in taking an attitude to routinization itself: that is to say, the notion of 'routine' is topicalized by actors themselves, and this is consequential in the production (or the flouting) of routine. The way people frame the very notion of 'routine' becomes, in these circumstances, 'ethical' in the old Foucauldian sense – it is part of that orientation to the self by which we organize our subjectivity through the conduct of conduct; it is part of how we take a strategic position on self and other.

I'd like to explore this ethical framing of routine through some examples, any or all of which might be deemed eccentric: they were chosen simply to invoke this particular level of analysis and to argue that it might add something to the study of routines. No particular typology is being suggested. However, the contrast between the three examples is very sharp, and suggests a central issue that might be germane to this kind of analysis: actions are being framed and evaluated – very differently in each case – in terms of their potential for expanding or contracting social agency, reflexivity and critical consciousness. What is ethically at stake in invoking the very idea of routine is the question of whether participants are reflexively in control of the flow of events. We therefore start with Western Marxism, in which 'routine' indexes the systemic reification or colonization of everyday life, and always constitutes a diminution of agency or increase of alienation. This is of course only one Western tradition, but it provides a very strong statement of a common modern rejection of everyday life as routinized and therefore debased. The idea of a hobby provides an example: to label and organize a practice in the form of a hobby came to symbolize the illusion of freedom and social significance experienced within a reality of constricted and routinized private obsession.

A second example is offered by 'Eastern practices' as assimilated in Western contexts – specifically Tai Chi and Buddhist meditation. These are practices based on a phenomenological *engagement* with routine: the endless but conscious repetition of the same few movements or breaths. In contrast to the first example, the aim is non-judgemental – neither to reject nor to embrace routines, but to enter into them with constant attention and consciousness. Routine is constituted as a technology aimed at increasing the 'skilfulness' with which one deals with the everyday, the inculcation of a kind of non-routinized response to the routine. The subject to emerge from this training is 'skilful' in that s/he is able to respond creatively to events rather than be overwhelmed by them or by habitual adaptations.

A final example – technology use in Ghana – contrasts with the first two in that unreflexive routine is highly valued. Routine and unthinking use of the internet in the North is treated as clear evidence of Northern superiority over Africa. Moreover, already-routinized Northern technology uses are stabilized and transmitted by official ICT (information and communication technologies) policies. By contrast, local technology use – however stably routinized – is negatively valorized as irrational and traditional.

Routine as Alienation

In critical theory, routine is part of a characterization of everyday life as reified and alienated. Particularly in the tradition that runs from Hegel through Marx, Lukács, Lefebvre and then Situationism and Baudrillard, the routinization of everyday life derives from a systematization of the world, which is experienced as natural and lawlike rather than historical and resulting from human agency (see, for example, Gardiner 2000; Lefebvre 1971, 1991 [1947]; Vaneigem 1979 [1963–1965]). Routine is therefore not just a subsumption under system constraints but also a loss of critical consciousness of the grounds of our own subordination. Routine constitutes a double loss of agency: we are caught up in a programmed flow of events; and we are unable to see that it is indeed a programme, and one we could change. In several variants, particularly in the work of Agnes Heller (e.g. 1984), the routine, the normal and the everyday are synonymous: it's all bleakly mechanized and devoid of critical consciousness. Any practices conducted on this terrain are in principle complicit with the system, as in Adorno's (1991) notion of the recuperative function of all consumption of culture industry products.

The opposite of routine, in this framing, involves radical and conscious rupture: revolutionary praxis, 'situations', Marcusian libidinal hedonism and Adornian autonomy – all forms of intransigent and reflexive non-complicity. There's also a strong dash of 'authenticity' running through this tradition: routine as alienation diverts the evolution of human species-being in directions that are warped and subordinated to systemic needs (as in Leo Lowenthal's famous characterization of mass culture as 'psychoanalysis in reverse' [cited in Jay 1996 [1973]: 173], as increasingly neurotic adaptations); whereas a radical rupture with everyday life presages human evolution pursued according to its own intrinsic logic. The romanticism at the root of this ethical vision is fairly clear, and comes to its full flowering in the 1960s, in often highly gendered ways. The hero of the 'revolution in everyday life', like the hero of artistic romanticism from the 1780s onwards, allows himself to be directed by forces – libido, history, spontaneity – that fracture routine and fracture his routine/routinized self. At the limits, this way of thinking and acting is not only anti-bureaucratic but contests the very notion of structure itself, of stabilization or normality – all of which are intrinsically oppressive (*because* they are stable structures). Poststructuralisms, particularly of the Deleuzian sort, persist in all this.

This ethical framing of everyday routine has consequentially framed consumption studies for many generations: consumption long appeared as the exemplary site of routinized alienation and oppressive normality, in which the appearance of constant change, variety, desire and satisfaction is unveiled, through critique, to be in reality the routine and eternal recurrence of the ever-same – a conveyor belt of programmed choices that is the very opposite of free choice. The move against older theories of consumption really starts with cultural studies, which was driven specifically by its desire to find radical political agency located in those spectacular sub-cultures that turned the everyday inside out. And yet, sub-cultures appeared as ruptural interventions, thus allowing the cultural studies analyst to persist in regarding normal, everyday life as dead, unconscious, conservative and without agency – in a word, routinized. By contrast, the emergence of contemporary consumption studies has been conditional on rejecting this problematic, and re-valorizing the everyday as a site of agency, negotiation, creativity and cognition.

Obviously, the tradition of alienation is only one route by which to arrive at this critical framing of routine. Crucially for this volume's attempt to open up routine as an object of social research, 'interpretative' (largely phenomenologically based) challenges to structuralist sociology have long relied on a view of everyday routine as taken-for-granted, unthinking, 'bracketed', and only brought to light

– reflection, critique, change – in extra-ordinary moments of rupture. Truth lies in those moments when we briefly awake; and this includes sociological truth, as exemplified in Garfinkel's famous routine-breaking experiments. Similarly, Latour – in this respect entirely true to his own ethnomethodological origins – defines his 'sociology of associations' as the tracing of associations in the process of their assemblage; he allows that a 'sociology of the social' is entirely appropriate for the already-assembled, 'to designate a stabilized state of affairs' (2005: 1). Only the not (yet) routine is sociologically or politically interesting.

Historically, the idea of a 'hobby' has often served as a symbol of everything the critical theorist takes joy in hating about routinized everyday life. Adorno's outraged response when asked by an interviewer about his hobbies tells pretty much the whole story:

> I have no hobby. Not that I am the kind of workaholic who is incapable of doing anything with his time but applying himself industriously to the required task. But, as far as my activities are concerned, I take them all, without exception, very seriously. So much so, that I should be horrified by the very idea that they had anything to do with hobbies – preoccupations with which I had become mindlessly infatuated merely in order to kill time – had I not become hardened by experience to such examples of this now wide-spread, barbarous mentality. Making music, listening to music, reading with all my attention, these activities are part and parcel of my life; to call them hobbies would make a mockery of them. On the other hand, I have been fortunate enough that my job … cannot be defined in terms of that strict opposition of free time, which is demanded by the current razor-sharp division of the two… (Adorno 1991: 163)

Adorno's patrician distaste rests on two interrelated sins of routinization, both conventional for critical thought. Firstly, the hobby can only be defined in relation to the banal routinization of everyday life in the modern world. Everyday life is constructed within a larger routine division between public and private domains; in the case of the hobby, this is manifested in the structure of work versus leisure. Under capitalism, both sides of this structure are largely organized into routine practices, alienated and non-agentic. However, leisure carries an extra ideological burden, and critical animus, because it appears as a domain of freedom (free time, free choice, autonomous relationships) and yet it is entirely determined by the needs of capitalist reproduction: leisure is structured into consumerist choices required for the reproduction of markets; and into domestic chores required for the reproduction of workforces. Hence, Adorno's view of everyday life as a sphere of recuperation, in which all forms of ostensibly autonomous pleasure are in fact deeply functional to systemic operation. What seems an expression of self-determination really immerses us deeper into neurotic and habitual adaptations to existing structures rather than producing an enhanced domain of consciousness and agency. At the same time, what critical theory finds most tragic about private activities, like hobbies and leisure, is their sheer insignificance: however important they are to actors experientially, they are socially inconsequential. We are therefore all trapped within private activities in which we seek our true meaning but which are trivial and socially marginal. Cohen and Taylor's (1976) book *Escape Attempts* (its title itself states the case) is a wonderful exploration of this paradox of meaning and meaningless. The inconsequential and the routine character of the everyday are strongly connected in authors like Heller (1984): the problem with everyday life is that it is *particularistic*, it does not transcend one's immediate environment in order to develop generic or species-specific human powers and capacities; rather, it is reified and habitual because of the structure of modern social conditions. In fact, Heller argues, everyday life does contain imaginative and creative practices, but these cannot be fully utilized within essentially repetitive and habitual mundane activities; this produces what she calls an unrealized 'cultural surplus'.

Secondly, the hobby is itself a routinized practice: 'preoccupations with which I had become mindlessly infatuated merely in order to kill time' versus 'reading with all my attention'. Listening to music as a hobby 'would make a mockery' of music as 'part and parcel of my life' not simply because of the resulting endorsement of modern structural features (work/leisure, public/private), but also because the hobbyist frame routinizes practice. 'Hobbies' are located in leisure 'free time' but are nonetheless structured, organized, bounded and pursued with seriousness and (purposeless) purposiveness. Any practice can be structured in the form of a hobby. Pretty much any object can be given a collectible value, for example; any activity can be given a competitive form (there are international associations for soap box racing enthusiasts, paper plane fliers, etc.) or accredited expertise (there is voluminous help for those pursuing hobbies like ant-farming, photography, etc.). By the same token, any practice can be commodified and hence sold as a hobby; conversely, the sale of many commodities requires the routine structuring of practices into a recognizable hobby. Any or all of these can be combined into a thing called 'a hobby' with definitions of approved/included and marginal/excluded variants of the activity or interest, and with organizations, specialist media, gatherings, hierarchies, archives, lobbyists, and so on.

The stabilization of practices in such forms is interesting enough, but it is the ethical framing that concerns us here. If you simply want to pursue or support an interest collectively, then these forms of routinization make complete sense – people organize themselves, and this involves complex and interesting forms of negotiation. However, notions like 'hobby' are not neutral descriptions of a social form; they are labels that accord a social status and cast social judgements on particular ways of doing the social. The word 'hobby' is never far from a battery of pejoratives like nerd, geek, anorak, twitcher, bubble-heads (an Australian label for scuba-diving enthusiasts), and so on.

These pejoratives have a long modern history that is entirely caught up in the romantic critique of everyday life that I sketched in terms of critical theory traditions.

I can only gesture at some key moments in that history. For example, the idea of a hobby first emerges as a popular label in the late nineteenth century from the English 'riding your hobby horse' – a persistent, almost uncontrollable, focus on a private obsession. Bicycle riding and snapshot photography in the 1890s and 1900s were structured, private activities that could attract obsessive involvement, and a work-like level of seriousness and commitment to what was – after all – a *merely* private and leisure enjoyment. In the 1930s, hobbies were prescribed for unemployed men to give structure and purpose to a life without public significance and pay. The hobby was both approved as socially responsible (an extension of nineteenth-century espousals of 'rational recreation' to both improve and control working-class men in the interest of public order) and at the same time seen to demean: to be involved in a hobby is to treat as serious and consequential what is really only a replication or simulation of 'real work', while at the same time the hobby structures and routinizes private, leisure time, and emasculates the working-class man. This latter theme continues strongly into the 1950s and 1960s, in which the hobby is seen as part of the feminization and domestication of the rising new middle-class men, as intrinsic to suburbanization: men are to return from the public world of work directly to their ideal home (and not by way of the pub); the hobby is designed to structure their time and activities in a home in which they have no purposive activity under the prevailing gender division of labour. Indeed, hobbies were routinely discussed in terms of therapy (office workers and junior managers need hobbies to unwind after work so they don't get ulcers) and in terms of keeping the man from getting in the way/under the feet of the home-making woman. The phenomenon of *Playboy* magazine in the late 50s and 60s is interesting in defining a new version of male consumerism that was libidinal rather than domestic, and not subordinated to the logic of suburban home-making routines (Ehrenreich 1983).

'Hobby' was therefore a judgement upon those who believed themselves to have found a self-defined sphere of free and purposeful activity contained within a freely chosen sociality: in fact their activities are densely and obsessively structured, and in ways that replicate the world of work but without its reality and consequentiality. Hobbies are rather silly 'escape attempts' by people who believe themselves to be doing something serious and free but are in fact constrained by much larger structures (unemployment, suburban domesticity). The very framing of practices as hobbies is – within critical thought – a judgement on the inconsequentially routinized nature of everyday life.

Routine as Technique

In critical thought, the figure of the hobby brings out the intrinsic silliness of routine as a potential site of meaning, agency, consciousness or rupture. Adorno's pride in 'reading with all my attention' inherently requires and asserts his rejection of the work/leisure dichotomy: to regard his own reading as a 'hobby' would routinize it as a stable practice within a stabilized diremption of the modern world. Even to frame his reading as routine – let alone to practise it as one – is a fatal surrender of critical consciousness.

Now for something completely different: Western Buddhist meditation and Tai Chi (which might themselves be treated, unkindly, as hobbies) methodically treat routine as the very ground of consciousness and as a technical means to maintain an alert and reflexive orientation to the world. Tai Chi is literally a routine. Students will take several years to learn a sequence of movements – a 'form' – that may comprise anything from 24 to over 100 individual moves. The practice of Tai Chi is simply the daily repetition of this routine over many years, and – more than this – constant and alert attention to the most microscopic nuances of each movement on each repetition. The essentials of progress are consistent and banal: you start by learning mechanical movements – this arm goes there, shift your weight onto the left leg, twist to the north now, and so on. Repeat several times a day with unwavering attention to the slightest shifts in breath, centre of gravity, balance, weight, intentionality. Over time and repetition, the movements are said to become increasingly 'internal' – you no longer move bits of your body; rather you move your waist (specifically your Dan Tien, a point just below the navel) and the rest of you will follow correctly and flowingly.

Daily repetition of Tai Chi is akin to an actor doing seven evening performances plus two matinees a week of the same show, or a musician rehearsing the same few pieces: how to infuse routine with *life*, how to treat each performance in an endless sequence as if it were the only one; and, of course, how to remain alert and alive doing what should, by rights, be numbingly boring. Tai Chi must be performed – over and over again – with total concentration (when it lapses, you might actually fall over). Moreover it is simultaneously a 'moving meditation' (accomplishment is partly defined by consistent clarity of focus on an object, as in any meditation); a mode of relaxation (but not rest – it can be very strenuous across the form, but each move must be performed without apparent effort); and a martial art (it must be performed as if your life depended on the proper focusing of energy in each repetitive move).

At the same time there is something wonderfully banal about Tai Chi. As I was informed in one class: when the master says, 'put your arm there', he simply means, 'put your arm there' – don't look for any deeper meaning. This gives an inkling of the deep seriousness of routine in Tai Chi: one does not think *about* routine, one enters into it entirely, so that one literally flows through the movements, and the movements (of your balance, centre of gravity, Dan Tien) move you. This is akin to the Western reception of Zen and the art of archery, motorcycle maintenance, guitar, flower arranging, calligraphy, whatever – any flow of events can serve as the vehicle for the same kind of immersion, the point being the merging of self (body and mind) into the flow. One is often told that you can do Tai Chi standing still, without moving, as long as you stand there in 'a Tai Chi way'. Routine is a way into what phenomenologists might call (here literally) a flow mentality; it stabilizes the very idea of movement into a structured form so that one can foreground and experience the notion of flow in itself.

Hence Tai Chi invokes very different relationships between routine and consciousness, and between routine and structure, than in the case of Western critical theory. The Tai Chi form is itself a technique, and its repetitive performance should inculcate an immersion that is in fact acutely and persistently conscious. It's a tricky dialectic: there can be no mastery without routine repetition; but each repetition is a unique event. The experience of Tai Chi over time is of an increasingly microscopic attention to the finest differences in movement. Each of the zillion repetitions is different, and awareness of that uniqueness, that now-ness, is integral to knowing that you are doing Tai Chi.

Discourses on Tai Chi rather pride themselves on being unable to express very much – 'Don't ask me about the Chi, just make sure your knee is positioned directly over your toes.' Western Buddhism, by contrast, is vociferous. As taught by the UK-based FWBO (Friends of the Western Buddhist Order), meditation starts with the learning of two routines that are to be repeated every day, forever: mindfulness of breathing and the metta bhavana (loving-kindness meditation). Mindfulness of breathing is just that: sit and focus on the flow of your breath, aided by a few techniques (count the in-breaths, then the out-breaths, then focus on the breath entering and leaving the tip of your nose). The central skill – as in Tai Chi – is staying alert, awake and interested throughout what is ostensibly extraordinarily, crushingly boring: following your breath for 30–45 minutes a day. There is constant joking about falling asleep during meditation, and snoring in the meditation room. Training conventionally starts by asking students to walk around the room and find something, anything, to be interested in, then to *cultivate* that interest – the corner of that cushion is blue with frayed tassels; is the material warm or cool?; who made it? Meditation normally starts with a body scan: focus on your toes, then legs, bottom, etc., in each case developing an interest and awareness in any aspect of your experience of those body parts – the feeling of gravity and weight, of temperature, the feel of your clothing, any discomfort, and so on. The point of this is to inculcate a clear and alert concentration on whatever counts as experience in the present moment. The body scan prepares you for the state of mind you are to bring to your breathing: an active interest in whatever is within the current fold of experience. This interest is ideally non-judgemental: its intention is not to do things better or criticize what you are doing or experiencing, but simply to monitor experience in order to be inside its flow, to be here, now. Similarly, in the constant discussion of how to bring meditation into one's everyday life, the ethical stance to be cultivated is one of disinterested interest: as you wash the dishes, think to yourself, 'I am washing the dishes', and bring this same ethically neutral, observational reflexivity to every move you make.

This routine alertness derives its point, and its difficulty, by contrast with routine distraction. We normally are *not* aware of ourselves washing dishes, and don't even want to be aware: we crave distraction, and we rely on habitual flows that do not require mental presence. A favourite example is driving: I can drive a considerable distance and get out of my car at the other end with no memory of anything along the way. Despite having accomplished something technically complex, dangerous and requiring an enormous coordination of skills, I seem to have been asleep.

Meditation replicates this yet asks you to stay awake and alert – mindful – throughout the drive, or in this case the fundamental act of breathing. It is therefore formally defined by a routine of concentration on a mundane focus, something that would otherwise – in the flow of routine experience – fall below the radar of consciousness. However, the core of mindfulness meditation is actually the experience of distraction and diversion from this flow. The teacher will constantly assure you that your mind *will* wander, that this is normal and that sometimes you will wander off for long periods of time, because you are worried about something, or extremely bored, or tired, or – in a lovely and often repeated phrase – because this is simply what minds *do*, they wander distractedly. Meditation is really about being able to see when you have drifted off, and then to calmly and gently bring your attention back to your breath, along with a brief, non-analytic acknowledgement of where it drifted off to. A 'good' meditation is not one in which you have maintained intense concentration on your breath for 45 minutes; it is not a virtuoso feat of mental discipline; to the contrary, it is a meditation in which your mind has constantly wandered off from the breath but you have just as persistently brought it back. It is in these moments that both consciousness and routine flow are entirely brought into view and you are entirely living in your present experience. Indeed both the wandering and the alertness are equally part of the experience that is to be experienced; the frame is part of the picture.

So what is the point of this for a Friend of the Western Buddhist Order? The routine of meditation offers a dialectic of awareness and distraction, boredom and interest that replicates everyday routines, and any everyday routine could – and ultimately should – be the occasion for cultivating the same kind of interested, alert awareness. Meditation offers a particular technique – or even laboratory – for dealing differently with the mundane flow of the everyday. For Western Buddhists, the aim of meditation as an ethical technique of the self is to achieve a 'skilful mind'. This is not about being good or moral, but rather about being capable of not harming self or other. This skilfulness essentially resides in the ability to remain alert in the flow of events, to retain a critical distance so as not to be caught up by the flow of action and emotion. And this flow is largely conceptualized not in terms of structures, drives or constraints but rather in terms of *habit*: the routinization of mechanical responses to events. In recognizing the moment of distraction within meditation we become aware of how our mind habitually works, and, rather than following the normal course of response, we can look at what we are doing, pause and perhaps find more creative or beneficial ways of doing things. 'Skilfulness' describes the inculcation of this moment of pause and reflection, the construction of a conscious opening in the flow of events, which allows us to respond to them differently rather than be overwhelmed and unconscious.

Like Tai Chi, then, meditation can be considered as a complex dialectic of routine and awareness, in which routine, and persistent alertness within a routine, is treated as the medium for exploring and inculcating different forms of awareness. Routine and awareness are not opposites but rather part of one developing experience of flow. Moreover, the logic of both Tai Chi and mindfulness meditation involves recognizing rather than denying structure. Meditation does not envisage a ruptural world without structure (or a world comprising nothing but meditation) but rather a technical distancing from structure in order to deal with it differently. Similarly, in Tai Chi it is only by passing through the mechanics of routine that one can develop more powerful responses to what the world (in the form of an opponent) throws at you. How, then, could we characterize this ethical framing of routine? Routine is the ground both of our awareness and of our unconsciousness; meditation is a formal technique to make its practitioners experience and develop this dialectic; and the formal technique presents itself as a prefiguration of the transformation of *all* routine into the same object of persistent awareness of skill and habit. Whereas in critical theory one can only awake from the routinization of leisure by rejecting it and the structures that constitute it, Tai Chi and meditation propose that routine must and can be the very grounds of our awakening, and of the cultivation of the strength to carry this wakening from the mat into everyday life.

Routine as Normativity

In our first two examples, routine is clearly unthinking; the issue is simply whether it can be a technology for deepening (hobbies) or transforming (meditation) an un-reflexive state. In our last example, unthinking habit is not only valued but regarded as a mark of (Western) superiority.

In studying the internet and mobile phones in Ghana, I used the idea of 'commun-icative assemblages' to think about how people bodged together the resources at hand into stable 'media' that could be used routinely by skilled communicators: for example, the flow of people and cassava to a district capital on market day involved the coordination of kin, roads, buses, market prices and much more. The presence of communicative routines testified to highly skilled, reflexive, determined and rational social construction by human agents who knew what they were doing.

Official ICT policies, by contrast, assumed black-boxed technologies – 'the internet', 'the computer' – which had a double connection to the idea of routine. Firstly, these technologies were expected to generate their own normative routines, and automatically. This is what we conventionally describe as 'technological determinism', and takes a very practical policy form: the expectation that placing well-specified kit in an air-conditioned room will generate appropriate practices among the 'beneficiaries'; and simultaneously the expectation that it will displace all existing routines, such as the communicative assemblages that were already maintained locally. Framed in this way, new technologies generate precisely the opposite view of routine from that which informed my ethnography: for most development practitioners, to develop Ghana into an information society literally *meant* entering into the routines dictated by the new technologies.

Secondly, the new technologies were obviously black-boxed via very complex processes of production and transmission through global circulations and framings by organizations from Microsoft to the World Bank and the US government. But the very idea of routine itself played a part: the supposed superiority of the official version of new technology over local media definitions was often demonstrated by the fact that it represented uses of the technology that were 'routine' in the North or amongst the educated elite. Idealized uses – e.g. the locally odd media-use model of one computer per person that structured the space of internet cafés – were legitimated precisely on the grounds that they were unthinking everyday technology use in the North. The communicative assemblages of local people, by contrast, were not considered to be 'routines', but rather the senseless, retrograde and obstructive chaos of village life. 'Routine' thus marked out a classic denial of the rationality of the other.

Hence, in my rural research I worked alongside a computer centre that was set up in the district capital, using UNDP (United Nations Development Programme) money, HIPC (Heavily Indebted Poor Countries) money and Ghanaian government money, and under the aegis of a quite visionary chief executive officer of the district. This was a high-spec internet centre, run by a very bright and innovative young man, but entirely defined within official discourses of ICT and development: it was a *centre* to which people were meant to come in order to become computer literate and to use the internet for 'information access'. All these terms were black-boxed – computer, internet, information – in that they were treated as given, complete and stable objects with already known and universal properties; these properties were expected to unfold automatically, anywhere, if implemented properly. The centre was almost always empty, largely because it did not connect to any of the surrounding communicative assemblages: no larger assemblages were formed.

I interviewed the regional director of the education department in her office, a computer proudly displayed on her desk surrounded by piles of bureaucratic rationality in paper form and by subordinates assembled around her to perform hierarchy. The first half hour of the 'interview' comprised her amusing anecdotes about the stupidity and backwardness of villagers and village life. In judging village life, forms of action could only be perceived by her either as irrational (literally, these people are ignorant and stupid) or as stabilized in traditional forms that were intrinsically retrograde (rational in my terms, but not in hers).

Routine played an interesting role in this discussion, and there were milder forms throughout this fieldwork: on the one hand, the internet and computers are seen as spectacular emergences, the latest revolution from the North, as yet another historical rupture, this time ushering in information society and globalized economies – notions that present new challenges that the South must meet from a position of backwardness. At the same time, ICTs as dramatic disruption sit alongside ICTs as a new routinization. It is considered obvious that mundane and unthinking use of these techno-marvels *must be* routine in every Northerner's life, as in that of the governmental and business elites in Ghana. Indeed, imaginations of what these routines might look like in London or New York, as well as experiences of everyday Northern technological life brought back from educational, business or government postings abroad, play a significant role in how people understand and frame these objects as they enter into their world. People like the education director make full use of this imagination of routine in order to align themselves – by way of education, class, urbanity, and so on – with perceived global transformation into a new kind of elite everyday life.

The notion of ICTs as routine in the North testified to the North's continued superiority: we backward Southerners marvel at what the Northerners already take for granted; we have to learn what the Northerner can do without thinking. Official ICT discourse and practice in Ghana was strongly based in a top-down flow of work habits from North to local elite to general population. But those outside the elites take a similar view. There is a phrase in Twi – *kwame obranyi* – which can be loosely translated as 'lucky or fortunate white guy', and which – in popular culture – is specifically linked to technological differentials. *Kwame* is the name for someone who is born on a Sunday, and is therefore blessed; *obranyi* is a white person, but often applied to Indians and Japanese, in so far as they are seen to come from technologically more advanced places. It is a phrase used in everyday life, but also in popular culture – there was a hit song by that name a few years ago, and it stated the conventional meaning: the *kwame obranyi* is able to create and appropriate new technical wonders that can do real good for people, and both the creation and appropriation are part of their normal way of being; whereas here in Africa either we don't have these things or we use them very badly, not for good.

Routine consumption of new technologies is treated both as demonstration of Northern or elite superiority, and as normative for the technology. The very aim of development policy is technology use that is mundane, unthinking, taken-for-granted, boring: that is the index of current Northern advancement and defines the goal of Ghanaian transformation. At the same time, this sense of routine ('naturalized', 'black-boxed') use is a form of denial of the existence or rationality of local routines, of the complex communicative assemblages that I found ethnographically.

Conclusion

'Routine' is a performative term in a fairly conventional way: it is not our neutral descriptor but is rather a term through which practices are structured and valorized. Given the history of critiques of everyday life from which we started, we need to regard it as a fairly strongly charged term. Obviously, this also raises the question of our own analytical use of the term: what new positions on practice, what ethical framings might arise from topicalizing routine in a volume and research agenda such as this one? What do we do to practices by researching them under the category of 'routine'?

The aim of this chapter has been rather more limited, simply desiring to highlight this performativity, and to explore some of the diversity of ethical framings that might arise in the process of acting on the notion of routine. In our examples, the respective framings might be described as critical, technical and normative: routine as the critical negation of agentic consciousness (the hobby); routine as technique for transcending unthinking routine (mindful meditation); routine as an identification of normative practices (everyday life in the North; chaos in the South). These framings contrast nicely but do not claim to exhaust the field or constitute specific dimensions to be applied elsewhere; they are just examples.

Nonetheless there are at least two central features running through the three examples which warrant treating their juxtaposition as more than simply random, as indicating themes to be pursued more generally. Firstly, in all three there is a concern with the 'quality' of experience, and in particular as this is manifested in different temporalities. The hobby is problematic for critics of alienation because it replicates the temporalities of alienated, mechanized labour on the very terrain of 'free time'. By contrast, the supposedly mundane character of Northern technology use testifies to its internalization of the temporalities of the 'new economy', to *kwame obranyi*'s capacity to be governed by such things as networking, digital efficiencies, efficient information circulation – to live in a new kind of temporal flow of practice that is allied to the future. The practitioner of Tai Chi or meditation inculcates a notion of cyclical time within an open-ended flow of experience: it disrupts 'normal' temporalities in order to transform the practitioner's relationship to them. Temporalities may be the symptom or the technique; what is at stake in the ethical framing of routine is the quality of everyday experience.

Secondly, the label of 'routine' assesses experience in relation to structure, constraint, something external and determining. However we might like, rightly, to cleanse our analytical languages of the structure/agency dichotomy, it is alive and kicking in the notion of routine: what is at stake is the way in which actors deal with the sedimentations of structure within everyday life. The critical take on hobbies tells a story about experience as colonized by structure, structured unconsciously so as to replicate and reproduce the capitalist system. The meditation story is about the reclamation of experience from habitual operations in an ordered world. The technology story is about how to achieve normative experience, experience structured by a desired future of global development. In this contrast, recurrent practices may be seen as variously tied to reproduction (they may keep systems alive, may contest them, may be central to anchoring them in a new place), but the very invocation of 'routine' as a way of seeing practices testifies to a concern with how different structures of experience mediate something big and out there.

References

Adorno, T. (1991). *The Culture Industry: Selected Essays on Mass Culture*. London: Routledge.

Cohen, S. and Taylor, L. (1976). *Escape Attempts: The Theory and Practice of Resistance to Everyday Life*. London: Allen Lane.

Ehrenreich, B. (1983). *The Hearts of Men: American Dreams and the Flight from Commitment*. London: Pluto Press.

Gardiner, M. (2000). *Critiques of Everyday Life*. London: Routledge.

Heller, A. (1984). *Everyday Life*. London: Routledge.

Jay, M. (1996) [1973]. *The Dialectical Imagination: A History of the Frankfurt School and the Institute of Social Research 1923–1950*. Berkeley, CA: University of California Press.

Latour, B. (2005). *Reassembling the Social: An Introduction to Actor-Network-Theory*. Oxford: Oxford University Press.

Lefebvre, H. (1971). *Everyday Life in the Modern World*. New York: Harper & Row.

Lefebvre, H. (1991) [1947]. *Critique of Everyday Life, Vol. I*. London: Verso.

Vaneigem, R. (1979) [1963–1965]. *The Revolution of Everyday Life*. London: Rising Free Collective.

Index

D

daily practices, *see* everyday practices
Dalby, Liza, 174
Daniels, Inge, 6
Dant, T., 25
Darier, E., 50
Deleuze, G., 93
Derrida, J., 95
Dewey, John, 9
diaries, 57
disruption, 67–81
  and political economy, 78–80
  power shortages, 68, 70, 71–6, 80,
    108–9
  of routines, 8–9, 10, 68–9, 107–10, 146
  traffic congestion, 68, 70
  water shortages, 67, 79–80, 108–9
dual burden for women, 49–50
dual-earner families, 49
Durkheim, É, 17, 144, 145

E

Ehn, Billy, 8
Eliade, M., 200
Elias, Norbert, 2, 100
embodiment
  and tea drinking, 199
  and wooden boating, 210–15
ethics of routine, 8, 217–30
everyday practices
  aggregation of, 44–6
  commuting, 85–96
  and coordination and synchronization,
    7–8, 25, 27–30, 35, 42–4, 46–7, 51,
    53–62
  disruption of, 8, 67–81
  elasticity of, 68–9, 71, 72–6, 78–81
  in Finland, 21, 23*f*
  in France, 21–2, 22*f*
  Mass Observation Project, 51–62
  practice-time profiles, 25–7
  practice-timescapes, 28–30
  relationships, 58–60
  and rhythms, 3–5, 10, 53–62
  rival practices, 21–4

tea drinking, 189–201
telephone use, 20
and time, 17–30
and time pressure, 49–51, 53, 60–1
and timespace, 35–47, 51
water consumption, 20–1
see also routines; social life
evolution, 136–8, 219
Ewen, Stuart, 145

F

Fabian, Johannes, 2
fads, 135–6, 139, 140
fashion
  cycles of, 7, 129–31, 140
  vs fads, 135–6, 139, 140
  vs innovations, 7, 134–5, 136, 139
  see also jeans
Finland
  everyday practices in, 21, 23*f*
  wooden boating in, 203–15
flea markets, 164–8
food, 56, 57
France, everyday practices in, 21–2, 22*f*
friendships, 60
funeral services, 176–8

G

Garfinkel, H., 220
Gell, Alfred, 2, 3, 146
Ger, Güliz, 9
Gershuny, J., 50
Ghana, technology use in, 218, 226–8
Giddens, Anthony, 36, 147
Global Denim Project, 161
Goffman, Erving, 38, 93
Gregson, N., 163
Gronow, Jukka, 7
Guattari, F., 93

H

habits
  and choice, 8–9, 100, 143–53
  cultivation of, 149–50
  disruption of, 68–9